Desert Storm

The War in the Persian Gulf

Desert Storm

The War in the Persian Gulf

By the Editors of Time Magazine

Edited by Otto Friedrich

A
TIME
Book

Distributed by

Little, Brown and Company

Boston   Toronto   London

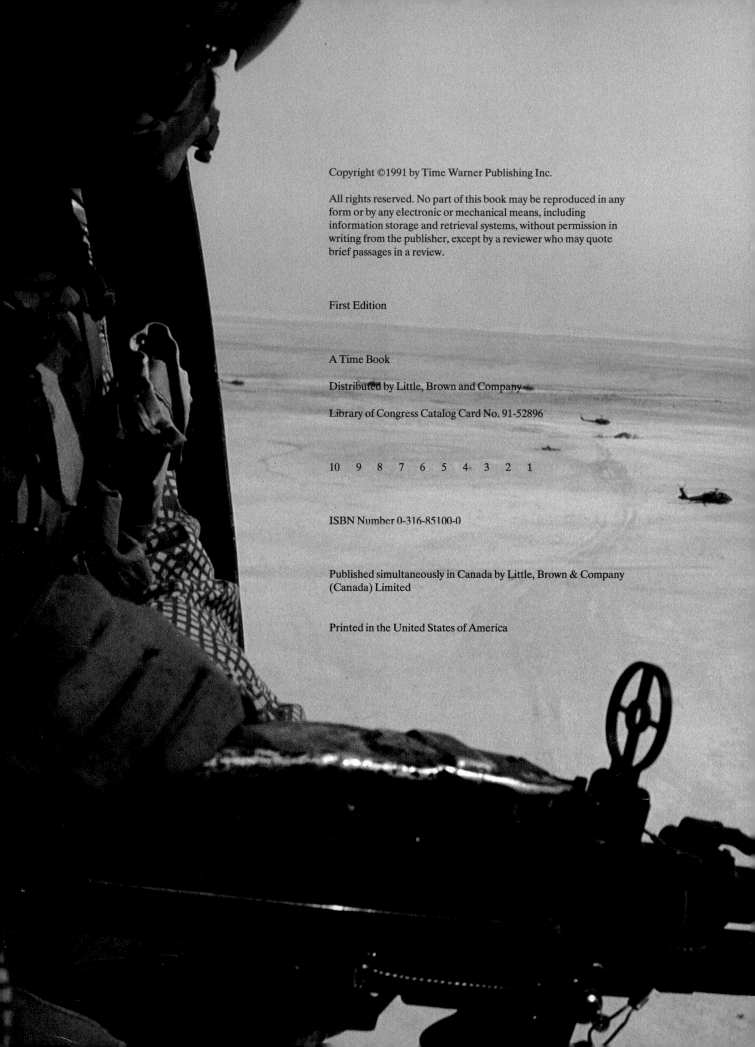

First Edition

A Time Book

Distributed by Little, Brown and Company

Library of Congress Catalog Card No. 91-52896

10   9   8   7   6   5   4   3   2   1

ISBN Number 0-316-85100-0

Published simultaneously in Canada by Little, Brown & Company
(Canada) Limited

Printed in the United States of America

Editor: Otto Friedrich
Picture Editor: Jay Colton
Designer: Robert K. Herndon

Writers:
I: Lance Morrow, senior writer
II: Christopher Ogden, diplomatic correspondent
III: Ed Magnuson, senior writer
IV: John Elson, contributor
V: Stanley W. Cloud, Washington bureau chief
VI: Jesse Birnbaum, correspondent
VII: Paul Gray, senior writer
VIII: Michael Kramer, special correspondent
IX: Jon D. Hull, Jerusalem bureau chief
X: Bruce van Voorst, senior correspondent
XI: William A. Henry III, senior writer
XII: Donald Morrison, assistant managing editor, ENTERTAINMENT
    WEEKLY
XIII: John Greenwald, senior writer
XIV: Ronald Kriss, executive editor
XV: Nancy R. Gibbs, associate editor

Principal Correspondents:
Amman: Scott MacLeod **Ankara:** Robert T. Zintl **Cairo/Saudi Arabia:**
William Dowell, Dean Fischer **Kuwait:** Lara Marlowe **London:**
William Mader, Frank Melville **Washington:** David Aikman,
Ann Blackman, Michael Duffy, Dan Goodgame, Jay Peterzell,
Michael Riley

Research: Nelida Gonzalez Cutler (chief), Ginia Bellafante,
Peggy T. Berman, Hannah J. Bloch, Anne Hopkins, Ratu Kamlani,
Valerie J. Marchant, Joe McGowan, Nancy C. Morgan, Ursula
Nadasdy de Gallo, Moira M. O'Donnell, Brigid O'Hara-Forster,
Ariadna Victoria Rainert, Susan M. Reed, Betty Satterwhite Sutter

Production: Trang Ba Chuong, Robert L. Becker

Pre-press Services: Raphael Joa, Project Manager, IMPACT
Center; Linda Parker, Project Coordinator, TIME Imaging

Desert Storm
The War in the Persian Gulf

When Victory Brings a Glow Of Righteousness

In the decades after World War II ended in a mushroom cloud over Hiroshima, the world got used to smaller wars with less decisive outcomes—a stalemate, Korea, or a quagmire, Vietnam—and to the chronic, glacial menace of the cold war.

Then at the end of the 20th century, history developed a brilliant, bewildering inventiveness that burst with transformations. In a period of 18 months, the old world order seemed to deconstruct. The Berlin Wall, Eastern Europe, the Soviet empire as a superpower, and huge, stolid Communism itself all came down like a massive old hotel being detonated, collapsing amid its billowing dust in a sort of historical dream sequence.

In the Persian Gulf there suddenly materialized a drama of dazzling display, brutal crispness and amazingly decisive outcome.

The war played like a movie before the world and seemed almost as brief. Like most movies, it was divided into three distinct parts, marked by decisive turning points of plot:

I. The Iraqi invasion of Kuwait and the coalition's formation and buildup.

II. The air war.

III. The ground war and coalition victory.

After the victory come the questions.

The war was what analysts called a "defining moment." What exactly did it define?

Rally in Montpelier, Vt.: a giddy mixture of pride and a renewed sense of the nation's worth.

▶ The end of the old American depression called the Vietnam syndrome, the compulsion to look for downsides and dooms?

▶ The birth of a new American century—the onset of a unipolar world, with America at the center of it, playing the global cop?

▶ The first postnuclear big war, almost as quick and lethal as one with nukes, but smarter, fairer, more selective in its targets, with no radioactive aftereffects?

▶ The first war epic of the global village's electronic theater?

▶ The apotheosis of warmaking as a brilliant American craft: a dazzling, compacted product, like some new concentrate of intervention—Fast! Improved! Effective!

▶ The dawn of a new world order?

The war defined all of those, and much, much more. But also somewhat less.

A daze of astonishment surrounded the enterprise: that it should have been so quick, so "easy," so devastating in effect. That coalition casualties should have been so light. That the cost to American taxpayers would be relatively small (if Japan, Germany and others honor their pledges of financial support). That Saddam Hussein should have been so cartoon-villainous (and so incompetent as a military leader), that his soldiers should have committed atrocities that took the moral onus off the carnage that the coalition left in its wake.

Americans may have sought a more innocent analogy: George Bush had—unexpectedly, miraculously—found the sweet spot. He and his men (Dick Cheney, Colin Powell, Norman Schwarzkopf) had performed a feat of concentration and grace under pressure after years when those had come to seem almost forgotten American talents.

The rest of the world watched the gulf war and its outcome, the riveting seven-month video, with expressions of admiration, awe, wariness, discomfort and, in the case of many Arabs, with a sense of rage and sorrow and betrayal.

What Bush accomplished had a feeling of conjuration about it: he created a sudden reality—vivid, dangerous, transforming—where none had existed before. Bush confidently assumed the role of deus—or *diabolus*—ex machina, like one of Homer's gods performing a flashy intervention from afar.

Americans welcomed home their returning soldiers with a giddy mixture of pride, relief and a renewed, almost stunned sense of the nation's worth in the world. Not since the end of World War II had Americans savored that glow of righteousness produced when mili-

Pro-Saddam demonstrators in Amman, Jordan, protest against U.S. intervention: a sense of rage and sorrow and betrayal.

tary power enacts the dreams of virtue and smites the forces of darkness.

The Pentagon had ordered 16,099 body bags to be sent to the Persian Gulf to bring home the American dead. Only 326 of the bags were used for that purpose. If the Iraqis had ordered body bags, they would have needed—what?—100,000? Or 150,000? More? No one knew or would ever know. Some Americans felt a moral unease that the war should have extinguished so many lives without producing, in the victors anyway, much sense of pain or regret: except for all those deaths, the American adventure in the desert might have seemed almost as innocent and exuberant as a cartoon—*Zap! Pow! Kaboom!*

Most Americans felt triumphant anyway. Bumper stickers showed an American flag with the words THESE COLORS DON'T RUN. President Bush's overall approval rating in the polls soared to 90%. He stood before a joint session of Congress and delivered a speech full of a patriotic pride and a sometimes wistful self-congratulation, urging on Americans the idea that they are a "caring people. We are a good people, a generous people . . . We went halfway around the world to do what is moral and just and right. And we fought hard, and—with others—we won the war. And we lifted the yoke of aggression and tyranny from a small country that many Americans had never even heard of, and we asked nothing in return. We're coming home now, proud, confident, heads high . . . We are Americans."

Bush had never been comfortable with what he calls the "vision thing." But in the context of the gulf war and its aftermath, he grew fairly visionary. Three times during his speech to Congress, Bush conjured up a phrase he had used much in recent months: "a new world order."

What does a new world order mean? In George Bush's mind? For the future of the world? Is it a harmless rhetorical flourish like his "thousand points of light"? Or does the phrase betoken some deeper American ambition—the pattern of the Persian Gulf intervention to be extended elsewhere in the world as occasions arise?

In his State of the Union speech earlier in the year,

Bush honored the collaborative aspects of his vision: "What is at stake is more than one small country. It is a big idea, a new world order, whose diverse nations are drawn together in common cause." But Bush's overall emphasis was on what the British used to call the "white man's burden"—America's mission as world policeman. His language and attitude sounded remarkably similar to the "pay any price, bear any burden" ethos that John Kennedy formulated in his Inaugural Address. "Today," Bush said, "in a rapidly changing world, American leadership is indispensable. Americans know that leadership brings burdens and sacrifices . . . We know there are times when we must step forward and accept our responsibility to lead the world away from the dark chaos of dictators, toward the brighter promise of a better day."

In another speech, before soldiers and their families at a base in Georgia, Bush expressed the thought more nakedly: "When we win, and we will, we will have taught a dangerous dictator, and any tyrant tempted to follow in his footsteps, that the U.S. has a new credibility and that what we say goes."

The U.S.S. *Wisconsin* fires its 16-in. guns from the Persian Gulf to pound Saddam Hussein's shore defenses.

The benign reading of Bush's N.W.O. is that with the end of the cold war, presumably the end of the old East-West struggle, the powers of the world can find new configurations. The United Nations may be able at last to fulfill the hopes of its founders as a mechanism for collective security. The gulf crisis, under Bush's masterly organization, brought together an extraordinary new coalition, including the U.S., the Soviet Union, Egypt, Syria, France, Britain and others, to confront an outlaw state.

The trouble was that new world order is a 19th century term that suggests Metternichian arrangements of large, heavy, somewhat static entities. History in the late 20th century seems to belong more to chaos theory and particle physics. It moves by bizarre accelerations and illogics, by deconstructions and bursts of light. It is global history with dangerous simultaneities at work. This bizarre new physics of history might argue for some kind of ordering. But the new world order, the American version as described by Bush, may not be new at all. It could be a revival of the old model of the U.S. as global intervener and savior of the world. If

so, then the world has a right to be somewhat nervous.

The coalition's brilliant desert campaign is probably not a repeatable exercise: history is very rarely so accommodating that it makes its dramas black and white, good guys and bad guys. Americans, liking to be liked, are sometimes astonished at the hatreds that they arouse—in the Arab world, for example, in Latin America and elsewhere—the hatred generally running south to north, from the have-nots to one of the gaudiest of the haves.

At the same time, America's status in the world was smudged and complicated by the realities of a long, slow rot at home.

"Today the world! Tomorrow America!" went the rueful joke. In America a new cliché sprang up, a variation on the '60s line that "if we can send a man to the moon, surely we can . . . " The new version held that the American talents demonstrated in the gulf war should be applied to the nation's social problems at home. Some had fantasies of daily White House briefings on the state of the war on drugs, of the struggle to subdue illiteracy and win an education victory. The

Getting ready for invasion, two U.S. Marines in Saudi Arabia practice the storming and defending of Iraqi trenches.

networks would dispatch their anchors to cities around the country to report live on the progress of the battle against recession. Schwarzkopf would stand in front of an enormous chart depicting the homeless problem and would say, "O.K., here is what we are going to do about it."

Neither political nor economic realities gave much hope that the nation's social problems—homelessness, health care, crime, drugs, a decline in industrial competitiveness—would be conquered soon, or even addressed. George Bush's approach would be basically to stand pat until the 1992 election, rather than risk his now enormous prestige in legislative battles he might lose.

Bush and his advisers calculated that the Democrats, leaderless and divided, badly damaged (for the moment) by the fact that most of them had opposed the war in the gulf, would offer no serious opposition for the White House, only a sacrificial token opponent. The Republicans would try to present the Democrats as part of the old, depressive crew: negative, carping, whining, pessimistic, unpatriotic.

But no one could safely predict either the national politics or the international order that would emerge in the aftermath of Desert Storm. Richard Nixon won the presidency in 1972 with 60.7% of the popular vote, and less than two years later, he left the White House in disgrace. Nixon once warned that the aftermath of victory is the moment of greatest danger. Americans might enjoy the moment of victory but then look beyond the war and consider that their country could not for very long assert its authority, moral or military, unless it could bring its realities at home into closer alignment with its persona in the rest of the world. Inside and outside must ultimately match, or be defeated by the contradiction.

British infantrymen take cover as one of their grenades wreaks havoc in an Iraqi Republican Guard trench.

"What is at stake," said President Bush, "is more than one small country."

How the U.S. Got into This War

Aug. 1 was a sultry, steamy day in Washington. Iraqi Ambassador Mohammad al-Mashat tugged at the collar of his white cotton shirt as the embassy's dark blue Cadillac, air conditioning blasting, disgorged him into the 3 p.m. heat at the entrance to the U.S. State Department. Summoned curtly by John Kelly, Assistant Secretary of State for Near Eastern and South Asian Affairs, the ambassador had guessed what was in store. No sooner was al-Mashat seated on the leather couch in the spacious sixth-floor office than Kelly warned him that the U.S. government was deeply concerned about the massive buildup of Iraq's forces on its southern border with Kuwait.

Nearly 100,000 soldiers—a force almost five times the size of the entire Kuwaiti military—were poised at the border. To intelligence analysts, a supply buildup looked complete. Exercises by the Iraqi air force suggested a ground assault was imminent. Anxiety was high in the region. Nonsense, said al-Mashat, it was Washington's rhetoric that was responsible for the increased tension. Preposterous, retorted Kelly. Iraq had put the soldiers on a war footing, no one else. Iraq, replied al-Mashat, had every right to move its troops as it pleased within its own territory. The burly Iraqi tried to calm Kelly, though, suggesting that press accounts of Iraq's recent oil negotiations with Kuwait were too pessimistic. "You don't need to worry," al-Mashat said. "We are not going to move against anybody."

The invasion: Iraqi T-72 tanks roll unchallenged down an empty highway into Kuwait City.

Two hours later, Kelly gathered with other officials from the White House, Pentagon, Central Intelligence Agency and Joint Chiefs of Staff one floor up in Secretary of State James Baker's mahogany-paneled conference room. Baker was half a world away, in Siberia, talking—and fishing on Lake Baikal—with Soviet Foreign Minister Eduard Shevardnadze. In an early test of post–cold war cooperation, he had told Shevardnadze that afternoon that Washington feared the Soviets' longtime clients in Iraq might soon invade their neighbor. "We hope you'll restrain these guys," Baker said. Shevardnadze didn't think it would be necessary. He doubted Iraq would cross the border.

Sitting at Baker's conference table back in Washington, CIA Deputy Director Richard Kerr thought differently. Having reviewed satellite photos and transcripts of radio intercepts, he predicted an invasion within six to 12 hours. No one else in the room was that pessimistic. When Kerr spoke, it was just after 5 p.m. in the U.S. capital, a few minutes past 1 a.m. in Baghdad. Less than an hour later, at 2 a.m. on Aug. 2, the Iraqi army swarmed south and smashed into Kuwait. Two commando units piled in from air and sea.

Advancing unchallenged in enormous Soviet-built T-72 tanks past the customs shed at Abdali and on down the empty six-lane highway—originally built by Kuwait as a token of friendship with Iraq—the troops took only four hours to cover the 37 miles to Kuwait City. Eight time zones west, the first reports of the invasion reached Washington at 6:30 p.m. George Bush was upstairs in his family quarters when Brent Scowcroft, his National Security Adviser, called from the Situation Room. Iraq had invaded Kuwait, but it was unclear how far Baghdad intended to go. Scowcroft told the President that most analysts believed President Saddam Hussein would only seize long-disputed areas along the border, perhaps the Rumaila oil field and Bubiyan Island. Bush turned on CNN and began devouring CIA reports.

In Kuwait City, machine-gun fire and the crumping of artillery shells awakened residents and set off panic in the capital. Helicopter gunships swarmed like wasps around the city's ultramodern high-rises. At 5:15 a.m.—9:15 p.m. the previous night in Washington—Kuwait's Crown Prince, Sheik Saad al-Abdullah al-Sabah, telephoned the American embassy. He asked for immediate U.S. help in turning back the invasion but also asked that his request not be made public. He was worried about Kuwait's image. An hour later, the Crown Prince called again. Forget the first call, he said. The Kuwaiti government was officially asking for help and no longer cared

who knew. The situation was desperate in Kuwait. The U.S. could do nothing. Its embassy had a tiny Marine security guard, nothing more. The closest U.S. forces of any consequence were on the island of Diego Garcia, 3,000 miles away in the Indian Ocean.

Iraqi rocket fire torched Dasma Palace, the residence of Kuwait's ruling Emir, Sheik Jaber al-Ahmed al-Sabah. As tanks closed in, he and his family leaped into a helicopter and fled to neighboring Saudi Arabia. Panicky Kuwaiti citizens attempted to follow their ruler. Iraqi soldiers forced them from their cars. Some had car phones. Troops ripped the instruments out, apparently anxious that they could be used for military communication. An estimated 300 tanks roved the city, growling up to the central bank, where most of the state's domestic gold bullion was deposited. Tanks and troops attacked and seized the Ministry of Information, home of Kuwait's television and radio station. They shut down the studios but not before a transmitter broadcast a plea. "O Arabs, Kuwait's blood and honor are being violated. Rush to its rescue," cried a voice. "The children, the women, the old men of Kuwait are calling on you." Then the transmitter broke off.

No help came. But Bush was already considering options with senior advisers. Kuwait seemed to be gone. Would Saddam be content with that, or would he keep moving south? Would Saudi Arabia be next? The U.S. embassy in Riyadh was instructed to ask the Saudis if they would like help. The cautious Saudis were not sure what, if anything, they wanted. When asked if they could use a squadron of jet fighters, Saudi officials said they would think about it and respond later. Bush went to sleep after midnight. When he awoke at 5 a.m., Scowcroft was outside his bedroom door with a sheaf of papers. Bush signed a pair of Executive Orders freezing all Iraqi and Kuwaiti assets in the U.S. and prohibiting trade with the invader. Dressing quickly, Bush was in the Oval Office by 5:30 a.m. Scowcroft joined him. The two men, friends since the early 1970s, ran over plans in their familiar shorthand. Get the allies to join in the assets freeze. Keep Israel quiet. Line up the Arabs to condemn the invasion. Work the U.N. Pull in the Soviets. Check out economic sanctions. Military options?

Summoning reporters before a National Security Council meeting later that morning, the President was asked whether the U.S. might intervene militarily. "We're not discussing intervention," Bush said. After the journalists were herded from the room, Bush listened to the analyses of his generals, spy masters, oil experts and diplomats. None was encouraging. When Treasury Secretary Nicholas Brady predicted oil prices

President Bush confers with British Prime Minister Thatcher in Aspen, Colo.; she impressed Bush by saying Saddam "must be stopped."

would jump and began to explain how the nation might adapt, Bush interrupted. "We're not here to talk about adapting," he said. "We are not going to plan how to live with this."

The President was frustrated. He felt misled. In recent days, he had talked to both Hosni Mubarak, President of Egypt, and King Hussein of Jordan about Iraq's intentions. The King, still considered an old friend at the time, had told Bush that Iraq would not invade. Mubarak said Saddam had told him personally that Iraq would work out its disputes with Kuwait through negotiations, not force. Bush set great store by his personal contacts. He felt betrayed. It didn't help that

none of his advisers had any good ideas about how to reverse the invasion. "What if we do nothing?" the President finally asked.

The consequences could be very dangerous. Saddam, with the fourth largest army in the world, had swallowed up a sovereign nation of 2 million people. Bush was convinced that Saddam had to be stopped right away, before he got stronger. The President, who had been skimming Martin Gilbert's *The Second World War,* repeated Winston Churchill's theory that if Adolf Hitler had been confronted and stopped in 1936, when he shoved into the Rhineland, World War II might never have needed to be fought. If Saddam were allowed to

Bush with Secretary Baker en route to Camp David: "What if we do nothing?" was the nagging question. Bush: "This must be reversed."

keep Kuwait, the fragile balance of power in one of the world's most vital regions would be wrecked. "This must be reversed," Bush said as the meeting adjourned.

What he didn't say was how he intended to do it. The President did not know. That afternoon the State Department tried asking Ambassador al-Mashat back to the office of a coldly furious Kelly. Fewer than 24 hours had passed since the envoy denied that Iraq had any intention of invading Kuwait. "Our national interest is at stake," the Iraqi started to explain. "We were forced to take military action." Kelly interrupted to insist that Baghdad pull out immediately. Al-Mashat stared through hooded eyes at the American diplomat, who was struggling to hold his temper. The Iraqi repeated the explanation, then sat silent. A reversal of the invasion would clearly not be easy.

Reversal would also involve a belated, 180° shift in U.S. policy toward Iraq, a policy that had its roots in the Iranian revolution of 1979. Until the Ayatullah Khomeini returned from exile early that year to overthrow the Shah, Iran had been Washington's strategic linchpin in the Persian Gulf. In 1953 the CIA had helped to topple Nationalist Iranian Prime Minister Mohammed Mossadegh and reinstate the deposed Shah Mohammed Reza Pahlavi. For the next 25 years, a succession of U.S. Presidents helped Iran to modernize and arm, while ignoring flagrant human rights violations by SAVAK, the Shah's secret police, and the regime's indifference to conservative religious standards. More important to the U.S. was Iran's role as a bulwark against possible Soviet expansionism from the north.

Iraq, a primitive state run by a military dictatorship, was virtually ignored during those years. Relations turned frostier when Iraq cut diplomatic relations with the U.S. after Israel's crushing victory in the Six-Day War in 1967. That chill ended on Nov. 4, 1979, when revolutionary fundamentalists in Tehran invaded the U.S. embassy and seized 66 American hostages. Instead of a strategic partner, America was suddenly the "Great Satan." Radical Shi'ite mullahs pledged to spread their fiery brand of uncompromising fundamentalism throughout the Middle East. The seismic event of the embassy seizure, turned into a national nightmare by the 444-day captivity of the hostages, forced Washington to reconsider its Persian Gulf strategy.

The fear of Islamic fundamentalism led the Carter Administration to turn to Iraq, a secular state headed since 1979 by Saddam Hussein. Saddam led the Baath

Socialist Party, which had close ties to the Soviet Union. Only weeks after the Tehran embassy was seized, Soviet forces had invaded Afghanistan, severely straining relations between Moscow and Washington. But Jimmy Carter was desperate. There seemed no alternative but to cultivate Iraq. In April 1980, Carter's National Security Adviser Zbigniew Brzezinski declared, "We see no fundamental incompatibility of interests between the U.S. and Iraq."

Under Iranian threats, Iraq invaded its neighbor that September, and the U.S. publicly remained neutral but privately favored Iraq. There were few illusions about Saddam Hussein though. "The intelligence reports all said he was a thug and an assassin," said Harold Brown, Carter's Secretary of Defense. But the prevailing view was that he was a man to do business with. His Iraq could provide a counterbalance to Iran. With 38 million citizens, compared with Iraq's 13 million, revolutionary Iran would be the dominant power in the region if it emerged victorious from the war. The prospect horrified Washington. When Ronald Reagan moved into the White House in 1981, the Administration's visceral fear of Islamic fundamentalism out-

weighed the new President's deeply felt anticommunism. Concerns about dealing with a recognized tyrant were put aside in the interest of advancing U.S. policy goals. Washington's support for Baghdad and Saddam accelerated.

When Israel destroyed Iraq's Osirak nuclear reactor in a stunning pre-emptive air strike, the U.S. voted at the U.N. to condemn Israel in June of 1981. The following year the State Department removed Iraq from its list of countries promoting terrorism. General Electric received permission to sell engines for Iraqi warships under construction in Italy. The U.S. launched Operation Staunch in 1983 in an effort to limit arms sales to Iran. No similar restrictions were placed on Iraq. On the contrary, arms flooded into Iraq from the Soviet Union, France and Egypt. Over the decade of the 1980s, arms sales to Iraq would total nearly $50 billion.

By 1984 the U.S. and Iraq had re-established diplomatic relations, and Washington was offering credit guarantees for agricultural exports. When the Iran-Iraq war slipped into a bloody stalemate in 1986, the U.S. began passing intelligence information to Bagh-

Skeptic: former Defense Secretary Schlesinger tells a Senate committee that U.N. sanctions are turning Iraq into a "basket case."

dad about Iranian troop movements. The Reagan Administration became more involved the next year, when it reflagged and escorted Kuwaiti tankers in the gulf. That operation made it more difficult for Iran to attack. The U.S. suffered when an Iraqi warplane attacked the frigate U.S.S. *Stark* with an Exocet missile, killing 37 American sailors. Saddam apologized for what he said was an accident and paid $27 million for death benefits and repairs. The incident was soon forgotten in official circles, which remained intent on giving Iraq what it needed to defeat Iran.

When Stephen Bryen, Deputy Undersecretary of Defense for International Trade and Security Policy, discovered an application to ship an advanced computer from a New Jersey firm to Iraq in 1986, he tried to halt the transfer. The computer was headed for a facility in Mosul called Saad 16, where researchers were working on developing a ballistic missile. The Commerce Department insisted on proceeding with the sale. According to Commerce's technical analysts, the computer was not advanced and fell into the "dual use" category, meaning it had civilian as well as military applications. Those sales were usually approved, as was this one. Only later did officials concede the error was a "mistake" that could have been avoided if it had not been U.S. policy to promote normal trade with Iraq. That policy allowed nearly $1.2 billion in sales during 1989 to Iraq from the U.S. alone. Thanks to Commodity Credit Corp. guarantees, Iraq had become the biggest foreign consumer of American rice and one of the top buyers of corn and wheat. Other nations followed America's lead. "We created this monster," said Bryen. "If you want to know who's to blame for all this, we are, because we let all this stuff go to Iraq."

Congress was not immune from blame either. When the Reagan Administration attempted to reach out to Iran as well as Iraq, the effort backfired badly in 1986. This secret initiative, providing U.S. arms in exchange for Iranian help in winning the release of several American captives in Lebanon, was amateurish, misguided and illegal. When Congress began investigating what came to be known as the Iran-*contra* scandal, one major political message to emerge was that any attempt to balance the pro-Iraq tilt by approaching Iran was doomed. Those analysts and officials who had encouraged the Tehran initiative soon left the Administration. Iraq could do no wrong, or so it seemed. In August 1988, when Iraq used poison gas to kill thousands of Kurdish civilians during the continuing war, U.S. official reactions were distinctly mixed. The Senate unanimously passed a bill condemning the gas attack and in-

stituting economic sanctions against Baghdad, but the Administration, supported by farm and industry lobbies, argued that sanctions would not work. It staged a counterattack on Capitol Hill that eventually killed the legislation. "Saddam had committed a horrendous act, the first use of gas since Hitler," wrote columnist Paul A. Gigot of the *Wall Street Journal.* "Yet his only cost was to have one of his senior aides politely dressed down by George Shultz."

Despite America's deepening involvement with Iraq, Washington had scarcely any more knowledge of Saddam Hussein and his regime when George Bush entered the White House in 1989 than it had had a decade before. Part of the problem was that the Reagan Administration tended to ignore the region following the U.S. evacuation of Beirut after the barracks bombing that killed 241 U.S. Marines in 1983. Washington's policy emphasis shifted to other areas. Central America captivated Reagan and his advisers. Mikhail Gorbachev's arrival in the Kremlin in 1985 put *glasnost* and *perestroika* at the top of the international agenda. Arms-control efforts were reinvigorated. The Middle East, a focal point for the Nixon, Ford and Carter Administrations, became a relative backwater under Reagan. Top Arabists retired from the State Department and intelligence services; the number of Arab linguists dropped. The quality of analysis of Arab issues declined.

Even with the best talent, analysis of Iraq's political intentions would not have been easy. Saddam ran a ruthless, highly centralized police state, riddled with informers. The penalty for disloyalty, real or perceived, was high. During one particularly difficult period of the Iran-Iraq war, a story made the rounds that the Minister of Health had suggested that Saddam step down temporarily. Saddam was said to have escorted the misguided minister from the room, personally shot him outside the chamber of the ruling Revolutionary Command Council, then had his body chopped up and delivered to his wife in a canvas bag.

Access to senior Iraqi officials, most of whom came from Saddam's hometown of Tikrit, was restricted. The regime operated more like a Mafia family with a don and capos than a government. The rumors fed such fear that contacts even with everyday Iraqis were difficult for Westerners. The U.S. had virtually no intelligence operatives inside Iraq. Embassy information gathering was almost nonexistent. Few Iraqi dissidents could be found within the country. Those who were known, or suspected, were arrested, tortured and killed. "The intelligence was limited, always has been, and still is today," said Richard Murphy, Assistant Secretary of State for Near Eastern and South Asian Affairs during the Reagan Administration. Information that the U.S. did manage to glean, particularly about Saddam's intentions, was often a welter of fragments, lies and contradictions. Under examination, it often caused more confusion than clarity.

The Israelis had the best intelligence estimates on Iraq, but their analysis was so unremittingly negative and hard-line that Washington tended to discount the most critical findings. Syria's President Hafez Assad, who considers Saddam a hated rival, was knowledgeable about Iraq, but his relations with the U.S. were considerably less than cordial; Washington accused him of harboring terrorists, including those who bombed Pan Am 103. Iran would have been a font of knowledge about Iraq, but by now had almost no contact with Washington.

Information from more moderate Arab governments in the region was easier to come by, but was often of dubious value. Egypt, Saudi Arabia, Jordan and the gulf states, like the U.S., all preferred maintaining Iraq as a counterbalance to Iran. Like Washington, they ignored Saddam's worst abuses and maintained that, despite his often bellicose rhetoric, he was getting more moderate and deserved continuing Western support. The Arab leaders were also uncomfortable with suggestions that Saddam was a liar. This tendency would prove a considerable liability when the Iraqi leader insisted to King Fahd of Saudi Arabia, King Hussein and Hosni Mubarak last summer that Iraq would not invade Kuwait.

As part of an overall strategic review, the incoming Bush Administration launched in 1989 an examination of U.S. policy in the Persian Gulf. The analysis, which dragged on well into autumn, was produced largely by junior officials who had worked on Middle East issues during the Reagan Administration. Neither Brent Scowcroft nor Robert Gates, the deputy National Security Adviser, had special expertise in the Middle East. Scowcroft, a former Air Force lieutenant general, was a generalist with primary expertise in U.S.- Soviet relations; Gates, the former deputy director of the CIA, was also a Soviet specialist. New Secretary of State James Baker knew almost nothing about the Middle East. He had never visited the region. The closest he came during his first year in office—while the policy review was underway—was a two-hour stop in Turkey. Richard Haass, the NSC staffer responsible for the Middle East, had no high-level experience in the field either. Dennis Ross, one of Baker's top advisers for the

area was another Soviet specialist with added expertise in Israeli affairs. He was not a gulf man. Nor was Assistant Secretary Kelly, whose only experience in the area was a truncated tour as ambassador in Beirut. Until then, his foreign service career focused on Europe. Only Haass spoke Arabic; Kelly, with two years in war-ravaged Lebanon, was the only one to have ever lived in the Arab world.

Not surprisingly, the strategic review recommended maintaining the status quo, the pro-Iraq tilt. On Jan. 17, 1990, George Bush confirmed the official policy of détente, declaring that expanded trade with Iraq was in the U.S. national interest. Precisely a year later, the first U.S. bombs would slam into Baghdad. The assessment was not unanimous. Opponents argued that Iran had emerged weaker than initially believed in 1988 from the eight-year war with Iraq and no longer posed the same kind of regional threat. Iran's economy was in tatters. Ayatullah Khomeini had died. Hashemi Rafsanjani, his successor as head of government, was believed to be less ideological, more pragmatic and, over time, probably more open to normalizing relations. The case for Iraq made much of CIA estimates that the Baghdad regime was equally weary of war. An international war debt of $70 billion made it likely, analysts argued, that Saddam Hussein would concentrate on increasing oil production and rebuilding Iraq's devastated economy rather than attempting other foreign adventures. His most probable targets, Kuwait, the United Arab Emirates or, at an unrealistic stretch, Saudi Arabia—all Sunni states—had helped finance the Iraqi war effort for the same reason the U.S. had backed Baghdad—fear of Iran's Shi'ites. The war payments were protection money, designed to keep both the fundamentalists and Saddam at bay.

There were other pro-Iraq arguments inspired by wishful thinking. Saddam had announced plans to promulgate a new constitution. It never happened, but the prospect was promising. Baghdad also relaxed stringent travel restrictions on Iraqi citizens, allowing many to travel beyond the nation's borders for the first time. Old worries about Moscow using Iraq to become more mischievously involved in the region faded. The Soviet Union was retrenching, too weak to exert any influence worth worrying about. There was one problem: Iraq's efforts to develop an arsenal of chemical and biological weapons. But that dark cloud was swept away by the rosier prospects of extended détente with Iraq. Bush signed off on the policy review that recommended quiet, behind-the-scenes pressure to move Saddam into the community of nations.

Getting Arab support for the U.S. plan was essential. Egyptian President Mubarak, here welcoming Bush to Cairo, proved a good friend and ally.

At the time, no one who mattered in the Bush Administration was paying the slightest attention to the actual situation in the Persian Gulf. In late 1989, Washington was totally absorbed by events in Eastern Europe. Mikhail Gorbachev dropped Soviet support for East Germany, the Communist regime of Erich Honecker toppled, and on Nov. 9 the Berlin Wall came down. Democratization swept the Continent and monopolized the political world. Bush, Baker and Scowcroft were preoccupied with Gorbachev, Chancellor Helmut Kohl and the accelerated unification of Germany. Kelly had been given the gulf responsibility at State mainly because the real Middle East action, the Arab-Israeli-Palestinian issue, was handled by another official, Ross. Kelly had only limited access to Baker at the best of times; now he had even less, and no influence to change U.S. policy even if he had wanted to.

Saddam Hussein, though, was watching Washington and did not like what he saw. On Feb. 15, he became enraged when a Voice of America editorial was brought to his attention. The broadcast praised the overthrow of dictators, most recently in Romania. In its sole reference to Iraq, the editorial noted that secret police "still operate in China, North Korea, Iran, Iraq, Libya, Syria, Cuba and Albania." U.S. Ambassador April Glaspie was called on the carpet in Baghdad by a Foreign Ministry official who protested America's interference in Iraq's affairs.

Glaspie reported Baghdad's fury to the State Department, which ordered her to apologize. "My government regrets that the wording of the editorial left it open to incorrect interpretation," she said, adding obsequiously that "President Bush wants good relations with Iraq, relations built on confidence." The State Department reprimanded the Voice of America. Kelly ordered that all VOA editorials that mentioned Iraq be cleared with State before being broadcast.

Saddam was not mollified by the U.S. apology. Nine days later, at a Feb. 24 meeting of the Arab Cooperation Council in Amman, he accused the U.S. of using the decline of Soviet influence in the Middle East as an excuse to dominate the gulf. In a fiery speech, he railed against the presence of U.S. naval forces in the gulf and called on Arabs to undermine the pro-Israeli American influence. Defeating Washington was an attainable goal, he argued in what Western experts would later identify as the Iraqi leader's first major miscalculation. "We saw that the U.S. as a superpower departed Lebanon immediately when some Marines were killed, the very men who are considered to be the most prominent symbol of its arrogance," Saddam said. "The whole U.S. Administration would have been called into question if the forces that conquered Panama had continued to be engaged by the Panamanian armed forces. The U.S. has been defeated in some combat arenas, despite all the forces it possesses, and it has displayed signs of fatigue, frustration and hesitation when committing aggression on other peoples' rights and acting from motives of arrogance and hegemony."

By spring, tough talk had turned to action. Britain arrested Iraqi agents trying to smuggle out triggering devices used in nuclear weapons. Security agents in Britain also seized parts of an extra-long-distance artillery gun bound for Iraq. Gerald Bull, the gun's Canadian-born designer, was assassinated in Brussels. Iraq arrested and executed as a spy Iranian-born British journalist Farzad Bazoft . On April 2, Saddam sounded

the most bellicose note of all. Announcing that Iraq had chemical weapons, Saddam said he was prepared to use them. "I swear to God we will let our fire eat half of Israel if it tries to wage anything against Iraq." He followed that threat by moving Scud missiles to Western Iraq near the Jordan border, within striking distance of Israel. State Department spokeswoman Margaret Tutwiler denounced the speech as "irresponsible and outrageous." Other than that, however, the Administration did little about the new mood in Baghdad.

Saddam received similarly contradictory signals 10 days later, when six U.S. Senators arrived on a fact-finding mission. Republican Bob Dole of Kansas told Saddam that George Bush intended to veto any efforts by pro-Israeli legislators to impose sanctions on Iraq and that "we in Congress also try to exert our utmost efforts in that direction." When Saddam complained about Israel's 1981 bombing of the Osirak reactor, Dole responded, "We condemned the Israeli attack." Democrat Howard Metzenbaum of Ohio praised the Iraqi leader as "a strong and intelligent man . . . You

The diplomatic payoff: Baker votes in favor of U.N. resolution 678, authorizing the allies to use force to expel Iraq from Kuwait.

want peace." Alan Simpson, the Wyoming Republican who would later criticize CNN correspondent Peter Arnett as a Baghdad "sympathizer," groveled when Saddam complained about such press criticisms as the VOA editorial. "I believe that your problem is with the Western media and not with the U.S. government," he said. "The press is spoiled and conceited . . . They do not want to see anything succeeding or achieving its objectives." The Senators' embarrassing remarks were released months later by Baghdad to illustrate the private messages that the regime had been receiving from Washington. The Senators complained that the transcript only covered excerpts of a three-hour conversation in which they also protested Iraq's use of poison gas on its Kurds and the threats against Israel. But Saddam drew a different conclusion: the Bush Administration and Congress would bend over backward to avoid a conflict with Iraq.

While the Administration continued to stroke Iraq, Saddam launched the first stage of his assault on Kuwait, which Baghdad has been coveting and threatening on and off for decades. He accused the wealthy Emirate, which boasts the world's third largest stock of proven oil reserves (Iraq is second), of secretly producing more than its OPEC quota and keeping oil prices low just when Baghdad was attempting to pay off its crippling war debts. Baghdad complained that Kuwait's excess pumping, combined with similar cheating by the United Arab Emirates, had depressed the price of OPEC oil by nearly $7 to about $15 per bbl. Iraq, which relies on oil for 95% of its export revenues, claimed that each $1 drop per bbl. cost the country $1 billion a year. By Saddam's reckoning, the Kuwaitis may as well have been stealing gold directly from his treasury. The practice, he said, using a phrase that was not fully appreciated until later, was an act of economic war.

Saddam had other complaints and demands too. He accused Kuwait of slant drilling into the Rumaila oil field, a finger-shaped deposit whose tip reaches into border territory claimed by both Iraq and Kuwait. Iraq officials argued that when it was fighting Iran in 1980, Kuwait secretly moved the desert border 2½ miles north to tap into Rumaila. Saddam demanded $2.4 billion in compensation for oil he claimed Kuwait had withdrawn. Baghdad also insisted that Kuwait forgive $10 billion to $20 billion in loans it had advanced during the Iran war. Ignoring that he had started the war and insisting that he had fought Iranian fundamentalists on behalf of all Arabs, Saddam argued that he was entitled to debt relief from the entire $40 billion he had collected from the rest of the Arab world.

Iraq also saw in Kuwait an opportunity to resolve Iraq's biggest disadvantage as an oil exporter, the fact that it was virtually landlocked. Despite its 169,235 sq. mi. of territory, Iraq has only 18 miles of shoreline, most of it blocked by Kuwait's Bubiyan Island. Baghdad had tried for years to lease the uninhabited island, little more than a mud flat. The Kuwaitis always refused, believing they would never get the land back. Finally, there was Baghdad's old claim that all of Kuwait belonged to Iraq anyway. It was part of the province of Basra under the Ottoman Empire, and Iraq has never acknowledged its sovereignty. When Britain, which had long maintained a protectorate over Kuwait, granted its independence in 1961, Iraq immediately threatened to invade. Britain sent troops, which were later replaced by Arab League forces. In 1973 and 1976 Iraq tried again, unsuccessfully.

The oil aspect of the dispute was supposed to have been settled in July at OPEC's midyear meeting in Geneva. To get the point across that he meant business, Saddam moved 30,000 troops of the Republican Guard, often described as his élite forces, to the Kuwaiti border. Kuwait and the United Arab Emirates got the message. They agreed in Geneva to stop overpumping, stick to their production quotas and support the first OPEC price hike in four years. But that wasn't enough for Saddam. He shifted an additional 70,000 troops to the border in late July in preparation for follow-up bilateral negotiations with Kuwait in Jidda. U.S. officials could not decide whether the troop movements were a bluff to pressure Kuwait into capitulation to Iraq's demands, a precursor to a limited invasion or an indication that Iraq was about to swallow the country whole.

On July 25, Ambassador April Glaspie was summoned to an early-morning meeting and was surprised to meet Saddam Hussein. A respected career foreign service officer, Glaspie had been in Baghdad for two years but had never met the Iraqi leader. Except for the Soviet ambassador, Saddam had stopped seeing resident foreign envoys in 1984, claiming he was "too busy." He accused the CIA and State Department of plotting against him. He said the U.S. was conspiring with Kuwait to keep oil prices low and destroy Iraq's economy. His threats to Kuwait, certainly in hindsight, sounded warlike. Blustering, he mocked Washington's reluctance to get involved in foreign wars. "Yours is a society," he told her, "that cannot accept 10,000 dead in one battle."

If Glaspie picked up any new nuances in the conversation, she did not incorporate or reflect them vigorously in her comments. Instead she stuck with the old policy she had advanced at the time of Saddam's VOA complaint in February. President Bush, she told Saddam, "personally wants to expand and deepen the relationship with Iraq." She assured him that "we have no opinion on the Arab-Arab conflicts, like your border disagreement with Kuwait. All we hope is that you solve those matters quickly." Glaspie would eventually be sharply criticized for her remarks, which Iraq had taped and later released. But the policy was not of her making. "She was an ambassador operating on the basis of instructions," said Representative Lee Hamilton, chairman of the House Subcommittee on Europe and the Middle East. She was reflecting a policy that Hamilton's committee colleague, Representative Tom Lantos of California, called "obsequious" and "based on fiction and fantasy." The fiction, George Bush conceded later, was that "there was some reason to believe that perhaps improved relations with the West would modify his behavior." In congressional hearings after the war, Glaspie said that she had warned Saddam (in their meeting) that Iraq should settle its dispute with Kuwait nonviolently. But had she told the dictator that if he crossed the border, the U.S. would fight? "No, I did not," she said. Such talk was not considered the best way to modify Iraqi behavior.

The same day the Administration erred through Glaspie's instructions in Baghdad, the VOA submitted, as ordered, another draft editorial on Iraq to the State Department. Taking note of Saddam's troop buildup, the statement adopted a different line. "The U.S. remains strongly committed to supporting the individual and collective self-defense of its friends in the Persian Gulf," the draft said. "The U.S. would take very seriously any threat that put U.S. interests or friends at risk." The Near East bureau at State, run by Kelly, killed the editorial.

On July 31, two days before the invasion, the Bush Administration was still committed to working with Saddam. Officials from State and the White House repeatedly called Representative Howard Berman, a California Democrat, to delay his efforts for a House vote to cut off trade with Iraq. That same day, State's Kelly was testifying before Lee Hamilton's committee. Congress wanted to know what was going on. "If Iraq, for example, charged into Kuwait for whatever reason, what would our position be with regard to the use of U.S. forces?" Hamilton asked. "That, Mr. Chairman, is a hypothetical or a contingency question, the kind which I can't get into," Kelly said. "We have no defense-treaty relationships with any of the [gulf] coun-

tries." Why wasn't the Administration talking tougher? Again, more bureaucratese. "We have historically avoided taking a position on border disputes or on internal OPEC deliberations, but we have certainly, as have all administrations, resoundingly called for the peaceful settlement of disputes and differences in the region." Hamilton's conclusion after hearing Kelly? "The Administration still believed Saddam was a guy they could work with." Glaspie said later that no one in the Administration ever suspected Saddam would take all of Kuwait. Baker admitted as much on the day of the invasion. Flying from Irkutsk to Ulan Bator, he walked back to tell reporters aboard his plane that he had just heard that Iraqi troops had crossed into Kuwait and had seized a border town. A few minutes later he was back. "I don't want to mislead you," the Secretary of State said. "It appears that their objectives are greater than we thought."

Bush had miscalculated. The Persian Gulf policy was wrong. As Kelly painfully admitted later under intense congressional questioning, "It did not succeed." Secretary of State James Baker conceded with lawyerly understatement that "with 20/20 hindsight, it's fair to say we would have done some things differently." Whether a tougher policy toward Iraq would have deterred Saddam will never be known. Iraqi Ambassador al-Mashat boasted that Iraq would have seized Kuwait whatever the U.S. had done. But by invading, Saddam Hussein miscalculated as well. He thought Bush and the rest of the world would stand idly by while he transformed the emirate into Iraq's 19th province.

When the President emerged from his first National Security Council meeting on the crisis, the guns had already fallen silent in Kuwait. The Emir's soldiers had resisted during a two-hour artillery barrage of the Dasma Palace, the nation's symbolic heart, but the Iraqi force was overwhelming. Bush termed the invasion a case of "naked aggression" and ordered three aircraft carriers to move to the region. Otherwise, his initial public demeanor was hesitant. He gave no indication in those early hours that the U.S. response would go beyond rhetoric.

Later that Thursday, he flew to Colorado, where he had long been scheduled to deliver a speech at the Aspen Institute. There he met British Prime Minister Margaret Thatcher, who had no doubts about what to do. "He must be stopped," she told the President. During a two-hour conversation, she drew the Saddam-Hitler analogy and reminded Bush of her Falklands experience in 1982, when she had sent a force to chase Argentine invaders out of the British-ruled islands. Thatcher doubt-

Iraqi TV Taped Broadcast

Saddam as the evil enemy. Having taken civilian hostages, he tries to seem paternal in a TV chat with Stuart Lockwood, 5. The West was appalled.

ed that any Arab political solution would work. What was needed, she said, was Western leadership, and if Bush decided to send troops, the U.S. could count on Britain's being alongside. Bush was impressed.

The President wondered about the other allies. "What about France?" he asked, since Paris has close ties to the Arab world. "Don't worry about France," Thatcher said. "When it gets difficult, you can count on her. She will be with you."

During their talk, King Fahd returned a call Bush had made to offer support for Saudi Arabia. The Saudi monarch reported his astonishment at the invasion because Saddam had promised him personally that Iraq would not move against Kuwait. But Fahd said nothing about any need for foreign troops. Bush told the King that he thought the Saudis were in danger.

The U.S. was willing, Bush said, to offer air support and more.

Fahd raised three questions: If the U.S. sent troops to protect Saudi Arabia, would they stay long enough to remove the Iraqi threat? When the threat was eliminated, would Washington speedily withdraw the troops? Would his Administration agree to sell Riyadh advanced weaponry, including jets, so the Saudis could defend themselves? Yes to all three, Bush responded. But King Fahd made no commitments.

Back in Washington on Aug. 3, Bush again summoned his National Security Council to define U.S. interests and explore the military option. The dangers of letting Saddam get away with aggression were sinking in. Satellite photos showed that the Iraqis had already moved south from Kuwait City to within five miles of

23

the Saudi border. The Saudis had stockpiled billions of dollars' worth of top-of-the-line equipment, including advanced fighters and AWACS reconnaissance planes, but their 65,000-man military was no match for Saddam's million-man force. If Iraq moved to seize the oil fields of northeast Saudi Arabia, Saddam would control more than 45% of the world's proven reserves.

At the Friday NSC meeting, Brent Scowcroft defined the terms of the in-house debate: the U.S. would not tolerate the invasion; too much was at stake. The West's oil supply was endangered; the world's economies, including those of the fragile democratizing nations of Eastern Europe, were jeopardized; Israel was threatened; Saddam already possessed chemical and biological weapons and was working on a nuclear bomb that might be deliverable in one to five years. The end of the cold war meant that it was now up to the U.S. to define the shape and structure of the world. Dick Cheney brought to the meeting General H. Norman Schwarzkopf, in charge of CENTCOM, the Florida-headquartered U.S. military command responsible for the Persian Gulf. Cheney had been unimpressed the day before with the modest options his military chiefs had proposed. Schwarzkopf presented an updated plan calling for the deployment of two divisions, a combat brigade, an air force of more than 500 planes, a multi-carrier battle group, plus scores of support warships. He was talking about 150,000 American troops, more than the U.S. had deployed in anger since the Vietnam War. Eyebrows went up around the polished table in the Cabinet Room. There was nervous coughing; bodies shifted uncomfortably in the high-back leather chairs.

Bush knew that putting any U.S. troops on the ground in an Arab country, particularly conservative Saudi Arabia, home of the important religious shrines at Mecca and Medina, would be a difficult political proposition. But the very possibility of an Arab solution was waning. The Arab League met, but only two-thirds of its members would even agree to a statement denouncing the invasion.

The President realized that King Fahd would have to be convinced. He directed Cheney and the Chairman of the Joint Chiefs of Staff, General Colin Powell, to brief Prince Bandar bin Sultan, Saudi Arabia's ambassador to the U.S., on the extent of the danger to the kingdom and on the proposed American response. Talking to Bandar first was an important decision that

A Florida Guardsman bids a tearful farewell to his children. Bush is doubling his troop strength to provide an "offensive military option."

went past protocol. Only 42, he had been Saudi Arabia's ambassador in Washington for nearly a decade. He is astute, brash and, a former jet pilot, knowledgable about military affairs. He is also well connected at home. The son of Prince Sultan ibn Abdul Aziz, the Saudi Defense Minister and No. 3 in the royal hierarchy, Bandar is considered to be the family member with the greatest influence on King Fahd.

In the Pentagon conference room, Cheney and Powell showed Bandar satellite photos of Iraqi armored divisions massing along the Saudi border, apparently poised for a strike at the oil fields near Dhahran, more than 200 miles south. He said the royal family was already debating the threat but wondered whether the U.S. had the will to take Saddam on in earnest. Bluffing would not work. When Cheney and Powell began outlining Schwarzkopf's initial plan, the Prince's eyes widened. He promised to call the King.

The President realized from the outset that a solely Western response would not work politically. That might look too much like Christians fighting Muslims for oil. Nor could the U.S. allow Saddam to argue that the clash was between Baghdad and Washington, patron of Israel. The Saudis could not accept U.S. troops under those circumstances. The U.S. needed a broad-based coalition of Arab states, the United Nations and the Soviet Union, in addition to the Western alliance. George Bush and his top aides were working around the clock to put it together.

In New York City, Ambassador Thomas Pickering spearheaded the effort to pass within hours a United Nations Security Council resolution condemning the invasion and calling on Iraq to withdraw. Secretary of State James Baker was by then in, of all places, Mongolia, for an official visit to be followed by two days of hunting in the Gobi Desert. He cut short the visit and flew home by way of Moscow, so that he could meet again with Shevardnadze. The Soviet minister told him that Moscow would back U.N. sanctions against Iraq but was not prepared to support U.S. military action. Baker replied that Bush did not intend to use troops unless U.S. citizens in Kuwait or Iraq were threatened. He wanted the Soviets to pledge not to resupply Saddam with weapons or parts for his largely Soviet-built war machine. Shevardnadze agreed.

In a compelling display of the new superpower relationship, the two men issued a rare communiqué, the first team effort by Washington and Moscow to muster support to solve a regional problem. Decrying the "brutal and illegal" Iraqi attack, the two countries called on all nations to join in an arms embargo against

Bush tosses out souvenir presidential tie clips during his Thanksgiving visit to U.S. troops in Saudi Arabia.

Baghdad. Baker was home in time for a weekend of strategy sessions with Bush at Camp David. Cheney, Powell and the Joint Chiefs were there. So was Schwarzkopf, who showed them a chart of "what it will take to defend Saudi Arabia" and another of "if you want to liberate Kuwait."

While the session was under way, Egyptian President Hosni Mubarak called Bush from Cairo to report that the Saudis had decided against accepting U.S. troops. Bush immediately called King Fahd. He repeated his previous arguments about the danger of an Iraqi attack and urged that Fahd allow Dick Cheney to fly over immediately to present a detailed briefing. Fahd thought about it for 14 hours and, under prodding from his nephew Prince Bandar, agreed.

Bush was by now convinced that he had to send troops. He was uncertain how many and what role they would play—strictly defensive, or offensive as well? Colin Powell warned that half measures would not work. The President understood. Both men were determined to avoid getting bogged down in another Vietnam. He also trusted Cheney and Powell and was impressed by Schwarzkopf, and they all recommended sending a large land, sea and air force.

Orders readying the first units went out on Aug. 6. Two squadrons of F-15 fighter planes took off for the gulf, and several giant, long-range B-52 bombers from the continental U.S. flew to Diego Garcia. They could go into action against Iraq in case Saddam moved into the Saudi oil fields around Dhahran before U.S. ground troops could arrive. For those ground forces, the U.S. still needed a go-ahead from Saudi Arabia, but Bush was already planning to send 200,000 troops. That total was kept secret, though, for fear of alarming the public. When press reports later in August predicted that 150,000 troops might be involved, officials derided the stories as exaggerated. But Bush was emphatic about the basic principle. "This will not stand," he snapped to reporters outside the White House. "This will not stand, this aggression against Kuwait."

The Saudis were still arguing. King Fahd, who knew Bush, was inclined to trust him. His brother, the less Western-oriented Crown Prince Abdullah, was holding out for some kind of Arab solution. Cheney arrived in Jidda with satellite photos, maps, intelligence estimates, a deployment program and a request that Saudi Arabia shut down the Iraqi pipeline that runs across the kingdom from Basra to Yanbu. After an extensive presentation, he sat back while the two brothers reviewed the possibilities in Arabic.

We must do this, Fahd said. Kuwait is being swallowed up. There is still a Kuwait, Abdullah replied, and as long as there is, we should try to settle this dispute among ourselves. Fahd broke in. Yes, there is still a Kuwait, but it exists only in our hotel rooms—a reference to the emirate's exiled leadership residing in a Sheraton hotel near Taif. Fahd turned back to Cheney. He would go along with Bush on two conditions: he wanted the President's promise that the U.S. troops would leave when the threat to Saudi Arabia receded, and a pledge that the U.S. would not launch a war without his approval. Cheney agreed and immediately called the Oval Office. Bush reiterated his assurances.

Establishing what Bush called Desert Shield was an extraordinary task. Bases had to be organized, airstrips built and hardened, hundreds of thousands of tons of supplies shipped in, and all at high speed. Temperatures in the desert in August reached 130° F. Equipment required redesigning, from sand filters on tanks to boots and camouflage uniforms. Soldiers based in Germany or North Carolina needed acclimatization to desert warfare, including learning to drink as much as five gallons of water a day to avoid dehydration.

The military needed time, and Bush was determined to use that time to build international support for his plans. He had spent considerable effort to develop personal contacts with the world's leaders, many of them as friends. He now turned first to the United Nations, primarily to give Saudi Arabia, Egypt and other moderate Arab nations and the Soviet Union diplomatic cover for joining with the "imperialist supporter of the Zionists." The U.N. followed its initial condemnation with more than a rhetorical flourish. On Aug. 6, the Security Council voted in favor of a trade embargo against Iraq, depriving it of imported supplies and export earnings. The President had already put a naval blockade in force to ensure that no Iraqi oil got out.

Next, Bush dispatched Baker on his second transatlantic journey in five days, to Turkey. Iraq's northern neighbor, a major trading partner and a linchpin in the strategy to isolate Saddam, Turkey is a poor country that had been getting about half its oil from Iraq while earning $300 million a year in oil-pipeline fees from Baghdad. The Emir of Kuwait promised to compensate the Turks for their financial damages, which Ankara estimated could total $2.5 billion annually. Because Turkey was so vulnerable, Baker wanted to deliver personally assurances that NATO would honor the alliance's commitment to back its fellow member in the event of an Iraqi attack. President Turgut Ozal agreed to enforce the full-scale sanctions. He also agreed that NATO could add fighter-bombers to the Incirlik air base near the border with Syria as a deterrent. That pinned down 100,000 Iraqi troops in the north, eliminating their use in Kuwait or southern Iraq.

With the deployment under way, Bush went on a planned three-week vacation to Kennebunkport, Me. Baker dropped out of sight at his ranch in Wyoming. Critics carped, but the President's plan was deliberate. He thought Jimmy Carter had made a serious error in disrupting most of his plans for more than a year while the American hostages were captive in Iran. That resulted in the Administration's being taken hostage. Saddam was holding more than 3,000 Americans and over 15,000 foreigners in Kuwait and Iraq. In grotesquely avuncular style, he called them "guests of the Iraqi people" but placed some at key military installations as "human shields" against coalition bomb attacks. Bush repeatedly insisted that the hostages would not deter him from taking action. He barred Administration officials from using the word hostage and drove the lesson home by fishing and playing tennis in Maine, supposedly giving the appearance of nonchalance while the struggle kept moving closer to war.

While on vacation, Bush monitored the military deployment and placed 62 calls to foreign government leaders. Baker too was working the phones. Both pressed Japan and Germany and the wealthy Arab states to provide emergency assistance to Turkey, Egypt and Jordan, nations hard-pressed by the effects of the embargo against Iraq. Bush called on Saudi Arabia and Venezuela to pump more oil to make up for the 4 million–bbl. daily shortfall caused by the blockade of Iraqi and Kuwaiti supplies.

Despite all his efforts to portray the conflict as the "whole world against Saddam," Bush was dismayed to find out how much support Saddam's emotional appeals seemed to have in the Arab world. Bush and other Westerners compared him (somewhat exaggeratedly) with Hitler, but many dispossessed Arabs regarded him as a hero who was taking on the "imperialists" and standing up for the poor against the wealthy oil sheiks of the gulf. To homeless Palestinians in the West Bank, and to others in Jordan, Yemen and the Mahgreb, Saddam seemed to offer a ray of hope—and not only to the poor and uneducated. "I love any Arab leader who will unite the Arabs, even by force," said Major General Yusuf Kawash, a retired Jordanian army officer who studied in the U.S. "We want to see one empire restoring our culture to its former glory."

Some educated Arabs ignored the invasion to seize upon Saddam's charge that the West was employing a double standard against the Arab world. The U.S. demanded that Baghdad give up territory it considered historically Iraq's; when it refused, Washington pressed for United Nations sanctions and made preparations for war. Why did neither the U.S. nor the U.N. force Israel to give up the West Bank and the Gaza Strip, seized in the 1967 war? Israel has held the occupied territories, in defiance of U.N. resolutions 242 and 338, for nearly a quarter-century. There have been no sanctions despite Israel's refusal even to negotiate. Israel's defense—in addition to military power—is that it captured those territories only after warning Jordan not to enter that war.

In Bush's coalition building, his appeal to Egypt had special urgency. Egypt, the only Arab state with a peace treaty with Israel, has been Washington's closest ally in the Arab world since Anwar Sadat made peace with Jerusalem in 1977. It receives $2.3 billion annually in military and economic aid from the U.S., second only to Israel. President Mubarak is a good friend of George Bush's, but he has to be careful to avoid charges that he is an American puppet. He was sincere in his outraged reaction to the invasion, all the more so since Saddam had told him, too, that Iraq would not invade Kuwait. Most Egyptians reacted angrily to the annexation of Kuwait, but Mubarak had to respond carefully because 1 million of them worked in Iraq and an additional 300,000 in Kuwait. Their expulsion could have devastating political consequences on the already tottering Egyptian economy. Bush pressed Mubarak to join the multinational force. As an added incentive, the Administration would ask Congress to cancel Cairo's $6.7 billion military debt to the U.S. Mubarak bit and promised to send about 5,000 troops and help raise other Arab forces. He also authorized U.S. aircraft to fly over Egypt en route to Saudi Arabia and cleared passage of coalition warships through the Suez Canal.

Syria was the other Arab country that received spe-

Preparing for battle: a long and winding convoy of the 1st Cavalry engages in a training exercise in the vast expanse of the Saudi desert.

cial presidential attention. Washington has long considered Syria a center of international terrorism, but Bush decided that he needed President Hafez Assad and intended to play on Assad's personal hostility to Saddam. During the long Iran-Iraq war, Syria openly supported Iran, which turned Syria into something of a pariah among other Arab nations. By agreeing to honor the U.N. embargo and casting its lot with the anti-Iraq coalition, Syria had an obvious aim: to reintegrate into the Arab world. Bush gave his personal endorsement to Assad by meeting him in Geneva, the first U.S. President to do so in more than a decade. Assad also got an estimated $2 to $3 billion from gulf oil states for his trouble.

At the end of the summer, with enough firepower in place to deter any immediate attack, if not to liberate Kuwait, Bush toned down his rhetoric and turned his attention to diplomacy. Saddam also issued a flurry of offers to negotiate, but his antics seemed intended mainly to avert a military showdown. A bevy of negotia-tors, including U.N. Secretary-General Javier Pérez de Cuéllar, began diplomatic missions, probing to detect flexibility on either side.

The U.S. had several choices: it could settle back and wait for sanctions—which had cut 90% of Iraq's imports and exports—to strangle Saddam. Proponents said this could take as little as six months, while opponents argued that years of deprivation were unlikely to force Saddam to give up. Or the U.S. could settle for a compromise whereby Iraq would retain a portion of Kuwait. That would not curb the proliferation of chemical, biological and missile weaponry that Saddam was developing, but the world had lived with that before. There were some U.S. strategists who considered any such compromise the "nightmare scenario," in which public opinion would oppose war, the coalition would disintegrate, and Saddam would remain in power, his aggression rewarded and his prestige enlarged. During the pause in September and October, both sides were stalling for time—Iraq to pry apart the coalition; the

On alert near the Iraqi border, British troops engaged in maneuvers pile out of a Puma helicopter and charge into the desert.

U.S. to get the military deployed and ready. Saddam tried his hand at public relations, declaring that he welcomed peace talks without preconditions. He promised to release women and children among the foreign hostages and said the men could leave too, if only the U.S. pledged not to attack Iraq. "It's a cat-and-mouse game," said British Foreign Secretary Douglas Hurd about the hostage ploy. "Now a little mercy, now some more ruthlessness."

Bush's diplomatic hand was strengthened by a September meeting in Helsinki with Mikhail Gorbachev at which the Soviet President supported U.S. demands that Iraq pull out of Kuwait unconditionally. Resisting all efforts by Baghdad to drive a wedge between the two capitals, Gorbachev reiterated that stance when Iraqi Foreign Minister Tariq Aziz visited Moscow in a search for openings. Aziz had better luck in Iran, where he negotiated the reopening of diplomatic relations after a 10-year break. There was talk of Iran's delivering food and medicine to Baghdad in exchange for embargoed Iraqi oil. Saddam also repatriated the last Iranian POWs and the last bits of Iraqi-held Iranian territory along the Shatt al-Arab, so he would no longer have to defend his Iranian border.

Not all the American diplomacy was successful either. When Baker departed on one trip, seeking allied contributions in troops and money, reporters with him presented the Secretary with a tin cup inscribed BROTHER CAN YOU SPARE A BILLION? Not everyone could, at least not right away. The biggest surprises were economic powerhouses Germany and Japan, who depend more on Persian Gulf oil than the U.S. does, and who balked when asked to help the coalition. Both maintained that their postwar constitutions—written by the U.S. in Japan's case—prohibited them from sending military units outside their own regions. The Administration then pressed both for such noncombat assistance as medics, supply specialists and engineers. Neither provided much. Germany's situation was particularly awkward, not only because the U.S. had helped Germany achieve unification, but because Iraq owed its chemical-weapons capability primarily to West German firms' illegally supplying it with the raw materials.

What angered U.S. officials most of all was the German and Japanese reluctance to contribute their financial share. Representative Carroll Hubbard, a Kentucky Democrat, spoke for many Americans when he said that Japan, which imports 70% of its oil from the gulf, was behaving predictably: "If there's no profit in it for them, forget it." Capitol Hill became so passionate

that the House of Representatives passed a bill threatening to pull America's 50,000 troops from Japan unless Tokyo paid all their basing costs. Japan responded swiftly, quadrupling its contribution to the gulf fund to $4 billion. Eventually, Tokyo would agree to pay $9 billion; Bonn came up with $5.5 billion. Some smaller nations dependent on imported gulf oil were also reluctant to contribute. When Washington asked for $450 million from South Korea, itself once a victim of aggression from the north, Seoul balked until warned that Congress would remember the next time it considered funding U.S. troops based in Korea. The Koreans dug into their pockets but contributed only half the request.

A sense of drift began to develop. Bush never believed sanctions would work, but he did not want to be accused of failing to take all possible steps to avoid war. He had asked Schwarzkopf to refine a package of offensive options, but the commander was still busy getting his defensive troops in place. He was not certain how many more troops he would need. Every time more Americans arrived in Saudi Arabia, Saddam supplemented his force in Kuwait. By the end of October, the U.S. had 210,000 soldiers in the region, well over 275,000 counting alliance troops. But from an original deployment of 100,000, Saddam had boosted his Kuwait contingent to 430,000. The U.S. could not consider a credible offensive option without a much bigger force.

Colin Powell flew to Saudi Arabia on Oct. 21. After reviewing Schwarzkopf's plans, he agreed that the U.S. had to think big. That meant doubling the number of American troops to 400,000 between early November and mid-January. Cheney and Powell took the proposal to Bush on Halloween; he approved. The President hoped the size of the buildup might finally convince Saddam that he was serious, not bluffing. The President reviewed the calendar. Barring complications, the troops would be "good to go" by Jan. 15.

Ramadan, the Muslim month of fasting, would begin on March 17, but that would not in itself pose an insuperable problem. Arab forces launched the 1973 war against Israel during Ramadan. The hajj, which brings about 2 million pilgrims annually to Saudi Arabia to the Great Mosque at Mecca, would cause more difficulties if fighting were still going on. And gulf weather turns bad in the spring. That all argued for a massive, decisive winter war. Bush agreed that an air campaign could start in January, followed, if necessary, by a ground war in February.

He had to tell the coalition leaders; he needed their support to go to war. He also wanted Congress's backing, but he didn't want to ask for it too far in advance, for fear of rejection. The best approach, the President and his advisers concluded, was to return to the U.N., which had already passed 11 anti-Iraq resolutions, and seek a 12th that would authorize the use of force. If the U.N. were ready for war, they reasoned, Congress would find it hard to oppose the President.

There were two things to do: start rounding up support for a United Nations vote in November, when the U.S., by coincidence, held the rotating chairmanship of the Security Council; and tell the American people about the decision to double the U.S. deployment for the sake of an offensive option. That could wait a week, the President decided, until after the Nov. 6 midterm elections.

Until Election Day, the President had been sending out mixed messages about his intentions, confusing Americans, allies and quite probably Saddam Hussein himself. He said he had "had it" with Iraq's mistreatment of hostages and cutting off of diplomats in the U.S. embassy in Kuwait City, but he quickly added, "I'm not trying to sound the tocsin of war." His claim that "we're prepared to give sanctions time to work" sounded almost soothing until he further bewildered listeners by saying that "the sand is running through the glass" for Iraq.

Some attributed the signs of vacillation to Bush's basic inability to articulate his views. But the confusion contrasted with his otherwise clear and oft-stated assertion of U.S. objectives: that Iraq withdraw completely and unconditionally from Kuwait; that Kuwait's government be restored; that U.S. citizens be protected and regional stability achieved. There were three reasons for the ambiguity. Some was deliberate. The Administration was, in part, bluffing. If it could scare Saddam out of Kuwait without a fight, so much the better. To avoid war, however, Bush had to threaten credibly that he was ready to wage one. Until he doubled the number of U.S. troops, there were no teeth in his threat. Saddam knew as well as Schwarzkopf that the coalition was in no position to take the offensive. Convinced that Iraq was not taking him seriously, the President announced the reinforcement to send a more forceful signal. Even as James Baker was hurrying through the Middle East, Soviet Union and Europe in pursuit of a diplomatic solution, Bush was announcing that the strategy had changed. The new buildup would give his commanders "an adequate offensive military option should that be necessary."

The second reason behind Bush's ambiguity was the necessity of addressing different audiences. For Saddam, the message had to be force. But for Middle Eastern coalition members fearful of the consequences of fighting an Arab brother, for jittery Europeans and also for Americans, who faced disproportionate risks, the U.S. had to be seen as pursuing every approach short of war. Third, Bush was really uncertain what he would have to do. He was receiving conflicting advice about the efficacy of the sanctions.

As soon as he announced the buildup, the threat of war hit home. Many Americans concluded that the Administration was rushing pell-mell into a conflict that some military analysts predicted could produce tens of thousands of U.S. casualties in the first few weeks. Despite the President's insistence that his main purpose was to resist aggression, polls showed that a majority of U.S. citizens believed the Administration's real objective was to preserve a cheap supply of oil for the West. Bush himself spoke vaguely of preserving "our way of life." Baker reinforced skeptics' suspicions by offering a glib rationale for the confrontation with Saddam: "If you want to sum it up in one word, it's jobs."

Antiwar feelings picked up. The prospect of war had not been a big issue during the political campaign. Announcing a major switch in strategy just after Election Day aroused some hostile reactions on Capitol Hill. With Congress in the middle of a two-month postelection recess, some legislators called for a special session to consider congressional authorization for a declaration of war. Support for the President began to unravel. He was scaring Americans more than he was frightening Saddam.

The President's maneuvers angered one influential Senator, Sam Nunn, the Georgia Democrat who chairs the Armed Services Committee. Nunn summoned his members back to Washington and opened public hearings to consider whether the U.S. was rushing too precipitously to war. Among the eminent witnesses were two respected former Chairmen of the Joint Chiefs, Admiral William Crowe and General David Jones, former Defense Secretary James Schlesinger, former Secretaries of State Henry Kissinger and Cyrus Vance and former National Security Adviser Zbigniew Brzezinski. All except Kissinger, who was hawkish throughout the crisis, argued for sticking with sanctions and diplomacy. According to Schlesinger, after only three months of embargo, Iraq's economy was "rapidly becoming a basket case." The embargo was "biting heavily," said Crowe, who added that the issue was "not whether an embargo will work, but whether we have the patience to let it take effect."

With domestic friction heating up, Bush and Baker

increased their efforts on the diplomatic front, pushing for a Security Council resolution to approve the use of military force. The President used a Paris summit for the Conference on Security and Cooperation in Europe to round up support from 33 other national leaders. He won quick agreement, as Margaret Thatcher had predicted, from France's François Mitterrand. Mikhail Gorbachev proved more elusive. The two Presidents dined together, but when Gorbachev appeared reluctant to endorse the force resolution, a planned joint news conference was scrapped to avoid underscoring the differences.

After Paris, while Bush visited U.S. troops in the gulf for Thanksgiving (and, on the way home, Syria's Hafez Assad), Baker split off in an effort to woo Security Council members as far afield as Yemen, Colombia and Los Angeles, where the Foreign Minister of Malaysia signed on. The extra pains that Bush and Baker took stood the Administration well when the U.S. called the vote on Nov. 29, just before rotating out of the council presidency. By a 12-to-2 vote, with only leftist Yemen and Cuba in dissent and China abstaining, the Security Council approved Resolution 678, authorizing the use of force to expel Iraq from Kuwait if Saddam failed to withdraw by Jan. 15.

Within 18 hours of the U.N. triumph, Bush made a surprise announcement to soften the impact of the action, which had now set the nation on a 47-day countdown to war. In a decision aimed as much at quieting domestic opposition as at finding a diplomatic solution, Bush invited Iraqi Foreign Minister Tariq Aziz to Washington and said he would send Baker to Baghdad to talk directly to Saddam. By offering to "go the extra mile for peace," Bush confounded many of his critics and punctured escalating congressional efforts to broker the crisis. Baker would not go to Baghdad to make any concessions, the President stressed, but solely to ensure that Saddam Hussein "understands the commitment of the U.S." to "implementing to a T" the U.N. resolutions. The President not only refused to give an inch but even hardened his position. Since Aug. 8, his stated objective had been to expel Iraq from Kuwait. Now he wanted more. The "status-quo ante will not be enough," Bush asserted. The U.S. wanted to cut down Iraq's military strength and abolish its potential to wage nuclear, chemical or biological warfare. And Bush knew that war was the only way to guarantee that.

Why the tougher stance? In large part, Bush had been reassured by the international vote of confidence given him by the U.N. But there was also a personal reason. The President had been reading Amnesty International's reports of Iraqi atrocities in Kuwait, not just hundreds of cases of murder but 38 types of torture, from electric-shock treatment to cutting out tongues and eyes. "Good God," said Bush, "it is so powerful, you won't be able to believe it." Saddam was evil, the President was convinced. He could no longer simply pull back with impunity.

Saddam responded, promising to free all his hostages. As many as 4,000, including 750 Americans, could be home by Christmas. The Iraqi leader appeared to be betting that his gesture would make it harder for Bush to gain support for an attack. It was another miscalculation. Bush welcomed the hostage release, but insisted that the gesture would have no impact on his decision. "I'm not in a negotiating mood," he declared. In private, he was more explicit. "One less thing to worry about," he told aides. But Bush wasn't above miscalculating either. In his Man of the Year interview with TIME, the President predicted, "My gut says he will get out of there."

Over the next two weeks Bush and Saddam jockeyed over dates for Aziz to come to Washington and Baker to fly to Baghdad. The President had erred in offering any date in the month between Dec. 15 and Jan. 15. When Saddam finally designated Jan. 12, Bush balked. Too close to the deadline. Iraq could not comply in three days with the message that Baker would be delivering. Pull out or else. Washington insisted on an earlier meeting, which caused yet more inconclusive fencing.

With the deadline looming, Bush passed up his annual Texas Christmas vacation and turkey shoot in favor of Camp David's proximity and tranquillity. Bush is not by nature contemplative, but on his return to the White House on New Year's Day, two weeks from the deadline, he had thought through his final doubts about sending the country to war. He no longer worried about criticism. He was convinced he was right. Saddam could not be allowed to succeed in any way.

European and Arab mediators were still attempting a variety of free-lance diplomatic initiatives. Too professional a politician to surrender his advantage, Bush offered Saddam one last chance. He would send Baker to Geneva to meet Tariq Aziz. Bush was confident, but his presidency was on the line. He wanted to deny any opportunity to outsiders to meddle in the crisis. The showdown was now between him and Saddam.

On Jan. 9, Baker and Aziz met for 6 hrs. 27 min. in the Salle des Nations, a spartan ground-floor meeting room in Geneva's Hotel Intercontinental. Because Bush suspected that Aziz would not pass on America's

real intentions to his chief, the President wrote Saddam a personal letter that was so uncompromising Aziz declined to deliver it. Instead, he complained at length that the U.S., the West, Israel and other Arab states had conspired against Iraq. Even the Soviet Union, its old mentor, had failed Baghdad. "If the Soviets had not collapsed, we would not be in this position," Aziz said. "They would have vetoed every one of the Security Council resolutions."

Baker called the President as soon as the meeting broke up. "No progress," he reported. The secretary hurried downstairs to tell journalists, who were speculating that the length of the meeting meant the two sides were doing more than reiterating rigid positions. No such luck. "Regrettably," Baker began to explain.

That same day, another call went from Geneva to Baghdad. This was from Barzan Tikriti, Saddam's half brother, who sat on Aziz's right throughout the meeting, making his own assessment. The Americans are weak, he reported. They have no stomach for a fight.

Baker flew the next day from Geneva to Riyadh to brief King Fahd and, as agreed, to get his approval for the coalition to begin the air war from Saudi territory. The monarch agreed. Two days later, on Jan. 12, both houses of Congress voted to back Bush if he chose to use force after the Jan. 15 deadline. The House vote was overwhelming; the Senate, by a margin of only five votes.

In the White House on Jan. 15, a relaxed and confident George Bush summoned Defense Secretary Dick Cheney to the Oval Office and, as Commander in Chief, signed the National Security directive ordering his troops to battle. He gave Saddam one full day's grace for face, so the Iraqi could explain, perhaps only to himself, that he had not caved in to a deadline. Then the skies over Baghdad erupted.

Heavy casualties were predicted; like generations of warriors before him, a solitary Marine waits and wonders.

A Massive Attack from Sea And Sky

For millions of people, the Persian Gulf war broke live just after the start of the evening TV news on Jan. 16. ABC's Gary Shepard was the first American correspondent to interrupt his broadcast from Baghdad to announce that he could hear explosions rattling Iraq's capital. The camera abruptly shifted to the night sky. It was filled with intermittent flashes, the spearing glow of tracer rounds from antiaircraft guns, sporadic flames on the distant horizon. The time in the gulf was 2:35 a.m., eight hours ahead of the White House. Before he lost contact with ABC anchorman Peter Jennings in New York City, Shepard declared, "An air raid is under way."

That was quite an understatement. The U.S. had just transformed Operation Desert Shield into Desert Storm— starting with a massive series of bombing strikes on Iraq's aerial defenses and communications centers. More than 100 Tomahawk cruise missiles, which the U.S. had never before fired in anger, blasted off warships besieging the Persian Gulf. Hugging the sea and flying at the speed of a commercial airliner, the missiles swept in below Iraq's air-defense radar to explode within 20 yds. of their targets. Equally elusive, scores of Air Force F-117A Stealth fighter-bombers lifted off from airfields in Saudi Arabia, streaked across the border and unleashed their smart bombs with lethal accuracy. Simultaneously, F-4G Wild Weasel planes picked up Iraq's search radar and released their

From the battleship *Wisconsin*, a Tomahawk cruise missile hurtles skyward toward Iraq.

Baghdad by night: bomb blasts and tracer rounds from antiaircraft fire. "I could see the outline of Baghdad

lit up like a giant Christmas tree," said one U.S. pilot. "The entire city was just sparkling."

A guard in gas mask examines the charred fuselage of a Soviet-built Iraqi Scud missile that landed in Riyadh.

HARM missiles to home in on the signals and destroy the ground stations. Other allied aircraft laden with electronics jammed any remaining defensive radar.

On a sixth-floor balcony in Baghdad's al-Rasheed Hotel, a British TV correspondent watched in amazement as a Tomahawk cruise missile glided past him at eye level. "I have covered many wars," he reported, "but this was the most extraordinary sight I have seen. It shot past with relatively little noise, unerringly streaking toward its target, which was the Defense Ministry, and scored a direct hit."

The first fierce air strikes left President Saddam Hussein's radar defenses blinded, crippled or bypassed. When antiaircraft batteries belatedly fired their conventional artillery ("triple-A") and surface-to-air missiles (SAMs) to challenge the air invaders, they could only spray the sky in uncoordinated and ineffective barrages. Incredibly, the allies' high-tech air attack had achieved on that very first day what General Colin Powell, Chairman of the U.S. Joint Chiefs of Staff,

would quickly describe as "tactical surprise." Rarely in history had a war started on such a precise and public timetable.

Taking full advantage of the Iraqis' initial shock and feeble response, wave after wave of allied planes struck priority targets deep in Iraq and occupied Kuwait. Such advanced American fighter-bombers as the F-15E Eagles and the F-16 Fighting Falcons attacked with laser- or TV-guided precision bombs. So did the Navy's F/A-18 Hornets, rising off carriers in the gulf and as far away as the Red Sea. The reliable A-6 Intruders, veterans of Vietnam combat, joined the assault. Even the high-flying and aged B-52 bombers that have been targeted against the Soviet Union for decades released their 750-lb. old-fashioned free-fall bombs. The French sent their Jaguar fighter-bombers to pound an Iraqi air base near Kuwait City. The British, employing low-flying Tornado jets, took on the dangerous task of ripping up enemy airfields with special JP-233 runway-cratering bombs.

The allies' initial air attacks had been so swift, numerous and accurate that few Iraqi pilots had even been able to get into the air to engage the attackers. Those that did were quickly shot down or fled to safer havens in northern Iraq. Demonstrating a mastery of air-to-air combat that would last throughout the war, the superbly trained allied pilots used their superior Sidewinder and Sparrow air-to-air missiles with deadly efficiency. They did not lose a single aircraft to Iraq's Soviet-built MiGs, Su-25s or French Mirages.

"I could see the outline of Baghdad lit up like a giant Christmas tree," said U.S. Air Force Captain Steve Tate after landing his F-15 at a Saudi base. "The entire city was just sparkling at us. They were shooting triple-A. You saw the concussions, the bombs going off and some fires." Tate had fired a radar-guided Sparrow missile at a Mirage F-1 from a distance of 12 miles. "When the airplane blew up, it lit up the whole sky. It was a huge fireball. You are so busy, you do not have time for feelings."

The allied airmen enjoyed another huge advantage: the constantly scanning electronic eyes of E-3 AWACS surveillance planes staring down from high altitudes to spot any emerging threat. Their crews instantly warned the friendly flyers. In darkened cockpits, sophisticated night-vision equipment turned the celebrated claim of U.S. pilots into more than just a boast. "We own the night," they had long declared—and they promptly proved it.

The Pentagon statistics on the first 14 hours of the air war were spectacular: more than 1,000 flights, or "sorties" in military language (about half of them were refueling, escort and other support missions), had been directed at the enemy; 80% of the combat sorties had been considered "successful." That meant the attackers had released bombs at their assigned targets, although the damage was uncertain. All told, a punishing 18,000 tons of explosives had been unloaded. That was only 2,000 tons less than the power of the atom bomb dropped on Hiroshima in the closing days of World War II. Only three allied jets (one American, one British and one Kuwaiti) had been shot down by ground fire.

The goal of all that firepower, of course, had been to seize control of the air. Both the radar facilities that could detect the attacking aircraft and the electronic equipment that could direct fire against them had been hit hard. So too had the command-and-control facilities from which any coordinated counterattack against the attacking aircraft would come. The same goal was pursued through bombing air bases, rupturing runways and tearing apart parked Iraqi jets, whether exposed in the open or protected in shelters.

It took Saddam Hussein's air-defense forces only a short time to realize that they were caught in a dilemma. If they turned on their radar so that they could accurately fire their SAMs, they risked sudden death from the allies' signal-chasing missiles. If they kept their radar off, their own antiaircraft missiles flew "dumb" with little effect.

"The day we launched the air attack, I said, 'We got 'em,'" General H. Norman Schwarzkopf, the gruff but eloquent four-star commander of the allied forces, was to recall much later. "We took their air away."

"Stormin' Norman" had been mulling the air-war strategy since shortly after Saddam barged into Kuwait on Aug. 2. By October the plan had been polished and perfected. "It was executable right down to a gnat's eyelash," Schwarzkopf declared. "It was ready to go." In mid-October he presented the scheme to President Bush and his top advisers in the White House. "The air-campaign plan watered their eyes, it was so good," he said. "It really was good."

The focus of the plan was to destroy what Schwarzkopf, citing Clausewitz, called Saddam's "center of gravity—that thing that if you destroy it, you destroy his ability to wage war. The centers of gravity were Saddam Hussein himself because of the highly centralized leadership. I don't mean personally destroyed. I mean the ability to function. No. 2, the Republican Guard. And No. 3, his chemical, biological and nuclear capability. It doesn't take a genius to figure out that if those three things are gone, his ability to wage war is to all intents and purposes finished."

Thus after blinding Iraq's air defenses, the bombers and Tomahawks (some from warships in the Red Sea and even from a submarine) blasted strategic targets all across Iraq. From the very first moments, the allies went well beyond the official mission of just forcing Saddam's troops out of Kuwait. His budding nuclear research facilities, chemical-weapons factories and biological production plants were pounded early and repeatedly. This would, of course, make him less menacing to the allied forces, although he was believed to have ample and well-dispersed stocks of chemicals in the field. More significantly in the long run, depriving him of weapons of mass destruction would make Iraq far less of a threat to its neighbors in the future.

The first allied attacks also crippled electric-power plants, disrupted radio and telephone circuits, and wiped entire floors off key government buildings in central Baghdad. The aim was to "decapitate" the Iraqi military by cutting off its commanders from their entrenched forces far to the south in Kuwait. "Command and control is the brain of a military system," explained a senior Air Force planner. "Without the brain, the hands holding the weapons can do nothing."

Some of the early targets, including Baathist Party headquarters, the Defense Ministry and Saddam's hometown of Tikrit, seemed, despite Schwarzkopf's denials, to have been chosen for a more personal decapitation mission. If so, it was one of the air war's few failures. Saddam survived.

The early stages of the aerial onslaught were so devastating that advocates of air power contended that, for the first time in military history, victory might be achieved without the need for ground troops to take heavy casualties as they rooted out the enemy. That argument has been heard before, but it has always proved deceptive. Hitler's great blitz could not break the spirit of London in 1940, nor could extensive Allied bombing defeat Nazi Germany. U.S. air commanders had talked of bombing Vietnam "back into the stone age," but that did not bring victory.

"There was a body of people in and out of government and throughout the world who thought the air option alone would do the job," Schwarzkopf said later. "However, Colin Powell and I understood very early on that a strategic-bombing campaign in and of itself had never won a war and had never forced anybody to do anything if they wanted to sit it out. I don't think he and I ever believed exclusively that that would be it."

Still, there had never been a purer test of what superiority in the air could accomplish. Unlike the jungles of Vietnam, the bleak desert stretching across much of Kuwait and southern Iraq offered troops, tanks and artillery few natural places to hide. Saddam's forces were dug in and dispersed, but they could not move without being seen. Never had such an open, exposed battlefield been under such total surveillance by camera-carrying aircraft and space-based spy satellites. Any substantial troop movement would be detected, even at night, and would invite quick destruction from the air.

The growing euphoria over the possibility that the war might be relatively painless led President George Bush to inject a more sober note. Said he: "There will be losses. There will be obstacles along the way. War is never cheap or easy."

The war was only into its second night, in fact, when Saddam managed to employ a weapon designed to inflict pain on civilian populations far from the battle-field. He launched eight Soviet-built Scud missiles from sites in western Iraq. Uncontrollable once in flight, they looped on ballistic trajectories over Jordan to re-enter the atmosphere above Israel. Six of the 350-lb. conventional warheads detonated in Tel Aviv and two farther north in Haifa.

While inconsequential as a military threat to the allied forces, the impact of the terror weapon was magnified as it, too, landed live on worldwide TV screens. The arcing trail of the Scuds, sometimes even the flash of their explosion, was caught by cameras as network correspondents rushed to put on their gas masks. Israelis, terrified at first, feared that the Scuds carried chemicals or biological weapons. Warned by wailing air-raid sirens, they hurried into rooms in their homes, which had been sealed at doors and windows with tape and plastic film. Fortunately, the first Scuds did little damage. But three elderly Israeli women and a three-year-old girl suffocated in their gas masks.

The Scud immediately became a political as well as a terror weapon—and one that was to divert a significant portion of the allied air strikes away from more militarily useful targets. In fact, nearly half the sorties flown in the first two weeks of the war were assigned to anti-Scud missions. That had not been part of the allied air plan.

Saddam obviously hoped to provoke Israel into retaliating. If Israel did so, there was a danger that such Arab nations as Egypt and Syria might pull back from their military commitment to the coalition of 28 nations arrayed against Iraq. Israel did indeed have plans to invade western Iraq both by air and with special ground forces to wipe out the Scud launchers. But U.S. officials exerted all the pressure they could to keep the Israelis on the sidelines. Washington promised new military and financial aid; it also vowed to search out the Scuds.

But finding and destroying the Scud launchers quickly became one of the air war's most vexing puzzles. Israeli intelligence estimated that Iraq had acquired 65 missile launchers from the Soviets. Just how many were designed to fire only from fixed sites was uncertain. Some could be moved, quickly set up to fire their missiles, then taken into hiding. In addition, the Iraqis had found a way to put rails on ordinary flatbed trucks and raise them to fire a Scud; then the trucks would scoot away. There was no way for allied airmen, even though relatively free to roam the skies, to be sure where all these various mobile launchers were, or how many Saddam had.

On just one day in the war's first week, the allies

An F-14 Tomcat roars off a carrier in the Red Sea to press the allied bombing campaign. Total of explosives dropped: 88,500 tons.

sent five waves of fighter-bombers to attack known or suspected Scud sites in western Iraq. The aircraft destroyed six. But just three days later, 10 of the missiles were lofted toward Riyadh and Dhahran in Saudi Arabia. One fell short in the gulf. All the others were intercepted by U.S. Patriot missile batteries, the converted antiaircraft system that was to become one of the high-tech marvels of the war.

The U.S. promptly sent two of the $1 million-a-shot Patriot batteries, operated by American crews, to help defend Israel. Its own army was still training to operate two batteries it had acquired earlier. This was the first direct military defense of Israel ever initiated by U.S. forces. And though Israeli officials repeatedly claimed the right to retaliate, they acquiesced in U.S. requests for restraint. Even though one Scud later destroyed more than 20 buildings in Tel Aviv, injuring at least 90 residents, a top Israeli defense official declared, "For us to attack Iraq now is like throwing a match on a bonfire."

"Christ, a missile has just gone right past my position!" yelled a startled British Royal Air Force corporal into his radio at a sentry post in Saudi Arabia. "It's sitting on its tail and climbing into the sky." It was a Patriot heading to intercept an incoming Scud. In R.A.F. slang, "a goat was on the loose" (translation: "This should not be happening"). The early Scuds, in fact, unnerved airmen in blast-proof shelters as much as they did civilians. Then there was an explosion in the sky. The Scud was blown to smithereens.

After just one week of the largest sustained air campaign in history on such a compact area, General Powell declared that the allies had achieved "air superiority." He reported that only five of Iraq's 66 airfields were still operational enough to send up an occasional jet. More than 10,000 sorties had been flown, and only 16 allied aircraft had been lost to ground fire. In 19 encounters between U.S. and Iraqi jets, the score in kills was U.S. 19, Iraq 0. But there had been one infuriating development: Iraq had captured at least seven allied airmen and had displayed them on TV. Bruised, dazed and speaking in stilted language that was clearly coerced, a few of them criticized the U.S. for attacking Iraq.

43

And Saddam still had a large fleet of combat aircraft, estimated at nearly 700, which included some of the Soviets' best: the MiG-29 Fulcrum, MiG-25 Foxbat and Su-24 Fencer. He even had two IL-76 Mainstays, airborne early-warning aircraft somewhat akin to the U.S. AWACS. But so far as is known, they never took to the air. Rumors quickly spread that Saddam was so angered at the performance of his air force that he ordered the execution of its top three commanders.

Still, the air power assembled by the allies was overwhelming—a fleet of more than 1,800 planes flown by pilots from no fewer than 10 nations: the U.S., Britain, France, Canada, Italy, Saudi Arabia, Qatar, Kuwait, Bahrain and the United Arab Emirates. The radar-evading F-117A Stealth fighter-bomber, which had botched a showcase assignment in the U.S. invasion of Panama, finally would earn its $42.6 million price tag. Defense Secretary Dick Cheney later was to say the low-profile bat-winged jet found its targets on 90% of its missions. Also effective were the American F-15s, F-16s, F-111s, A-6 Intruders and A-10 Thunderbolts (which are so hideous that airmen call them Warthogs). The British Buccaneer, Jaguar and Tornado fighter-bombers also starred. The French Mirage proved far more effective when piloted by the French than when flown by the Iraqis, who lost the two they committed to aerial combat.

The low-level Tornado attacks on airports had a high cost. Six Tornadoes were lost early in the war. The daylight missions were the worst because the Iraqi triple-A gunners could see the attackers. "There is a great deal of difference between the veil of darkness and a spring morning in a desperately flat open desert," said R.A.F. navigator Gary Stapleton after a sortie in which one Tornado was shot down. "We went in that far and survived, but we came back in tears. We work together, play together, live together. Hopefully, we won't die together."

Some of the air strikes had already shaken up Saddam's Republican Guard, the reputedly crack troops posted mainly astride the Iraq-Kuwait border. The B-52s, in particular, pounded Guard positions with their thunderous bombs. They also dropped 500-lb. bombs with delayed fuses. The noses penetrated the Iraqi shelters before the warheads exploded. "It makes life in the bunkers very uncomfortable," said a Pentagon official. If the Republican Guard could be demoral-

ized, the U.S. commanders seemed to assume, Saddam's lesser forces might fold.

An old Vietnam observer showed up in Dhahran and rebutted arguments that the B-52s would be no more effective now than they had been in that war. He remembered that the Viet Cong had sometimes climbed right out of their holes after a B-52 raid to fight as ferociously as ever. But he added, "The difference is that the V.C. were mostly armed with small weapons that they could carry with them. The Republican Guard depends on heavy armor and tanks. It is hard to take that kind of equipment down into a bunker with you."

Gradually, Powell said, the air strikes would spread to interdict supplies flowing from the Baghdad area to the southeastern center of Basra and on to the troops in or near Kuwait. In one of the war's most chilling, and prophetic, statements, he predicted what would happen to the army occupying Kuwait: "First we're going to cut it off, and then we're going to kill it."

The precision of the allied bombing was dramatized by American and British press briefers, who showed videotapes of the attacking airmen's view. A laser beam fingered the target. The weapons officer centered his cross hairs on the pinpoint of light. He released his bombs. They raced unerringly to follow the beam—recording their own approach by means of TV cameras.

In one case a bomb flew right down the air shaft of the Iraqi Defense Ministry. In another strike the explosives found the very center of a tall air-force building, and its top floors suddenly disappeared. "This is my counterpart's headquarters," said a proud Lieut. General Charles Horner, commander of the U.S. Air Force, as he pointed out the devastation on a video screen.

The shows were meant to prove that allied bombing was not indiscriminate. Military installations were the targets, and the smart bombs rarely missed. As unusually cloudy weather moved into the area, allied air crews were even ordered to bring their expensive ordnance back from their runs rather than risk releasing the explosives on obscured ground facilities that might be inhabited by civilians. While the weapons' infrared- and TV-guidance systems could generally find their targets through clouds and fog, the air crews had a self-protective reason for aborting these missions. The pilots could not see the SAMs that the Iraqis still sometimes fired. In good weather the way to escape a SAM was to zig and zag out of its closing path.

When the skies did clear, the allies sharply in-

At dawn, a deck crew readies an F/A-18 Hornet for flight. Said a general: "We've got plenty of targets and plenty of airplanes."

44

creased their air campaign. They had been averaging about 2,000 sorties a day. On one day in the second week they flew 2,700—without losing a single aircraft. The lack of serious resistance to the rolling waves of attacking bombers was explained by one of President Bush's top war advisers: "Saddam is hunkering down and not fighting an air war that he can't win. We know how to keep most of his aircraft from taking off, and when they do, they get picked off one by one."

Captain Ayedh al-Shamrani, a Saudi pilot flying an F-15, spotted two Iraqi Mirage F-1 jets racing barely above the gulf toward British ships. They carried Exocet missiles, the potent French-made weapon that nearly had sunk the U.S. frigate Stark *in a mistaken attack in 1987. Shamrani closed to within 3,000 ft. of the Iraqi jets. "They started breaking in front of me, but it was too late," he recalled afterward. "You know the F-15. Nobody can beat it." Shamrani blew up both Mirages with his missiles. "I just rolled in behind them and shot them down," he said. "It was easy." He became the air war's first hero.*

Saddam was so leery of engaging allied air power that he began sending some of his best aircraft on short hops across Iraq's eastern border into Iran. The first flights, one or two at a time, led to speculation that the pilots might be defecting. But the number swiftly grew and eventually reached 147. It was obvious that Iraq had reached some kind of agreement with its bitter enemy to provide a refuge for the planes.

"It's definitely not defections," a U.S. intelligence official told reporters. "Some of them have been escorted into Iran by Iraqi planes, and then the escorts have flown back." Iranian officials insisted that the planes and their crews would be detained until the war was over. But U.S. military commanders feared that the parked jets might yet join the battle when, and if, the allies launched a full-scale ground offensive. Saddam might be saving them to fight when they could serve his purpose best. There was always the possibility of a last, desperate suicide attack by Iraqi pilots.

Schwarzkopf never relaxed. He knew that the allies still had what he called "several Achilles' heels." He ticked them off: "Take Riyadh air base. AWACS after AWACS after AWACS lined up next to refueler after refueler after refueler. You know, three good fighter planes making a run down there could have taken out huge assets. I can't tell you how many nights I turned to

Laden with deadly missiles and night-fighting infrared equipment, a team of F-16 fighter planes prepares for a takeoff at sunset.

An F/A-18 Hornet flies on patrol over toxic clouds spewing from Kuwait's devastated oil wells.

Said an American: "Saddam has lost his marbles."

Chuck Horner and said, 'Now, you guarantee me they can't come through, right?' " Schwarzkopf also fretted about the massive supplies being stockpiled near Dhahran: "All you have to do is to stand in Dhahran and look at the huge amounts of equipment we were bringing in there." It presented an inviting, if well-defended, target. But Saddam's pilots apparently had no kamikaze zeal.

The freedom of allied aircraft to fly virtually unchallenged over Kuwait proved invaluable when Saddam suddenly began spewing oil into the gulf. The spill was originally estimated by the Saudis at 460 million gals., which would have been the worst oil pollution in history. But later estimates placed it at 126 million gals., smaller than the 1979-80 spill in the Gulf of Mexico but still one of the biggest ever. The oil began spreading southward from Sea Island terminal, a tanker-loading facility 10 miles off the Kuwaiti coast. Then, in another display of pinpoint accuracy, four U.S. F-111 fighter-bombers attacked the two land stations that controlled the flow to the underwater pipelines feeding the off-shore terminal. Their laser-guided bombs, in effect, turned off the spigots. Now the oil seeped into the porous ground instead of the sea.

But just what had the awesome display of aerial firepower, the sheer numbers of combat missions and the wizardry of the weapons accomplished? The allied commanders had no way of being certain. While pilots told of seeing flames sometimes still visible 200 miles from the targets they had hit, no airman ever belittles his exploits. Interpreters pored over fighter-aircraft films, air-reconnaissance photographs and satellite pictures. But bomb-damage assessments remained murky.

Even after the devastating allied attacks on air-fields, the Iraqi engineers were proving more proficient than expected in repairing the surfaces. Many of the scattered air bases required continual revisits from the bombers. One expert on land warfare explained, "Saddam has a secret weapon: the bulldozer."

No less troublesome were the clever tricks adopted by the Iraqis to deceive their tormentors. They deployed fake tanks made of plywood or fiber glass. They set heaters inside empty concrete tank and aircraft shelters to attract missiles by simulating the infrared signature of engines. They ignited pails of oil inside or on top of protective bunkers to fool pilots into thinking the contents already were ablaze. And black circles painted on roofs of military installations, or even on runways, depicted bomb damage that had not occurred.

The Iraqis were not always smart. On one night a line

of Iraqi tanks, armored personnel carriers and supply trucks rolled across the open desert just north of the Saudi Arabian border. A patrolling squadron of U.S. Marine Harrier jets attacked the exposed column. In the first major strike at moving Iraqi armor, they destroyed 24 of the vehicles. Allied troops across the border could still see the flames the next morning. Said Marine Colonel Ron Richard: "They were sloppy, and they were caught."

Marine Lieut. Colonel Dick White spotted a similar column of 20 vehicles from his Harrier jet. He led strikes that killed them all. "We rolled in and made two bombing passes and strafed with 25-mm cannons and left the entire column in flames," he said. "Saddam has lost his marbles. It's opposed to all military logic."

Yet the air war, however splendidly successful, had its human costs. The worst single American loss was that of an Air Force AC-130H Spectre. The large plane, a gunship version of the troop transport, was shot down by ground fire over the northern portion of the gulf. The 14 servicemen in it were missing and later presumed dead. Still, after nearly 30,000 combat sorties, flown at a rate of one per minute, the U.S. had lost only 12 aircraft. All were hit by triple-A or SAMs, none by an opposing jet fighter.

Inevitably, just as in peacetime training, there were noncombat—but equally fatal—accidents. In one especially bad day, the U.S. lost three airplanes to what appeared to be mechanical problems. A B-52 Stratofortress returning from a bombing run to its base on the island of Diego Garcia ditched in the Indian Ocean. Three of its six crewmen were rescued; the others were lost. Two helicopters, an AH-1 Cobra carrying two Marines and a UH-1 Huey with four Marines, crashed in Saudi Arabia. There were no survivors.

Allied airmen forced to eject behind enemy lines were not abandoned. In the first such rescue, U.S. pilots saw a truck carrying Iraqi soldiers heading toward a downed American airman. As it got closer, a U.S. helicopter and two A-10 Warthogs swooped down on the site. One of the Warthog pilots cut loose with his modernized Gatling gun. The truck turned into a lump of twisted metal. The chopper swiftly landed, picked up the pilot and carried him to safety. Multiservice rescue teams were always poised to perform this kind of mission.

Harder to accept were the deaths of U.S. soldiers and Marines who were mistakenly attacked by American air crews. An ever-present danger anytime aircraft operate in close support of troops, the fatalities bore out an Army aphorism expressed by Lieut. General Thomas Kelly, the Pentagon's top operations officer: "Once a bullet leaves a gun, it has no friends."

The first death by friendly fire occurred during the initial serious ground clashes of the war. Iraq had sent four battalion-size probes across the Kuwait border into Saudi Arabia, one of them driving to occupy temporarily the vacated coastal town of Khafji. Farther to the west, U.S. Marines on the ground and Air Force jets swung into action to repel them. The pilot of a tank-killing Warthog directed a Maverick missile at a moving ground target. It turned out to be an armored personnel carrier containing seven Marines. All died.

U.S. commanders warned their air crews against such accidents and took steps to improve the identification of friendly ground vehicles. Fluorescent orange sheets were rigged on the top of various APCs. Some U.S. troops began wearing armbands that emitted infrared signals so the airmen above them would know not to attack. But the problem was to persist throughout the war.

At one point an Army lieutenant colonel was removed from command of an Apache helicopter battalion after the officer's unit had reportedly fired 100 Hellfire missiles at trucks and other "soft" targets. More important, the colonel had personally aimed Hellfires at two vehicles that, unknown to him, carried U.S. soldiers. Two died and six were wounded. In addition to his concern about air crews' attacking the wrong army, Schwarzkopf warned his subordinates against the extravagant firing of costly missiles at relatively insignificant targets.

At a base in Saudi Arabia, U.S. Army Colonel James Riley, an Apache squadron commander, lectured his pilots. "You use a flyswatter on a fly," he said. "You save your best ammo for appropriate targets." The Hellfire missiles are so expensive ($53,000) that his air crews had rarely been allowed to test-fire them. But the Apache is designed to attack from long distances, which makes identification of small ground targets difficult. Lieut. Colonel Bill Hatch, another Apache leader, predicted grimly, "If I start shooting, I am going to take out some friendlies."

Still, the casualties were minimal in relation to the scale of the air operations. And despite the uncertain-

The Iraqis achieve little success with their French-built Mirages: one lies in ruin in a devastated hangar near the Kuwait border.

ties, the successes were significant. At the halfway point in the air war, Iraqi fuel supplies had been so depleted by the bombing that civilians could no longer buy gas for cars, cooking or heating. All was saved for the military.

"We decided at the outset that we did not want to destroy the oil-production capability of Iraq," Schwarzkopf later explained. "We did not want to bomb it back into the stone age. When this was over we wanted Iraq to continue to be an economically viable country. What we did want to destroy was their ability to refine petroleum products and to continue to deliver gasoline to the military so the military could conduct the war."

The nightly pounding of facilities near Baghdad knocked out all electricity in the capital except that produced by emergency generators. Saddam and his top commanders were forced to use unsecure short-range radio or slow alternative means, including couriers, for getting messages to and from troops in the Kuwait theater of operations. Saddam began moving his command-and-control facilities to the city's fringes, even into schools. Some aircraft, too, were shifted to civilian neighborhoods.

"We will not target civilian areas," declared U.S. Major General Robert Johnston at a briefing in Riyadh. Schwarzkopf added his assurance. "Yes, sure, it gives them an advantage," he said. "But we are not going to reduce ourselves to that level of immoral conduct."

As the bombing focused increasingly on interdiction of military supplies, 33 of 36 targeted bridges crossing the Euphrates and Tigris rivers were attacked. The Iraqis struggled to span the water with pontoon replacements, but truck convoys backed up. One such line of stalled vehicles along the main supply route from Baghdad to Basra extended for 15 miles. U.S. commanders estimated that the normal daily movement of 20,000 tons of military food, fuel and other supplies to Kuwait had at times been slashed to a mere 2,000 tons.

At sea, U.S. Navy and Marine jets not only roared off carriers to join the bombardment but also strafed and sank numerous Iraqi minelaying vessels and gunboats. British ships, too, dispatched fighter aircraft and helicopter gunships to nullify Saddam's small navy. When Saddam ordered his naval captains to emulate much of his air force by taking their ships to safe harbors in Iran, few made it. They were spotted from the air and sunk or

Sunlight pours through a gaping hole made by an allied bomb in the reinforced-concrete roof of a building on Saadun Street in Baghdad.

disabled. Midway through the war, American commanders declared that the Iraqi navy was no longer a serious threat. Twenty-four vessels, some equipped with Exocet and Soviet antiship missiles capable of crippling all but the largest warship, had been destroyed. Another 31 had been heavily damaged.

Saddam's air force, too, had been sharply depleted. U.S. commanders in Riyadh reported that 99 Iraqi planes had been blasted on the ground. Nineteen had been knocked out of the air in dogfights. An additional 89 had darted off to Iran. And an unknown number of planes had been hit but not certifiably destroyed. Thus nearly a third of Iraq's air fleet was out of action. The allies had seized clear control of both the air and the sea.

There was one not so incidental by-product of all the bombing: Schwarzkopf revealed that "the Baghdad nuclear-research center has been leveled to rubble." But some 540,000 entrenched Iraqi troops, presumably armed with chemical weapons, had still to be overcome. Schwarzkopf reported that the air pounding was shaking the will of Saddam's troops. "We began to see a cracking of his military," he said. "We had many reports of mass desertions. We got reports that his people were being kept in the trenches at gunpoint."

It was time to assess the air war's progress at the highest levels. President Bush announced on Feb. 5 that he would send Secretary Cheney and General Powell to the war theater to find out whether air power alone "will get the job done." Bush said he was "skeptical" about the possibility of avoiding a final all-out land-air-sea assault to dislodge Iraqis from Kuwait.

En route to Saudi Arabia, Cheney told reporters that a "next stage" in the war probably would be necessary. Some air strategists still argued that the high risks of a ground offensive need not be undertaken. Yes, it would take longer for air power alone to crush the Iraqis, but they could eventually be isolated, starved and shaken into submission by bombing. Advocating patience, U.S. Air Force Brigadier General Buster Glosson said of Saddam, "Time is not on his side; it is on our side." U.S. Air Force Colonel John McBroom insisted that the Iraqi forces could be "almost completely obliterated" from the air.

Cheney faced a hangar full of U.S. airmen in Saudi Arabia. "You are heart and soul of the most enormously successful air campaign in the history of the world," he declared. Powell addressed a tactical U.S. Air Force wing and drew ringing cheers with another of his terse predictions: "We told Saddam Hussein, 'Move it or lose it.' He wouldn't move it. Now he's going to lose it."

For a time, advocates of air power prevailed. After being briefed by Cheney and Powell, President Bush announced, "The air campaign has been very, very effective, and will continue for a while. We are going to take whatever time is necessary to sort out when a next stage might begin." Explained one of the President's top advisers: "We hoped the pounding would lead the Iraqi army in the Kuwait theater to crack and just give up. It appears that is not going to be the case." But it was still possible, he said, that whatever ground offensive is launched "will be nothing more than a mopping-up operation."

As if eager to prove the validity of their arguments, the allied air commanders increased the already furious tempo of their assault. On one day in the war's fourth week, the daily sorties rose to a record 3,000. Explained General Kelly at a Pentagon briefing: "We've got plenty of targets and plenty of airplanes. The wise thing to do is keep on doing what we are doing."

That meant seeking out any remaining strategic targets that had been missed earlier. Baghdad's residents got no respite from their sleepless nights. Fireballs rose high above the center of the city when U.S. fighter-bombers scored direct hits on two five-story buildings housing the Justice Ministry and the Ministry of Local Government. One of the buildings collapsed.

The allied pilots fought off the tendency to become complacent, or careless, because they were so rarely challenged. They worried about how many SAMS Saddam might have saved. "We go out every night," said Marine Major Thomas McElrath. "And every night we ask ourselves, 'Is this the night he's going to turn it all on and bag us?'" Marine squadron leader Robert McCarthy expressed the same fear: "Is this the night he's just suddenly going to decide to light the sky up?"

Jordanian officials complained bitterly that the allies were even attacking truck tankers used to import oil from Iraq. Refugees along the main Baghdad-to-Amman highway confirmed the air strikes. A score of drivers were reported killed. The allied command insisted that Iraq had been moving its mobile Scud launchers and missiles along the highway, interspersing them with civilian truck convoys.

The brunt of the allied air power turned increasingly toward tactical targets, including what the military calls "battlefield preparation." From Baghdad to Basra, planes struck at bridges the moment there was any sign that repairs had made them usable. They repeatedly blasted the Republican Guard and their tanks and supply depots. Yet a high Administration official conceded, "The numbers and dispersal of ammunition dumps and supply locations have been higher than expected and have required more sorties than expected."

Iraqi tanks, too, were well protected. The Guard had spaced their armor in earth revetments three to four miles apart. Each circular shelter held about 35 tanks. Effective hits on such targets demanded the kind of precision that only the allies' most sophisticated weapons provided. Explained U.S. Air Force Major General Richard Hawley, one of the key allied planners: "You don't kill dug-in tanks by dropping a bomb 30 meters away in the sand."

The air generals shifted tactics to meet the Iraqi innovations. Unhappy about their slow rate of destroying tanks, they divided the battlefield into square "kill boxes." The squares were scouted in daylight by F-16 pilots, who spotted the sometimes nearly buried tanks. With the targets pinpointed ahead of time, the nightly raids by F-15s and F-111s, using laser-guided bombs and special heat sensors, became much more efficient. The New York *Times* reported that on some nights as many as 200 tanks were knocked out by about 60 attacking jets.

The U.S. employed another high-tech air system with little publicity but great results. Two J-STARS aircraft quickly deployed from Florida watched ground movements as keenly as the AWACS detected and tracked planes in the sky. Thus whenever the Iraqis tried to shift their tanks and supplies in a major way, the allies quickly found out.

Having learned the hard way, the Iraqis began moving supplies a few trucks at a time. The allied response was to let pilots simply "troll" for anything in motion on the ground rather than stick to specific assignments. One surprisingly effective trolling aircraft turned out to be the Marines' plump gray subsonic Intruder. Its two-man crews often flew alone with their lights out, then surprised the Iraqis by releasing 500-lb. Rockeye cluster bombs that broke into 247 "bomblets." The troops called it "steel rain."

On the U.S. aircraft carrier Ranger *in the gulf, pilots at times reported finding so many "targets of opportunity" that the ammunition elevators on their ships could not*

The Iraqis claimed that this destroyed building was a baby-milk factory, but the allies said it was a chemical-weapons plant.

bring the proper weapons to the flight decks fast enough. Their bombs were so specialized for specific targets that the airmen talked about using the "bomb du jour." But now they just loaded their jets with whatever ammo happened to be at hand and took off to strike again. To keep all hands in a martial mood, loudspeakers on the Ranger *blared the Lone Ranger music of the "William Tell" Overture during takeoffs and landings.*

Also pounded ever harder were the frontline troops waiting behind minefields and oil-filled antitank trenches for the long-anticipated ground war to begin. The Iraqis were absorbing a punishment that "no army in history had to endure," observed General Hawley. "It demonstrated that you cannot prevail if you cannot control the air."

Along with bombs, the allied armada dropped 14 million leaflets urging the Iraqi soldiers to surrender and explaining just how to do so. The instructions were explicit: "1—Remove the magazine from your weapon. 2—Sling your weapon over your left shoulder, muzzle down. 3—Have both arms raised above your head. 4—Approach the multinational forces' positions very slowly, with the lead soldier holding this document above his head. 5—If you do this, you will not die."

More than 1,000 took the bait during the first four weeks, relieved to end their nightmarish ordeal. More would have done so, they told their captors, but execution squads from the Republican Guard roamed their ranks, shooting anyone who tried to desert. Even listening to foreign radio broadcasts could mean a quick death. There would be mass defections once the ground war started, some predicted. Said one: "If you kill Saddam Hussein, all this will end."

The early Iraqi defectors straggled across the border in small groups, holding the surrender leaflets high. Then some dropped to their backs and waved their arms and kicked their legs to show that they had no weapons. The bemused allied soldiers came to call this "the dying cockroach mode."

Radio Baghdad had long accused the allied airmen of blasting civilian targets at will, but it cited few specifics or numbers of casualties. Suddenly Saddam decided to escalate this propaganda war. His announcers charged that 150 people, including 35 children, had been killed by bombing raids on Nasiriyah, a southern Iraqi town near the Euphrates River. The broadcasts began claiming that civilian deaths from air raids had soared into the thousands—statistics no one could check.

Then, on Feb. 13, the war's worst tragedy handed Saddam a propaganda windfall. Two U.S. F-117A Stealth fighter-bombers, assigned to destroy a low structure in the Baghdad neighborhood of Amiriya, once again displayed the devastating accuracy of their laser-guided bombs. The two pilots, attacking in predawn darkness, easily found their target. Their warheads tore through the 10-ft.-thick reinforced concrete roof and into several subterranean floors below. There they exploded with terrible consequences.

The next morning, smoke was still seeping from the ruins when TV crews were led to the scene. Charred bodies were dragged out in blankets by rescue workers who had descended through choking fumes and rising water to find them. Even hours after the blast, the heat drove the emergency crews back from the deepest level. The recovered bodies were placed in rows outside what was left of the shattered building. Relatives of the victims cried and pounded the earth in anger and despair, some cursing the reporters. One woman asked in English, "Why? Why?" The scenes appalled viewers throughout the world.

Iraqi officials reported that more than 400 civilians, including many women and children, had been killed in what they insisted was an air-raid shelter. Iraqi Health Minister Abdul-As-Salem Muhammad Saeed denounced the bombing as "a well-planned crime."

U.S. military commanders contended just as firmly that the structure was a bunker housing an active military command-and-control facility. They cited the facility's tall chain-link fence, topped with barbed wire, as incompatible with a civilian shelter. They claimed to have intercepted radio signals from the bunker and to have photographed military vehicles and soldiers outside it. They also said the roof had been camouflaged and painted with dark circles meant to signify previous bomb hits.

But reporters interviewed civilians who said they had been spending nights in the shelter almost since the start of the war. Signs in both Arabic and English marked it as an air-raid shelter. American officers could never adequately explain why, if their surveillance had detected the military movements, it had failed to see such a large number of civilians using the facility.

"We didn't know civilians were in there," said General Kelly at the Pentagon. "We struck it. We suffer remorse as a result." He charged that the placing of civilians in a military structure was not only a violation of the Geneva war conventions but might also have been "intentional."

As much of Baghdad lies in ruins, inhabitants continue a search through the wreckage.

One elderly Iraqi woman was especially effective as she denounced the bombing in English while TV cameras rolled. She was dignified and controlled while eloquently expressing her outrage. TV viewers in France later saw her castigating them just as forcefully at another bomb-damage site—in French. She seemed to be trailing the reporters as Saddam's officials led the way.

A few days later British press briefers candidly admitted that one of their bombers had inflicted casualties on a residential area west of Baghdad. They showed films of a highly accurate strike on a bridge in the town of Fallujah. But one smart bomb, they conceded, had proved to be dumb. It lost its way and slammed into nearby apartments and a marketplace. The devastation was promptly shown to foreign TV cameramen. Iraqi officials said 130 people had died.

American commanders responded by pointing to examples of Iraqi trickery. After the Iraqis charged that allied bombers had attacked a mosque in Basra, Pentagon briefers displayed sketches and an aerial photo of the site. A U.S. bomb had indeed fallen near the

mosque. The crater it left was clear. But the mosque was then undamaged. In a later photograph, the mosque's dome was gone. The arrangement of debris suggested that an explosion had been touched off from under, rather than above, the dome.

There were other deceptions. After leaving Baghdad, a British TV cameraman reported from Amman that he had been taken to an Iraqi hospital to interview "civilian" casualties. But when he discovered that some of the patients were wearing parts of their military uniforms under the bedcovers, his film was confiscated. Some of Iraq's cities, notably Basra, had been badly damaged during the eight years of the Iran-Iraq war. Foreign reporters could not always tell whether the destruction they were shown was fresh.

The few bombing errors by the allies and the ability of Saddam to exploit them increased political pressure on President Bush to speed up a ground offensive. It should not have affected the military planning, but Schwarzkopf admitted that it was "on the back of my mind." He later explained that he kept asking himself a question: "How long would the world stand by and watch the United States pound the living hell out of Iraq with the bombs before saying, 'Enough is enough'?"

Almost lost in the furor over the civilian tragedies was the fact that the air war was steadily weakening the Iraqi military forces. The American command on Feb. 14 released statistics showing a sharp increase in the number of tanks, artillery pieces and armored personnel carriers destroyed by the bombing. The military's numbers: Saddam had lost 1,300 of his 4,280 tanks in the Kuwait theater; 1,100 of his 3,110 artillery pieces; and 850 of his 2,870 APCs. Thus nearly a third of the Iraqi tools of war had been knocked out. General Kelly described the state of the Iraqi army as "perilous."

The Iraqi soldiers who began giving up in small but growing numbers seemed to agree. Said one: "Every night is bomb, bomb, bomb. When we fought Iran, we had breakfast, lunch and dinner every day. Here, there's no water and hardly anything to eat." Noted another: "And when there was a lull in the bombardment, we felt lucky and went out only to find a place to bury our fellows who were killed."

On Feb. 15 Saddam's five-man Revolutionary Command Council made the unexpected announcement that Iraq was ready "to deal" with the U.S. resolution requiring that it withdraw from Kuwait. It set off premature celebrations in Baghdad but had no impact whatever on the pace of the air war. Increasingly, the bombing concentrated on softening up Iraq's frontline defenses. One priority target: the artillery pieces that could fire shells containing chemicals at attacking allied troops. And for the first time, the U.S. used "fuel-air" bombs, a fearsome weapon in which the warhead first releases and then detonates a flammable liquid just above the ground. The resulting horrendous explosion is similar to that of a small battlefield nuclear weapon. The bombs were dropped from low-flying helicopters to clear minefields along the Kuwait border.

As the war's fifth week ended, the number of combat missions flown had passed 88,000. There had, of course, been losses. Twenty-two American and nine other allied aircraft had been shot down by ground fire. Among the 29 U.S. servicemen and one servicewoman missing in action, nearly all were from air crews. There had been 15 combat deaths among Americans and 37 lost in noncombat accidents. Again, the casualties were mostly the result of air operations.

On another particularly bad day, four American

aircraft went down. An Army UH-60 Blackhawk medical evacuation helicopter crashed in northern Saudi Arabia while trying to land in bad weather. Seven of its occupants died. A Marine CH-46 chopper was destroyed in another crash landing, but its more fortunate crew survived. An engine failed on an Air Force F-16 as it was refueling, forcing the pilot to eject. He was not hurt. The Iraqi ground gunners caused the other loss. They shot down an OH-58 Kiowa scout helicopter, killing its two-man crew.

Unfortunately, American soldiers continued to be killed by their colleagues in the air. The toll rose when U.S. Apache helicopters found an Iraqi ground patrol and attacked. They also hit a U.S. M113 APC and a Bradley fighting vehicle. Two Americans died and six were wounded. At this point in the war, only four U.S. soldiers had been killed by enemy guns or shells, while 10 had died under fire from their buddies in the air.

The Apache crews had far more successes than failures. Two of them came across a complex of Iraqi bunkers and were startled to see 52 Iraqi soldiers jump out of their shelters, some waving white cloths. One of the pilots, Warrant Officer Charles Cunningham, later offered an explanation for the surprising surrender: "They probably never saw an Apache before. It's so ugly."

The unprecedented phenomenon of troops giving up in large numbers at the mere sight of approaching helicopters grew. Four U.S. Air Force choppers on a scouting mission flushed an astonishing 421 Iraqis out of their complex of 15 bunkers. All that was required were some pointed suggestions from a helicopter loudspeaker and a few missile bursts. Large Chinook transport choppers had to be called in to ferry the prisoners into Saudi Arabia. As the sixth and final week of the air war began, such incidents seemed to bear out General Schwarzkopf's then controversial declaration that the Iraqi forces were "on the verge of collapse."

In just a few more days of intensified bombing, the attrition of the Iraqi armor and artillery once again jumped dramatically. The new numbers: Iraq had lost 1,685, fully 39%, of its tanks; 1,485, an imposing 48%, of its artillery pieces; and 925, or 32%, of its APCs. In the air, the allies' dogfight dominance remained complete: no Iraqi pilot had been able to shoot down a single opposing fighter. (The final score in aerial combat would be allies 40, Iraq 0.)

Beyond that, 35% of Iraq's combat aircraft were now out of the war. Gone were the 140 parked in Iran and 98 destroyed by the allies (56 on the ground and 42 in combat). The whereabouts of the other 65% remained something of a mystery. Some were sitting in residential areas, even in schoolyards, for protection. Two were sighted next to one of Iraq's most prized archaeological treasures, the more than 50-centuries-old city of Ur. Allied intelligence officers still watched for any signs of a large, desperate Iraqi attack.

Now the sorties flown in the Kuwait theater alone jumped from the normal 700 to 1,000. Nor were the frequently hit earlier targets ignored. The overall air missions were running at just under 3,000 a day.

Returning from an F-111 mission over Kuwait, Air Force Captain Bradley Seipel reported, "It's amazing flying up there. You look at Kuwait, that whole area, it's just fire. The whole military establishment is burning." Said his fellow crewman, Captain Mike Russell: "It's like constant explosions, constant fires. It's just awe-inspiring night after night how we ripped them up."

Then came a different kind of fire. Intercepted radio messages indicated that Saddam had ordered the torching of Kuwait's vast system of oil wells and oil-production facilities. Even in the early days of the Iraqi occupation of the country, refugees had reported that the invaders had begun to wire the oil fields with explosives. Now they began going off. The number of fires reported by Pentagon intelligence officers quickly grew. First it was 145, then 190 and finally more than 500. (After the liberation of Kuwait, the actual count rose past 1,000.) Fully a fourth of Kuwait was covered by clouds of black smoke that turned noon virtually into night.

President Bush was to describe Saddam's tactics as a "scorched earth" policy. American military commanders belittled its significance in the air war. But British officers told reporters that their Jaguar fighter-bombers had to cancel all their missions against Iraqi artillery positions in Kuwait on one morning because they could not spot their targets through the thick smoke. "For those aircraft without night-vision capability," said Group Captain Niall Irving, "it is a problem." As the winds shifted to blow northward, the sometimes toxic fumes may also have been a problem for the Iraqi troops. The pall even reached Baghdad.

The allied briefers continued to emphasize the strikes against the Republican Guard. They claimed that one of the Guard's four mechanized divisions had lost 70% of its vital equipment and that the fighting ca-

A G.I. explores debris of Dhahran barracks, where 28 Americans died from a Scud-missile hit.

pacity of the other three had been cut in half. If true, that level of attrition was approaching the point that would render the Guard vulnerable to an all-out ground assault.

But while publicly highlighting the punishment of the Guard, the allied commanders were actually directing more and more of their air assault at the sections of the frontline fortifications they intended to breach. Swarms of helicopter gunships buzzed across the border to join the B-52s and fighter-bombers in bombing and strafing the confused Iraqi defenders. The entrenched Iraqis had no way of knowing when they might be hit or from what direction. They could only huddle in their holes.

"I just didn't quite envision going up there and shooting the hell out of everything in the dark and have them not know what hit them," said Apache pilot Ron Balak. "A truck blows up to the right. The ground blows up to the left. They had no idea where we were."

There was one telltale sign of the imminence of the final offensive: allied aircraft for the first time dropped napalm—the flaming weapon that had torched Viet Cong bunkers and whole villages in the Vietnam War. Now the flammable gel was used to set oil on fire in the tank-trap trenches along the Kuwait border. The purpose was pre-emptive; instead of waiting for the Iraqis to ignite the wall of flame, the allies would burn off the oil before the ground onslaught began. The jets even took out the elaborate complex of pumping stations and pipelines created by the Iraqis to keep feeding oil to the trenches.

A U.S. Marine near the border watched the trenches burn. He listened to the horrible racket of allied multiple-rocket launchers, howitzers and air-delivered cluster bombs rock the positions of the defending Iraqi troops. Said he: "It's like perching on the rim of hell and waiting for orders to jump in."

Crowds mourn the victims from a bombed Baghdad shelter, which allies said was a military post.

"The Mother Of Battles": 100 Hours

"We're going to go around, over, through, on top, underneath and any way it takes to beat them."
—General H. Norman Schwarzkopf

The countdown to G-day began on Thursday night, Feb. 21. President Bush summoned his top aides to set a final deadline for Saddam Hussein to get out of Kuwait or face a gigantic U.S. ground attack. That evening, as he often does in moments of crisis, the President did a little "prudent recreating." He attended a performance of *Black Eagles,* a drama about black aviators during World War II, at Ford's Theater. The handsomely restored building, about five blocks from the White House, is best known as the place where John Wilkes Booth shot Abraham Lincoln on April 14, 1865. Bush enjoyed the play, applauding vigorously, but his companions could tell he was distracted.

At 10:20 that night, Bush met with the war cabinet in his private study on the second floor of the White House. It was warm for February so the fireplace was dark. On hand were Joint Chiefs of Staff Chairman Colin Powell, Secretary of State James Baker, National Security Adviser Brent Scowcroft, Vice President Dan Quayle, Defense Secretary Dick Cheney, White House press secretary Marlin Fitzwater and other top aides. Quayle and Cheney wore tuxedoes; they had just left a dinner hosted by visiting Queen Margrethe II of Denmark at the Danish ambassador's residence. On the agenda for discussion now were two documents. One was a list

Destruction: U.S. convoy passes Chinese-made T-59 tank blazing in its dugout.

of criteria by which the allies would judge whether an Iraqi withdrawal from Kuwait was unconditional and hence worthy of a cease-fire. The other was a statement explaining why an agreement on Iraqi withdrawal, reached earlier that day by Soviet President Mikhail Gorbachev and Iraqi Foreign Minister Tariq Aziz, was inadequate.

Bush proposed that the two drafts be combined. "It's not enough just to say we don't accept the Soviet plan," he said. "I went through this with Gorbachev on the phone, and he knows it's unacceptable, and he knows the specific reasons why, and we ought to lay them out to the whole world."

"Well, let's set a date and set a time," suggested Powell.

"I think that's a good idea," Bush replied immediately.

Powell then explained that a deadline would be "helpful to the military because then my guys in the field know what to expect. They know exactly what to be looking for and when." Bush wanted the deadline for Saddam's compliance to come as soon as possible; so did Powell. Baker cautioned that the U.S. ultimatum must have allied support and must be seen as allowing a reasonable time for Baghdad to accept.

Powell suggested that noon on Saturday, Feb. 23, be the deadline. "I think that's a good idea," said Bush.

Noon in Washington was 8 p.m. in Kuwait, and the allied forces' superior technology gave them a distinct advantage in night combat.

"It's good for me too," said Baker, "but it is a new item that the allies don't know about and [that] we need to get back to them about." It was now around 11:15 p.m.

"O.K., we're agreed then," said Bush. "It's noon Saturday." The meeting broke up around midnight, and Baker returned to his office to start telephoning the allied foreign ministers.

On Friday morning, in the dappled sunshine of the White House Rose Garden, Bush formally announced the new deadline. On Saturday night, several hours after Saddam had failed to comply, the President again appeared on camera, this time to declare that the Iraqi leader had ignored his "one last chance" to quit Kuwait. The warning was clear: a new stage in the gulf conflict had arrived.

The plan that the U.S. would follow had been worked out in immense detail by General H. Norman Schwarzkopf. "Make no mistake," one top Pentagon official said later, "this was Norman's plan from A to Z." In a sense, however, the general was simply going by the book. A relatively obscure (and unclassified) U.S. Army publication, *Field Manual 100-5,* lays out the

principles of "AirLand Battle," a post-Vietnam military doctrine that has been gospel for every war-college student since the early 1980s. "Don't give me a meat grinder," Schwarzkopf repeatedly warned his planners. Instead of the World War I–style frontal assault that Saddam was preparing for, AirLand doctrine calls for air attacks on the enemy's rear areas to cut off supply lines, destroy command-and-control centers and strike at reinforcing units, in order to isolate the battlefield.

The strategy is aimed as much at the enemy's mind and morale as at his weapons and troops. After air attacks softened defenses, armored units would make deep, rapid thrusts through enemy lines; troops would take advantage of the combined effect of artillery, air support, naval bombardment and armor on carefully chosen targets to throw the enemy off-balance by spreading fear and confusion. U.S. Air Force Lieut. General Charles Horner, commander of the combined air forces in the gulf war, worked closely with the Army in updating *Field Manual 100-5.* "The idea," he said, "is to feed the enemy in bite-size chunks to the ground forces to devour."

The AirLand scheme was devised as a battle plan for World War III. Its origins go back to the 1970s, when NATO strategists were trying to figure out how to defend Europe from an attack by overwhelming numbers of Soviet tanks. The key was to fall back on the front while trying to disrupt Soviet supply lines from the rear. A 1979 study by military consultant Joseph Braddock said U.S. intelligence could predict the location of Soviet armor units as they moved up toward the front. Even modest success in slowing the flow of Soviet reinforcements could tip the balance just enough to give NATO forces temporary battlefield superiority.

For an AirLand battle to succeed, commanders must stage operations in sequence, so that the effect of a deep attack on Day One will be felt when the opponent's crippled forces are later needed at the front—on Day Five, for example. Relying less on brute force than on operational elegance, AirLand strategy requires commanders to concentrate their efforts on attacking the right thing in the right place at the right time. The enemy's crucial "center of gravity"—a term borrowed from Prussian strategist Karl von Clausewitz—is the target whose destruction will have the greatest ripple effect on the enemy's overall military operations.

AirLand doctrine explains why the allies gave first priority to war in the skies—achieving combat suprema-

Dangerous search: U.S. 1st Cavalry trooper warily explores the dark entry to an abandoned Iraqi outpost.

Fire fight: troopers of the 1st Marine Division's Task Force Ripper encounter resistance near Kuwait's

International Airport and open up with M60A1 tanks and automatic weapons.

Direct hit: the 20-mm Vulcan gun on an M113 armored personnel carrier blows up an Iraqi ammunition truck on the horizon.

cy there and destroying Saddam's strategic capabilities. Nonetheless, Schwarzkopf said, "we were talking about ground options in August. In one of my very first briefings with the President, we discussed ejecting Iraq from Kuwait. I gave the President terrible advice because I told him [at the time] that in order to do the job I needed about five times more force than I ended up getting. I told him it would probably take about seven or eight months longer than it actually took to do the job."

Schwarzkopf began kicking around ideas with General Powell, who also discussed various scenarios with Secretary Cheney. As Schwarzkopf recalls it, "I was continually being asked how I would kick them out [of Kuwait]. We tried to develop offensive options based on the forces we had available, but at that time my problem was that the troops available did not equal the mission.

"By the middle of October, we had a completely robust strategic air campaign. We went back to Washington to brief the President, and we were told, 'Oh, by the way, brief the ground plan at the same time.' Well, the ground campaign left everybody saying 'Umm, gee, uh,' because my assessment was, given the troops available, you can't get there from here. So then the deci-

sion was made to send over the remainder of the forces.

"Almost immediately after I was given the additional forces, I brought all the division commanders that were going to be involved over here, and we sat down in Dhahran, and I said, 'O.K., folks, here now is my commander's intent. Here is what the campaign plan has to be.' At that time the strategic air campaign became Phase 1. I briefed them on how I saw Phase 2, Phase 3, Phase 4 evolving, and so we proceeded to put the ground campaign together." Just before Christmas, the ground-war plan was ready, as far as Schwarzkopf was concerned: "There comes a time when you freeze it. We're not going to change another damn thing; we're going to go with what we've got now." In fact, some details kept changing almost until the assault began, as planners drafted contingencies to take account of possible Iraqi responses.

Once the air war had begun on Jan. 17, there were several factors that affected the timing of a ground war. One was Ramadan, the Islamic month of dawn-to-dusk fasting, which this year began on March 17. Combat during this period of prayer and reflection would have been intensely difficult for the allied Arab forces as well as the Iraqis. Another factor, Schwarzkopf noted, was the coming of summer: by May, daytime temperatures in the desert regularly rise above 90° F. The general was also aware of what he called the "diminishing returns" of the air campaign.

One major factor in the timing of G-day was the readiness of the allied forces: waiting, waiting, waiting. "Our troops had been honed to a very fine edge," Schwarzkopf recalled later. "Every time I went out to the field, the commanders told me, 'Sir, let me tell you my unit has never been better trained, the morale has never been higher.' I had never seen a combat force more ready to go to battle than these guys were. But you can't keep a unit at that level forever. It's like getting ready for the Super Bowl. Some people get ready too early, and when the [game] rolls around, it's all over."

For many of the grunts in the northern desert, the prospect of battle brought feelings of relief as well as anxiety. Some of the troops had been on line for six months; at least the boredom of their routine was finally to be broken. Especially at night, when temperatures dropped below freezing and ice began to form inside canteens, it was hard to remember the white heat of summer. Up at the front, the motto was "Travel light, freeze at night." Soldiers slept in parka linings, with socks on their hands if their mittens were missing.

Lugging around gas masks and other protective gear was also a nuisance, though complaints were few. The troops' greatest worry was a chemical attack, a strike by an enemy they could not see. Said Private First Class Myra Camacho of Brooklyn, N.Y.: "You imagine walking around, and your buddy is lying on the ground having convulsions, and you have to inject him with atropine."

That is why the troops loved the chickens scattered around their bases. There were gas-monitoring machines with sirens that would sound if chemical agents appeared in the air, but the chickens—counterparts of the canaries that miners used to carry with them to detect poisonous gases down in shafts—were the backup. One airbase named its newspaper *Buford Talks,* after its chicken. The theory was that as long as the bird was talking, the troops were safe. Some soldiers daydreamed: when peace comes, let's have a barbecue.

Close to the front, nerves sometimes got raw. But there was also an adrenaline change from seeming to be closer to action. "When we moved farther north," said one soldier, "it helped morale because it broke the routine. We got T rations, which are hot and a lot better than MRES." MRES, or Meals Ready to Eat, were the soldiers' most accessible enemy. Everyone hated them.

Egyptian soldiers refused them. Only ravenous Iraqi prisoners of war would wolf them down—even the chewing gum.

Up front, where lead scouts of the 82nd Airborne Division kept watch against possible enemy troop movements, fires for heating or cooking were outlawed; hot coffee was made on tiny butane heaters hidden in cardboard boxes. Nights were so quiet that a cough could be heard 400 yds. away; the land was so barren that a single twisted piece of brush became a landmark known as the Tree. "It's easy to get lost out here," said Captain Scott Barrington of Chester, Va. "There are no terrain features. It's like the K Mart parking lot."

Roughly one-tenth of the U.S. force were women, universally known as the "females." Some were in such traditional support roles as cooks, clerks and nurses. But they also served as armorers, fire fighters, strategic planners and intelligence officers, serving close to the fire zone. Enlisted women had their own tents and latrines, but those concessions to gender did not guarantee much privacy. Most latrines were just plywood outhouses with wire screens from the waist up.

The men took the women's presence in stride. "Once you work with them enough, they realize that you're a soldier like they are," said Lieut. Lynnel Bifora of Mohawk, N.Y., who was serving with the XVIII Airborne Corps. "I won't let them carry gear for me. I like to tell them that a bullet has no gender. Combat has no gender. You can kill the chivalry bit."

All along the northern line, the days were passed with digging. Everyone, from the lowest privates to the officers—even the chaplains—took their turns with the shovels. "Each shovel I scoop out means I might save an arm," said Private Gregory White of the 82nd Airborne, a native of Los Angeles. "The next shovel means I might save a leg." The first holes were called "hasties" or "run and dives." With each passing day, the hasties grew deeper, until they were armpit deep. Then they were flanked with sandbags.

Every day brought some new test of ingenuity. The Army's combat engineers were masters of improvisation—as they had to be. When the ground war began, their task would be about the most perilous of all: to clear the way across the flaming trenches, minefields and berms that the Iraqis had built all along the Kuwaiti frontier with Saudi Arabia. It was handy to know how to hot-wire a bulldozer. So Colonel Robert Flowers, commander of one engineers' brigade, distributed homemade hot-wiring kits for trucks and other vehicles.

Scrounging became a way of life. Supplies have a

Invaders: a 1st Marine Division amphibious force heads for Kuwait City. "What we're doing is an off-tackle

play," said a general, "where you apply all the power you can at one point."

way of not keeping pace with soldiers on the move: the bureaucratic term for material with no forwarding address is "frustrated cargo." This makes for frustrated soldiers, unless they learn the time-honored military art of swapping what they have for what they need. One inventive maintenance officer, Major Frank Timmons, traded some spare plywood for long underwear, better rations for his troops and five trucks. The local Saudi merchants were not much help. Soldiers complained that prices doubled and tripled between visits to the small shops—from $6 to $15, for example, for a pack of Snickers bars that Stateside would cost $2 or $3.

Saudi Arabia is a strict Muslim country that recognizes no religion other than Islam. So church services for the troops were held discreetly in tents, out of Arab earshot, and chaplains took off their denominational insignia. But one of the devils of the desert was sheer boredom. Beginning in mid-September, Desert Shield Radio, a network of four FM stations, played news and music around the clock. DSR was a welcome replacement for "Baghdad Betty," who used to taunt soldiers that their wives back home were being unfaithful. (She darkly claimed that one of the seducers was Bart Simpson.) Happily, "Betty" went off the air when the bombing started. By and large, musical tastes seemed fairly sedate, perhaps reflecting the fact that the soldiers were older than troops of past wars (an average age of 27 years, compared with 21 in Vietnam). "We got a lot of requests for soft and sentimental songs," said Sergeant Major Bob Nelson, DSR's program director. "When it heats up, we slow down."

The most precious distraction—and also a source of irritation—was mail. About 400 tons arrived in Saudi Arabia per day. Letters were read and reread until pages crumbled. Mail from home not only punctuated the waiting but also moved time forward, as many soldiers discovered from one letter to the next that their children were growing up in their absence. "It's like an exam," Marine Sergeant H.B. McDuffie of Tallahassee said of the frustration of waiting. "You can only study so long, and then you're ready to take it. The whole thing is personal to me now. I missed Christmas. I missed New Year's Day, and now Valentine's Day, because of this war." McDuffie and his buddies did not have long to wait.

Caution and common sense dictated that Powell and Schwarzkopf be pessimists, preparing for the worst. That was why frontline troops had to struggle with gas masks and other cumbersome protective equipment, and why the U.S. forces had prepared about 10,000 beds, aboard ships and three field hospitals, to receive the wounded. But well before G-day, a few military experts were disputing the widespread predictions of high allied casualties in a lengthy war (often estimated at 30,000 to 40,000 within the first few weeks). In a Feb. 8 op-ed-page article for the New York Times, for example, political scientist John J. Mearsheimer of the University of Chicago argued that "the U.S. military can liberate Kuwait in less than a week and suffer relatively few casualties—probably less than 1,000 fatalities." His reasoning: the Iraqi army is "inept at fighting mobile armored battles." In reality, even before the ground campaign began, the war had been won to a greater extent than Schwarzkopf and his commanders dared hope. Five weeks of virtually day-and-night bombing had destroyed much of the Iraqis armor and artillery. Just as tellingly, allied chiefs had evidence from the battle of Khafji that Iraqi soldiers were not the equal of their coalition enemies.

On Jan. 29, nine brigades of Iraq's 5th Mechanized Division—which U.S. intelligence had touted as one of Saddam's stronger units—swept into Khafji, a practically deserted town six miles south of the Saudi border with Kuwait. By the next night the Iraqis had occupied the town, but troops from Saudi Arabia and Qatar, supported by U.S. air and artillery attacks, retook Khafji on Jan. 31 after fierce fighting.

Saddam may have intended the raid to lure allied forces prematurely into a ground war, but if that was the goal, he clearly failed. Not only did the allied Arab forces repel the invaders, but U.S. military planners also got their first opportunity to see how Iraq's troops operated against American-style mobile tactics. The Iraqis performed badly, surrendering en masse when counterattacked by U.S. Marines who had been held in reserve while the allies retook Khafji. "[The Iraqis] showed us they couldn't handle combined operations," said a senior Pentagon official. "They maneuvered but couldn't work effectively as a unit." Post-battle inspection also disclosed that Iraqi tanks and armored personnel carriers (APCs) were in poor condition. "Until that time," said Schwarzkopf, "we had been led to believe that [the enemy's] artillery was absolutely magnificent, but at Khafji he couldn't put it together worth a darn. It was a nonfactor." The battle of Khafji, the general added, "led us to believe that we were really going to kick this guy's tail."

Some postwar reports suggested that U.S. intelligence, which relied heavily on photographic evidence from satellites, spy planes and drones, seriously overestimated both the solidity of the Iraqi defenses and the numerical strength of Saddam's army. For example,

Advancing: 1st Cavalry soldiers seize key positions along the Euphrates River valley to cut off Iraqi retreat routes.

Pentagon officials constantly stated that there were about 540,000 Iraqi soldiers in the Kuwait area when war began. But this figure was based on the assumption that the units involved were at full strength: as it turned out, many Iraqi commands were at less than two-thirds of their scheduled manning levels.

By the time of the Khafji fight, Saddam had, in a military sense, no eyes. Lacking aerial reconnaissance, Iraqi commanders could not see what was going on behind enemy lines. Thus Schwarzkopf was able to hoodwink Baghdad into concentrating its forces in the wrong place until the very end. Six of Iraq's 42 divisions were massed along the Kuwaiti coast, guarding against a seaborne invasion. A force of 17,000 U.S. Marines repeatedly and conspicuously practiced amphibious landings in an exercise portentously named Operation Imminent Thunder. To judge from a huge military map the allies later found in a former Iraqi command center, Saddam was persuaded that the Marine force would attack Failakka Island in the northern gulf about 25 miles east of Kuwait City. As zero hour approached,

Marine and Navy forces patrolled off the island, as if preparing for a landing, and bombers subjected it to intense attacks. An armada of 31 ships moved close to the coast, and the battleships *Missouri* and *Wisconsin* took turns firing 16-in. shells at Iraqi shore defenses. But it was all a feint: the war was nearly over when the Marines disembarked to help mop up the scattering of Iraqi troops still in Kuwait.

That was not the only allied deception. For several days before the assault began, a phantom Marine "division," consisting of 460 troops, patrolled the Kuwait border. The goal of Task Force Troy was to persuade the Iraqis that a division of 16,000 men was chafing to attack. The real division was on the move to a new assault position 100 miles to the west. Task Force Troy was "armed" with loudspeakers that broadcast tank noises; the artillery pieces and tanks in the berms defended by the unit were dummies.

Most of Iraq's frontline troops—an estimated 210,000 remained hunkered down behind minefields, barbed wire and oil-filled trenches along the 138-mile

Saudi-Kuwait border. There they waited for what Saddam predicted would be the "mother of battles," in which the allied invaders would "drown in their own blood." But on Jan. 17—the day the U.S. launched the air attack—Schwarzkopf started what other allied officers described as a "left hook." More dramatically, the general called it his Hail Mary play, referring to a game-ending football tactic: the quarterback on a team that is narrowly behind lobs a pass in the general direction of his receivers in one corner of the end zone, hoping that one of them will catch the ball for a touchdown or draw a penalty, which would allow one more play.

In Schwarzkopf's version of the Hail Mary play, more than 200,000 U.S., British and French troops swiftly and secretly moved as much as 300 miles westward from the gulf, setting up bases across the border from a desert area of southern Iraq. Part of the allied force, spearheaded by units of the 101st Airborne Division, was to drive northward to the Euphrates River, cutting off retreat routes for the Iraqi forces in Kuwait—and, incidentally, blocking any possible reinforcements from Saddam's units stationed near Baghdad. Another part of the allied force was to turn east and hit Republican Guard divisions along the Kuwait-Iraq border, taking them by surprise on their right flank.

Fearing that a frontal assault on heavily dug-in Iraqi defenders could result in thousands of allied casualties, Schwarzkopf had first proposed the Hail Mary maneuver in November. His tactical commanders were initially skeptical. They argued that 200,000 troops could not be moved so far and so fast, with all their armor, artillery and 60 days' worth of ammo, fuel and supplies, over a desert with rudimentary roads. "I got a lot of guff," the general said later. "They thought that Schwarzkopf had lost his marbles." For example, Major General Ronald H. Griffith, commander of the 1st Armored Division, was concerned about a possible shortage of spare parts and chemical-protection garments; he also worried about whether his armored vehicles might outrun their fuel supplies and whether he had enough ammo. So stiff was their resistance that Schwarzkopf ordered his logistics commander, Major General William G. Pagonis, to sign his name to a pledge that the troops and their equipment would be in place by their deadline. Schwarzkopf reasoned that if his own subordinates doubted the plan would work, Saddam's generals would feel certain that such a move was impossible and would leave "this big, open flank" undefended.

One of Schwarzkopf's inspirations was the 1942 battle at El Alamein, which he vividly recalled from a West Point course called the History of Military Art. At El Alamein, Field Marshal Bernard Montgomery employed a decoy operation that persuaded the Germans the main British thrust was taking place somewhere else. Schwarzkopf was also influenced by Saddam's obsession with the threat of a Marine amphibious landing. As the general recalled later, "When I saw the way he had stuck all of his forces in this one bag down there [near the coast] . . . I was worried about the barrier they were building and the troops they were digging in behind them. The worst case would be for our troops to go in there and get hung up on the wire and having chemicals dumped on them. [But] as long as they weren't moving troops out to the west, as long as they weren't sending that barrier out to the west, we were in great shape. I knew we had the ability to defeat them by this turning movement."

Schwarzkopf's battle plan—again in keeping with AirLand strategy—also called for narrowly focused thrusts through the main Iraqi defensive works. Concerned that his troops might get caught in deadly barrages from Iraqi artillery firing poison-gas shells, Schwarzkopf ordered a shift in the bombing campaign during the last week to concentrate on knocking out the frontline guns. Success was spectacular: the sorties destroyed so much Iraqi artillery that its fire was neither as heavy nor as accurate as had been feared. Meanwhile, special-forces commandos, who had been operating deep inside Iraq, used hand-held lasers to pinpoint, for allied air bombardment, mobile Scud-missile launchers in Western Iraq.

As the Feb. 23 deadline approached, allied tanks equipped with bulldozer blades cut openings through the sand berms that Iraqi troops had built as their first defensive wall. Tanks and troops began probing attacks—in some cases well before G-day. (After the cease-fire, allied officials acknowledged that at least 3,000 Marines had moved more than 10 miles inside Kuwait to prepare for the beginning of the ground war. But Major General Michael Myatt, commander of the 1st Marine Division, insisted that his instructions were "to do nothing that is irreversible," and that he was prepared to retreat to Saudi Arabia if Saddam had acceded to Bush's demands.) During the night, B-52s pounded Iraqi positions and helicopter gunships swept the defensive lines, hitting equipment with their rockets and using machine guns to decimate Iraqi units in the trenches. Allied artillery opened an intense bombardment that included multiple-launch rocket systems,

Casualty: an APC rumbles along the road to Basra, its crew ignoring the slain Iraqi soldier lying near the highway.

"The Mother of Battles": 100 Hours

which released thousands of shrapnel-like bomblets over the trenches. Here as elsewhere during the war, the allies' night-fighting capability proved critical—and shattering to Iraqi morale.

And finally, G-day began. Between 4 and 6 Sunday morning, allied forces jumped off at selected points all along the 300-mile front. The weather was far from the stereotype of the desert: torrents of rain turned the sand into mud. In addition to the clouds and fog, thick black smoke from about 600 torched Kuwaiti oil wells drifted over the battlefields.

The first troops over the frontier wore bulky protective garb, since allied commanders dreaded Iraqi use of poison gas, but the Iraqis never fired any chemical weapons. Though there were various theories in explanation, the main reason seems to have been that the Iraqis never managed to deliver their chemical weapons from storage sites deep inside Iraq to the front lines.

Troops from Saudi Arabia, Egypt and other Arab states hit the strongest Iraqi fortifications near the coast. To their left were the U.S. 1st and 2nd Marine divisions, which attacked points on the so-called elbow of Kuwait, where the border with Saudi Arabia turns sharply to the north, and on the "armpit," where it shifts westward again. The Marines were led by Lieut. General Walter Boomer, whose daring operational plans for the assault had raised eyebrows at the Pentagon when the plans arrived there 16 days earlier. But they worked. Some units of the 2nd Marine Division, wearing full chemical gear, cleared two barriers of berms in just under two hours. "We're not going to do anything fancy," said their commander, Brigadier General Russel Gutton. "What we're doing is an off-tackle play, where you apply all the power you can at one point to defeat your opponent."

While waiting for D-day, allied troops in Saudi Arabia had built replicas of the Iraqi entrenchments and endlessly practiced breaching them. Now remotely piloted vehicles (RPVs) and pilotless drone planes guided soldiers to the most thinly defended areas of the Iraqi lines. Combat engineers fired off 100-yd.-long strings of tubing laced with explosives, known as line charges, to blast paths through the minefields. Tanks and APCs drove through those paths in long, narrow files, observing radio silence and communicating only by hand signals to avoid Iraqi detection.

The allied attackers had also figured out ways to counter the Iraqi threat of setting aflame their oil-filled

Mopping up: victorious U.S. troops search through an abandoned Iraqi radio outpost in the Euphrates River valley.

trenches. In the Marines' sector, U.S. planes burned off the oil by dropping napalm. The Saudis, for their part, used bulldozers and tanks fitted with earth-moving blades to collapse the trenches and fill them with dirt. Within hours, allied forces had burst through these supposedly impregnable defenses, sweeping past heavy concentrations of enemy troops and armor and calling in air strikes and artillery fire whenever the Iraqis fought back. That was seldom necessary, since the frontline Iraqi troops proved to be of poor quality and, as a British military spokesman put it, "ridden down by the bombing." During the 100-hour combat, there was virtually no closeup infantry fighting—a major reason why allied casualties were so low.

On the far western flank of the allied forces, the French 6th Light Armored Division crossed the Iraqi border before dawn Sunday. In company with the U.S. 82nd Airborne Division, the French moved rapidly toward the fort and airfield at As Salman, 105 miles inside Iraq. Along the way, American artillery and French Gazelle helicopter gunships armed with HOT antitank missiles attacked and subdued a force of Iraqi tanks and infantry at a strongpoint code-named Rochambeau. Many of the Iraqi soldiers surrendered—thus becoming among the first large contingents of what would soon total perhaps more than 80,000 prisoners of war.

To the right of the French, the U.S. 101st Airborne Division mounted a combined land-air assault deep inside southeastern Iraq. Chinook helicopters, some of them piloted by women, "sagebrushed" in, only 50 ft. above the sand, ferrying half the 4,000 troops with some of their vehicles and equipment into the desert. (The remaining troops and their supplies came by land.) The force established a huge refueling-and-resupply base roughly 50 miles from the Saudi border and then moved deeper inside Iraq toward the Euphrates River. It was an operation that some members of the 101st compared with the Division's famous landing in Normandy ahead of the D-day invasion in June 1944. "The only difference is there's no water below, and we're moving in helicopters, not gliders," said Major Robin Sellers.

In his Feb. 27 press conference, Schwarzkopf said the actions of the 101st should have dispelled any suspicions that America's real object was to destroy Iraq. "When we were here," said Schwarzkopf, referring to the 101st's positions along the Euphrates, "we were 150 miles from Baghdad, and there was nobody between us and Baghdad. If it had been our intention to take Iraq, to overrun the country, we could have done it unopposed for all intents and purposes."

Farther southeast, other units—including the British

1st Armored Division; seven U.S. Army divisions; and Egyptian, Saudi and Syrian units—attacked at various times throughout the morning and early afternoon along the Saudi-Iraq border into western Kuwait. Allied units achieved or exceeded virtually all their first-day goals, as Iraqi defenses began rapidly collapsing. By Sunday night, for example, the 1st Marine Division had reached the outskirts of al-Jaber military airport, half the 40-mile distance from the Saudi border to Kuwait City.

The first day's triumphs, among other things, resolved one of the uncertainties of the war: whether a multinational, multilingual force, with differing military traditions and weaponry, could mount an effective, coordinated attack on an enemy that had the theoretical advantage of fighting under one flag. U.S. forces were the backbone of the operation, but it was politically essential that they served as part of a multinational effort, to demonstrate that the whole world opposed Saddam. As it turned out, virtually all allied units that saw combat fought with distinction. (Privately, though, some officers reported that the performance of the 15,000 Syrian troops was disappointing.) Schwarzkopf's warmest praise for non-Americans under his command was for the British, whom he called "absolutely superb members of this coalition from the outset." As part of the allied flanking maneuver, Britain's 1st Armored Division had to take on Saddam's proud Republican Guard. One of the division's components was the 7th Armored Brigade, heirs of World War II's Desert Rats, who fought at El Alamein and helped drive the Germans out of North Africa. The British, unluckily, were victims of one of the war's most tragic incidents: nine soldiers lost their lives to friendly fire when an American A-10 fighter-bomber hit two armored vehicles by mistake.

As for the other allies, Saudi troops, who had launched the assault against the feared "Saddam line" of fortifications into eastern Kuwait, had an unenviable double duty: to deceive Baghdad into thinking that all of the allies were massed for a frontal assault, and to deflect Iraqi defenders from the U.S. Marine crossing farther west. The Saudi-led Arab forces "did a terrific job," Schwarzkopf said, in breaching "a very, very tough barrier system." The 38,500 Egyptians, second in number only to Saudi Arabia's 40,000 among the allies, ran into Saddam's dreaded oil-filled fire trenches. Although the trenches were not aflame, it was a position the general called "not a fun place to be."

On Monday, troops continued moving rapidly: the Saudis and U.S. Marines directly north toward Kuwait City; American airborne units toward the Euphrates;

British, American and allied Arab forces to the east. After taking As Salman in 36 hours, the French halted at midday on Schwarzkopf's orders to set up a defensive bastion against a possible Iraqi attack from the northwest. France's only deaths of the war took place unexpectedly at As Salman. A paratrooper stooped to pick up a greenish, tangerine-shaped object; it exploded in his face, killing him and a soldier standing nearby. Would-be rescuers tripped a similar explosive device, wounding 25. The explosives turned out to be antipersonnel cluster bombs that had been dropped on the base earlier by U.S. aircraft.

Monday also saw the worst allied calamity of the war. It took place, ironically, about 200 miles behind the front lines. At 8:23 p.m., the warhead of an Iraqi Scud missile, which had broken apart in flight, landed on a warehouse near Dhahran that had been turned into a U.S. military barracks. Twenty-eight soldiers died and approximately 100 were wounded. Many of the troops were eating dinner; some were asleep. According to Radio Baghdad, the attack had been directed against "coward traitors who mortgage the sacred places of the nation and turn Arab youths into shields of flesh."

Mass surrenders began almost as soon as the Iraqi lines were breached on Sunday. In fact, the biggest obstacle to the allied advance proved to be the waves of surrendering soldiers. By Tuesday, the total had passed 30,000, and the allies temporarily stopped counting. The Iraqis came out of tanks and collapsed bunkers, waving handkerchiefs, underwear, anything white. Some of the surrender stories were bizarre. In one instance, about 40 Iraqis tried to turn themselves in to an RPV guided missile, turning round and round and vainly waving their arms while the pilotless drone flew circles above. In another, a lone U.S. soldier driving a Humvee, the latter-day version of a jeep, got stuck helplessly in the mud. When an Iraqi tank and APC rumbled by, they first pulled the Humvee from the mire—then their crews surrendered.

Many of the POWs were starved, thirsty, often sick. Many had been terrorized by their own commanders, who used roving execution squads to shoot or hang troopers suspected of wanting to desert. (All the allied units set up checkpoints, in hopes of finding Iraqi soldiers who might have been guilty of committing atrocities.) Some of the POWs quickly volunteered to show the advancing allies where mines had been laid.

Unarmed prisoners, despite their overwhelming numbers, were relatively easy to cope with; bunkers were another matter. Advancing allied troops generally left them unexplored for fear of booby traps. Engineering units eventually came along to open them, collect any weapons and blow up the ammo. The U.S. Army's 307th Engineer Battalion used grappling hooks to open bunker doors as a protection against hidden mines or explosives. Then the engineers collected grenades and other munitions, set them with charges that had 30-to-45-second delays and blew the hatches. Some of the weapons were found in boxes labeled "Jordan Armed Forces," but officials in Amman insisted that they had been shipped before the United Nations' embargo went into effect.

Almost until the end of the war, Radio Baghdad was broadcasting bizarre claims of splendid Iraqi victories. On Monday, however, the radio announced an order, purportedly from Saddam himself, for Iraqi forces to withdraw from Kuwait. Bush refused to accept that as an authentic Iraqi surrender. A few Iraqi units still tried to challenge the pursuing allied forces. They were cut to ribbons. That afternoon the 1st Marine Division encountered Iraqi units in the Burgan oil field near Kuwait International Airport and flushed them out with what is called "time on target" fire. Translation: all guns in the division open up, laying down a devastating simultaneous curtain of explosives on a limited target area. Emerging into the open after that barrage, the Iraqis were hit with more fire from tanks, artillery and Cobra attack helicopters. About 60 Iraqi tanks were destroyed in the brief but deadly encounter. On Sunday night, well before Radio Baghdad's order to retreat, Iraqi forces had begun to pull out of Kuwait City. By Tuesday afternoon, the withdrawal was virtually complete. The retreat spared the city, its inhabitants and the advancing allies the potential destruction of house-to-house fighting. By midafternoon, Kuwaiti resistance forces claimed to be in control of the city. But sniper fire continued for a while, and Saudi and Kuwaiti troops did not stage their victory parade into the city until Wednesday. (Schwarzkopf thought it symbolically important that the city should be seen by the world as liberated by Arab forces.) For the rest of the week, in fact, the Kuwaiti resistance kept busy flushing out isolated squads of Iraqi soldiers who had either missed the radio order or who had taken cover in hopes of eventually melting into the populace.

Outside the city, the Iraqis were scrambling to "get out of Dodge," said one U.S. briefing officer. Although a few Iraqi units managed to carry out something resembling an orderly retreat, it was mostly a pell-mell flight. Roads leading north to Basra, Iraq's second largest city and military headquarters for the Kuwait operation, were so jammed with vehicles and

Friends in Battle
A Photo Essay

As often happens in armored units, where soldiers live and train in close quarters, Sergeant Ken Kozakiewicz, 23, of Buffalo became good friends with the driver of his unit's Bradley armored vehicle. During a fierce battle in the Euphrates Valley, the Bradley took a direct hit from a mortar. The driver was killed instantly. Army medics quickly put the dead man into a body bag and evacuated the survivors. They did not at first realize, in the confusion, who the dead man was.

To the rescue: a shocked Sergeant Ken Kozakiewicz of the 24th Mechanized Infantry Division gets help from medics.

A waiting helicopter is prepared to evacuate all the injured and the dead—one soldier in a body bag.

Only after being handed the dead man's dog tags does the sergeant learn that the corpse in the body bag

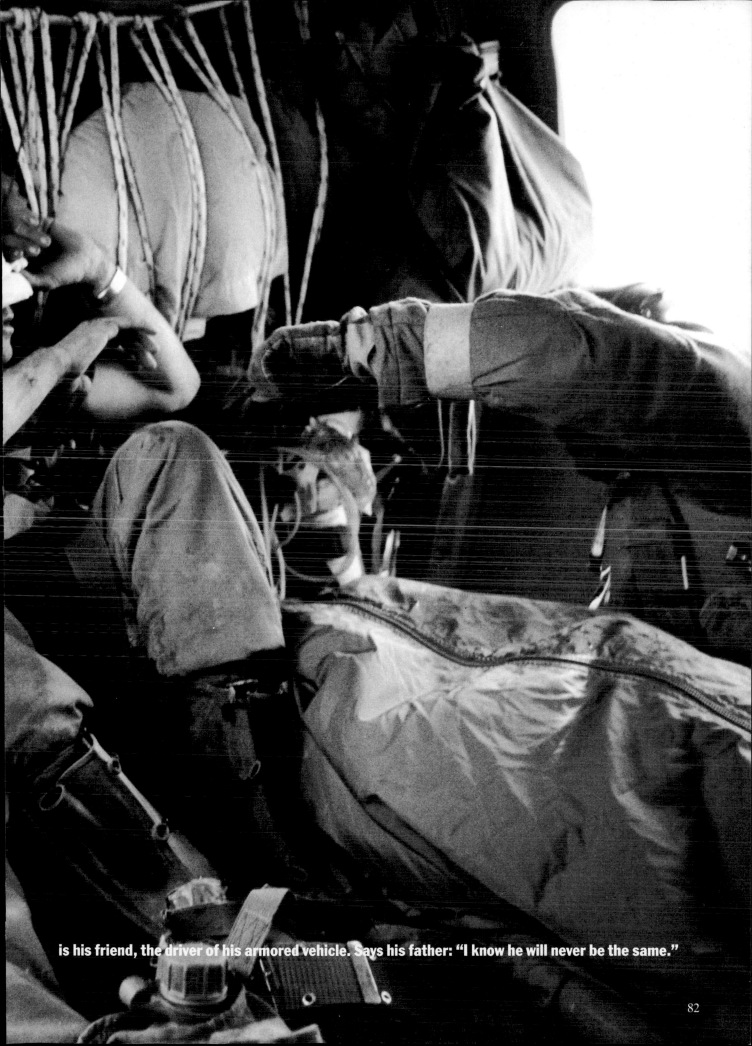

is his friend, the driver of his armored vehicle. Says his father: "I know he will never be the same."

Life and Death in the Sand
A Photo Essay

War is often described in terms of high strategy, vast armies clashing on vast battlefields. But much of war is more commonplace: small bands of soldiers engaged mainly in just passing the time, talking together, doing chores, marching, performing drills and exercises, eating, sleeping, thinking of home. These are some pictures of how many ordinary G.I.s spent their winter in the sands along the Persian Gulf, from the boredom of the field camp to the first, sudden, shocking bursts of gunfire.

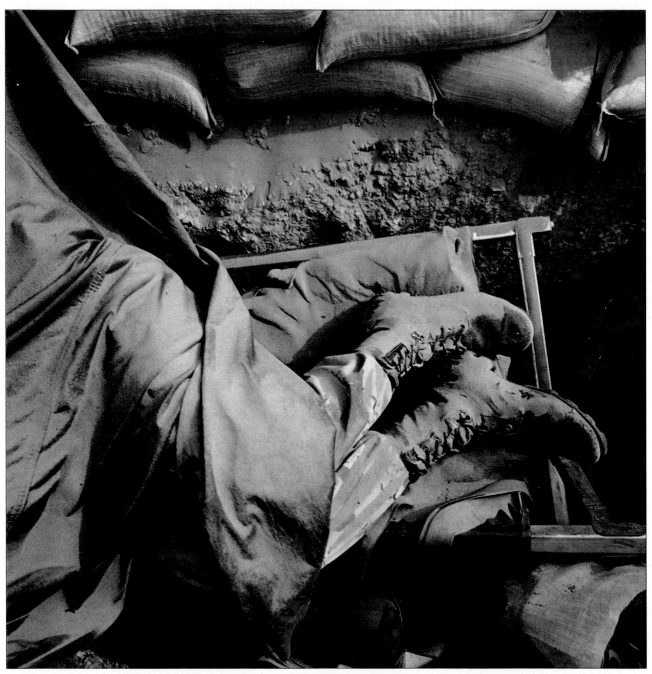

The best way to sleep through a Saudi Arabian sandstorm is to keep your boots tightly laced.

When you want to take a bath in the desert, what you need is a bar of soap, some water and a few sandbags.

The most precious pastime—writing and receiving letters.

Keeping fit is part of a soldier's job, an important part.

Now in Iraq readiness is all: something is moving on the distant horizon.

On the lookout for anything suspicious in the area.

MRE stands for Meals Ready to Eat, but you have to be very hungry.

A multiple-rocket-launching team gets briefed for its next firing across the desert.

In Iraq a 155-mm howitzer can be a man's best friend.

At a guard post a soldier can only wait, and then wait some more.

Hands tightly bound behind him, an Iraqi prisoner of war watches an allied convoy heading north.

The battle is over: Iraqi captives clustered near Nasiriya.

U.S. troops watchfully stand guard over captured Iraqis.

Dead Iraqi still sits at the wheel of this gutted vehicle while a dozen more corpses lie scattered nearby.

An Iraqi in the twisted sprawl of death.

Dust unto dust . . . U.S. soldiers bury Iraqi casualties in the sand.

troops that one U.S. Navy pilot said it looked like "the road to Daytona Beach at spring break." Soon it began to look like the world's longest junkyard. Allied bombing of roads and bridges led to mammoth traffic jams, and the trapped tanks and APCs were a temptingly easy target for allied fighter-bombers.

One eyewitness to the wreckage was TIME Rome bureau chief Robert T. Zintl, who observed mile after mile of abandoned, twisted, burned and shattered tanks, trucks and other vehicles. Alongside the road, cars were propped up on crates, their tires stripped off and engines cannibalized. An occasional corpse, its head torn open and arms blown off, could be seen wedged beneath a car.

"What is truly disconcerting is the stuff everywhere," Zintl reported, "the personal possessions and pieces of day-to-day life that the Iraqis looted even as they were trying to get out of town. A green telephone sits among the wreckage, its receiver off the hook as if a call had been interrupted. A mattress and blanket lie next to a tank; an orange candy bar is stuck in the treads. Kitchen skewers lie on top of ammo clips. Cassette tapes blow across the highway. A chandelier is on display on the road shoulder. It's as if the Iraqis took part in that TV show where people were turned loose in a supermarket and given one minute to grab as much as they could. Scavengers gather around the back of an APC to pry souvenir bullets out of a cartridge belt; inside the front door there is a pile of clothing, including a child's pink dress with ruffles and sequins."

By Tuesday afternoon, U.S. Marines had reached the main highway linking Kuwait City and Basra; the next morning, British units broached that highway farther north. Meanwhile, other allied forces, including units of the 101st Airborne and the 24th Mechanized Infantry Division, had taken up strong positions along the Euphrates River to block any retreating Iraqi units. Saddam's forces were now trapped. The battle had entered what one military briefer called a "pursuit and exploitation phase."

Some commentators saw the U.S. air attacks on the retreating Iraqis as the moral equivalent of shooting fish in a barrel—a bullying slaughter of an obviously defeated and demoralized foe. But in the dispassionate view of legal scholars, the attacks were justified by international law. U.S. troops are trained to pursue a retreating enemy by fire, and Saddam had left his forces vulnerable by refusing to accept clearly the U.N. conditions for a cease-fire. Nor had he ordered his troops to surrender, which would have entitled them to protection under the Geneva convention. Said Colonel Dew-

ey E. Helmcamp III of the National Defense University in Washington: "We are under no obligation to allow them to walk off the battlefield because they say they want to. That is different from a surrender."

In the midst of the rout—at last—came the two largest tank battles of the war. U.S. Marines encountered on Tuesday the Iraqi 3rd Armored Division at Kuwait International Airport. Because of the heavy smoke from oil wells set afire by the Iraqis, the sky was so dark that Marine Major General Michael Myatt had to read a map by flashlight. The Marines took advantage of what light there was and late in the day reported that all 100 Iraqi tanks they had engaged were destroyed. Regarding the performance of Iraqi frontline troops during the battle, Lieut. General Walter Boomer said, "I expected them to fight harder than they did . . . My view is that their heart wasn't in it." The Marine losses: 18.

A far larger clash took place along the Kuwait-Iraq border, where U.S. tanks that had carried out Schwarzkopf's flanking maneuver finally met Saddam's 96,000-man Republican Guard as it pushed eastward. Schwarzkopf had defined the Guard, which Saddam had held back from the first stage of battle, as the "center of gravity" of the Iraqi forces. "The whole campaign," said a senior Army staff officer, "was designed on one theme: to destroy the Republican Guard."

As early as Monday night, British troops had encountered some Guard units, destroying one-third of their armor with artillery fire and aerial attacks. American troops also encountered Guard units and by nightfall Monday reported that one of the seven élite divisions in the area had been rendered "basically ineffective."

The main battle raged all day Wednesday, with some 800 U.S. tanks of the 101st Airborne, 24th Mechanized Infantry and 3rd Armored divisions attacking about 300 tanks of the Guard's Medina and Hammurabi armored divisions. Numerically, it was the world's largest tank battle since the great Soviet-German combat at Kursk in 1943, but this one was not nearly so close. Some allied officers said the Guard fought about as well as could have been expected of troops who lacked air cover, had minimal communications and were subject to intense allied bombing. The Guard's basic tactic was what one U.S. officer called "a delay posture, a descend and delay." What they did, he explained, was to fight, withdraw, then fight and withdraw again, with a rear battle line providing cover as a forward line retreated past it. Another officer col-

Manhunt: ready for trouble, a Marine challenges anyone who may be hiding inside this fortified bunker.

Giving up: hands raised, fear and fatigue stamped on their faces, Iraqi soldiers emerge from their foxholes

91

in the desert to surrender to advancing allied forces.

orfully summed up the American forces' tactical response: "We are chasing them across the plains, shooting as we go."

One U.S. commander called the Guardsmen "good soldiers," but the two attacked divisions fared no better than other Iraqi units, and not just because of allied air supremacy. The U.S. M1A1 tanks were far superior in both maneuverability and firepower to Iraq's best, the Soviet-built T-72s. In one duel between an M1A1 and a T-72, the American tank backed up, outside the Soviet vehicle's range. After the Iraqi tank fired a round that fell short, the M1A1 fired its longer-range cannon and scored a direct hit that put the enemy out of action.

That evening in Riyadh, Schwarzkopf conducted an extraordinary press briefing in which for the first time he spelled out the allied strategy and gave a blow-by-blow account of the fighting. By this time, he said, Iraq had lost more than 3,000 of the 4,700 tanks it had deployed in the Kuwait theater at the start of the war. "As a matter of fact," the general added, " you can add 700 to that as a result of the battle that's going on right now with the Republican Guard." Saddam's forces lost comparably high quantities of their other armored vehicles, artillery and trucks. As a result, Schwarzkopf said, Iraq was left with only an infantry army incapable of carrying out offensive operations against any other country in the region. Destroying Saddam's offensive capability fulfilled one of the two principal war aims; the other, clearing the Iraqis out of Kuwait, was by now just about accomplished.

On Wednesday at 9 p.m. (5 a.m. Kuwait time), Bush went on the air to announce that he was ordering a suspension of all offensive action, to take effect three hours later. It was not officially a cease-fire, since it was unilateral action and not an agreement negotiated with the Iraqis, but it had the same effect. At 8 a.m., the shooting officially stopped, although there were still sporadic incidents. Some Iraqi units appeared not to get the word at first; allied troops set up loudspeakers blaring over and over again the message in Arabic that Iraqis would not be attacked if they held their fire. There was a stern warning to those troops that failed to heed: on Saturday, a column of 140 Iraqi tanks and other vehicles ran into a U.S. force and began shooting. The Americans counterattacked, destroying 60 Iraqi tanks and capturing the other 80.

The winding down of the war found G.I.s relieved that the toll of dead and wounded was so low. "When I first heard that the ground war had begun, I had to walk

Corralled: U.S. Special Forces capture and disarm stragglers. Iraqis were scrambling to "get out of Dodge," said one American officer.

away to be alone for a few moments," Marine Corporal Charles R. Phelps told a reporter. "All I could think of was how many people would die. I am glad it ended like this." How many actually did die remained a matter of considerable uncertainty. Estimates of the Iraqi military dead ranged wildly between 25,000 and 100,000; the captured, approximately 80,000. The civilian casualties in a month of bombing added uncounted thousands more. But the allied casualties were almost miraculously low. The U.S. lost 124 dead and 357 wounded.

After a war that had lasted a scant 100 hours, the formal cease-fire agreement was signed on Sunday, March 3, at Safwan, an Iraqi air base on a drab desert bluff, less than five miles northwest of the Kuwait frontier. The U.S. Command chose the site, much to the dismay of Iraqi military leaders, who would have preferred a locale in Kuwait. U.S. Army Captain Ken Pope of LeNoir, N.C., commanded one of two companies from the 1st Armored Division that drove to Safwan to inform the Iraqis of the decision. There was some tension in the encounter. The purpose of choosing Safwan, Pope told a reporter, was "to show them that, hey, we're in Iraq. We won the war, and you're going to have to come to terms with us."

Schwarzkopf and high-ranking officers representing the other allies landed by chopper at Safwan, which by then had been cleared of all Iraqi forces. Later, a delegation of Iraqi officers led by Lieut. General Sultan Hashim Ahmad, drove up in Humvees, after having passed through a U.S. Army checkpoint; their escort included two Bradley APCs and two M1A1 tanks, chief instruments of their defeat. The Iraqis were searched and checked by a metal detector but well out of press scrutiny. "I don't want them humiliated," Schwarzkopf was overheard telling an aide.

The general made it clear that he was not at Safwan to negotiate. "I'm here to tell them exactly what they have to do," he said. The talks between the two sides lasted for about two hours, and the Iraqis agreed to all allied demands. These included understandings on how to avoid accidental engagements between Iraqi and allied units and on exchanging information about soldiers missing in action. The Iraqis also agreed to help the allies locate the countless thousands of mines that had been laid in the battlefield area. Afterward, the Iraqis had no comment on the discussion. Not so Schwarzkopf. "I think," he said, "we have made a major step forward in the cause of peace."

Bursting through the door of an empty outpost, soldiers look for Iraqis.

The end: hungry, demoralized and defeated, swarms of Iraqi soldiers surrender en masse.

"Their heart wasn't in it," said a general.

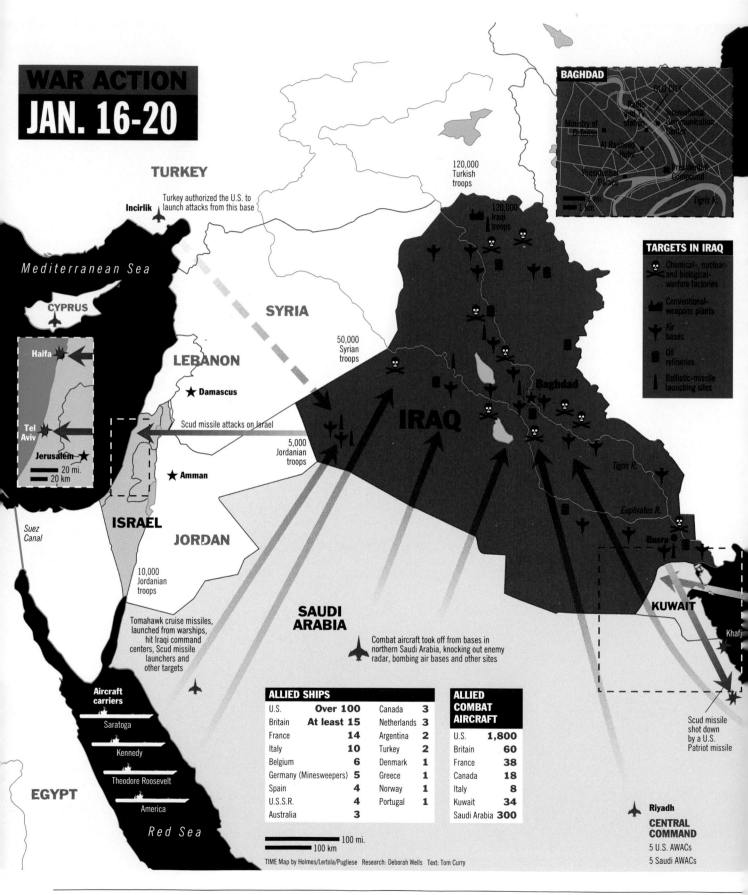

WAR ACTION
JAN. 16-20

TURKEY

Incirlik — Turkey authorized the U.S. to launch attacks from this base

Mediterranean Sea

CYPRUS

BAGHDAD

OLD CITY
Ministry of Defense
Radio and TV station
International Communication Center
Al Rasheed Hotel
Presidential Palace
Presidential Compound
Tigris R.
1 km

120,000 Turkish troops

120,000 Iraqi troops

SYRIA

LEBANON

★ Damascus

50,000 Syrian troops

5,000 Jordanian troops

Scud missile attacks on Israel

Haifa

Tel Aviv

Jerusalem ★

20 mi.
20 km

★ Amman

ISRAEL

Suez Canal

JORDAN

10,000 Jordanian troops

Tomahawk cruise missiles, launched from warships, hit Iraqi command centers, Scud missile launchers and other targets

IRAQ

Baghdad

TARGETS IN IRAQ

- ☠ Chemical-, nuclear- and biological-warfare factories
- 🏭 Conventional-weapons plants
- ✈ Air bases
- Oil refineries
- Ballistic-missile launching sites

Tigris R.

Euphrates R.

Basra

KUWAIT

Khafji

Scud missile shot down by a U.S. Patriot missile

SAUDI ARABIA

Combat aircraft took off from bases in northern Saudi Arabia, knocking out enemy radar, bombing air bases and other sites

Aircraft carriers

Saratoga

Kennedy

Theodore Roosevelt

America

EGYPT

Red Sea

ALLIED SHIPS			
U.S.	**Over 100**	Canada	**3**
Britain	**At least 15**	Netherlands	**3**
France	**14**	Argentina	**2**
Italy	**10**	Turkey	**2**
Belgium	**6**	Denmark	**1**
Germany (Minesweepers)	**5**	Greece	**1**
Spain	**4**	Norway	**1**
U.S.S.R.	**4**	Portugal	**1**
Australia	**3**		

ALLIED COMBAT AIRCRAFT	
U.S.	**1,800**
Britain	**60**
France	**38**
Canada	**18**
Italy	**8**
Kuwait	**34**
Saudi Arabia	**300**

Riyadh

CENTRAL COMMAND

5 U.S. AWACs
5 Saudi AWACs

100 mi.
100 km

TIME Map by Holmes/Lertola/Pugliese   Research: Deborah Wells   Text: Tom Curry

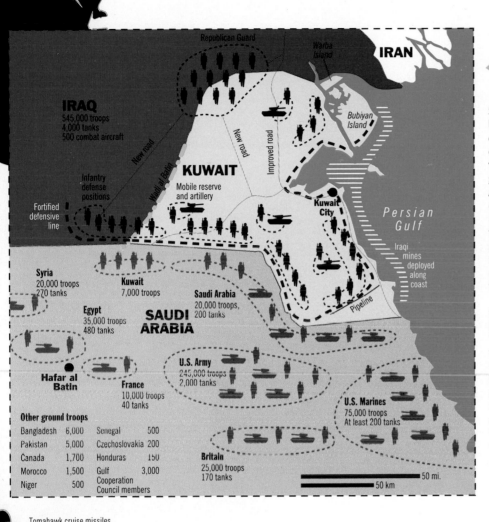

IRAQ
545,000 troops
4,000 tanks
500 combat aircraft

Republican Guard

Warba Island

IRAN

Bubiyan Island

New road

New road

Improved road

Infantry defense positions

Wadi al Batin

KUWAIT
Mobile reserve and artillery

Fortified defensive line

Kuwait City

Persian Gulf

Iraqi mines deployed along coast

Syria
20,000 troops
270 tanks

Kuwait
7,000 troops

Saudi Arabia
20,000 troops,
200 tanks

Egypt
35,000 troops
480 tanks

SAUDI ARABIA

Pipeline

Hafar al Batin

France
10,000 troops
40 tanks

U.S. Army
245,000 troops
2,000 tanks

U.S. Marines
75,000 troops
At least 200 tanks

Other ground troops

Bangladesh	6,000	Senegal	500
Pakistan	5,000	Czechoslovakia	200
Canada	1,700	Honduras	150
Morocco	1,500	Gulf Cooperation Council members	3,000
Niger	500		

Britain
25,000 troops
170 tanks

50 mi.
50 km

At 12:50 a.m. Thursday (4:50 p.m. Wednesday EST), the first fighter planes took off from the Dhahran air base in Saudi Arabia. In the Persian Gulf, U.S. warships launched Tomahawk cruise missiles to land the first blows on Iraq, destroying concrete-reinforced aircraft shelters and other targets. Before 3 a.m., a radar-evading Air Force F-117 Stealth fighter dropped its first bomb, demolishing a Baghdad telecommunications center. Over the next four days, the planes of the U.S.-led coalition flew more than 4,000 sorties, targeting command-and-control centers, airfields and Scud missile launchers.

Shortly after 2 a.m. Friday local time, eight Scud missiles, fired from mobile launchers in western Iraq, hit Tel Aviv and Haifa. Twelve Israelis were wounded. While allied pilots tried to destroy the remaining mobile Scud launchers inside Iraq, another missile volley pounded Tel Aviv Saturday morning. The U.S. immediately dispatched Patriot antimissiles to Israel, and Sunday dawned without further Iraqi attacks.

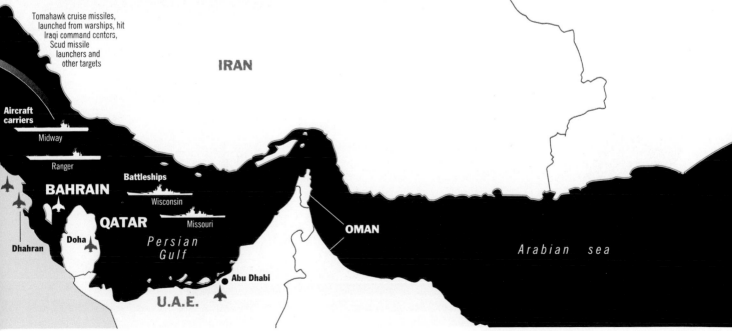

Tomahawk cruise missiles, launched from warships, hit Iraqi command centers, Scud missile launchers and other targets

IRAN

Aircraft carriers
Midway
Ranger

Battleships
Wisconsin
Missouri

BAHRAIN

QATAR

Doha

Dhahran

Persian Gulf

OMAN

Arabian sea

Abu Dhabi

U.A.E.

WAR ACTION
JAN. 21-27

THE TORNADO IDS

BA

Tornado fighter-bombers are capable of flying close to the ground, under radar, at 100 ft. (30 m). This has enabled them to crater Iraqi airfields. They fly in total radio silence until they are back in friendly territory, and the flight pattern is computerized before takeoff.

TURKEY

Incirlik — U.S. attacks launched from this base

U.S. confirmed two nuclear facilities destroyed

Mediterranean Sea

CYPRUS

TARGETS IN IRAQ

Chemical-, nuclear- and biological-warfare factories

Conventional-weapons plants

Oil refineries

Main air bases

Airfields

Scud launch areas

Haifa

SYRIA

IRAQ

Samarra

★ Damascus

LEBANON

Tel Aviv

Continued Scud missile attacks on Israel

Baghdad

Jerusalem ★

20 mi.
20 km

★ Amman

Tigris R.

Intense bombing of Basra and the Republican Guard

ISRAEL

Suez Canal

JORDAN

Euphrates R.

17,500 allied combat and supply missions in first eight days of war

Basra

Submarines in Red Sea and Mediterranean launched Tomahawk cruise missiles

KUWAIT

Sea I.

SAUDI ARABIA

Wells and storage tanks set ablaze at Al Wafra oil field

More Scud attacks on Riyadh and Dhahran

Iraq dumped oil into the gulf from pumps at Sea Island terminal

Aircraft carriers

Saratoga

Kennedy

Theodore Roosevelt

EGYPT

America

100 mi.
100 km

THE PRICE OF WAR U.S. daily cost of running the war is about $500 million. If a ground war breaks out, the cost could escalate to $1 billion per day. Here are the costs for some of the weapons:

1 hour of flight time for A-10 Thunderbolt $1,306

1 hour of flight time for B-52 bomber $7,730

"Smart" bomb (GBU-15) $100,129

Patriot missile $500,000

Tomahawk cruise missile $1,000,000

Red Sea

TIME Map by Hart/Holmes/Lertola/ Pugliese/Wells

SADDAM'S AIR-FORCE BUNKERS

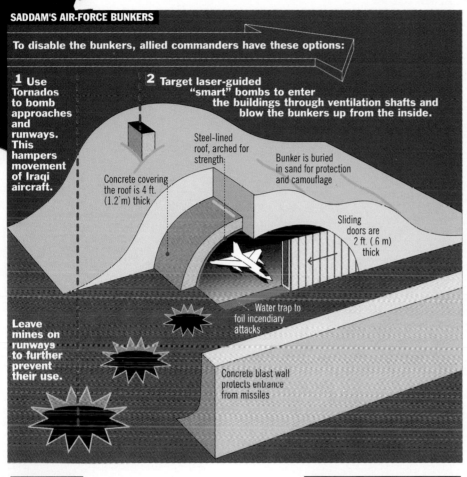

To disable the bunkers, allied commanders have these options:

1 Use Tornados to bomb approaches and runways. This hampers movement of Iraqi aircraft.

2 Target laser-guided "smart" bombs to enter the buildings through ventilation shafts and blow the bunkers up from the inside.

Steel-lined roof, arched for strength

Concrete covering the roof is 4 ft. (1.2 m) thick

Bunker is buried in sand for protection and camouflage

Sliding doors are 2 ft. (.6 m) thick

Water trap to foil incendiary attacks

Leave mines on runways to further prevent their use.

Concrete blast wall protects entrance from missiles

After a brief lull, allied bombers stepped up the air war, shifting their focus to military targets around Basra, the supply gateway to Kuwait, and Republican Guard troops and positions along the Iraqi-Kuwaiti border. Iraq intensified its Scud-missile bombardment of Israel and Saudi Arabia. Although U.S. Patriot antimissiles knocked down most, six warheads hit Tel Aviv or Haifa, and one exploded in Riyadh, destroying buildings and causing a total of five deaths and 160 injuries in the two countries. Allied forces captured the tiny Persian Gulf island of Qaruh, which the Iraqis had used as a forward observation post; it was the first bit of Kuwaiti territory freed from Iraqi control. In a rare dogfight, a Saudi pilot shot down two Iraqi planes trying to launch Exocet missiles. In what could be the start of a scorched-earth policy, Iraqis set fire to Kuwaiti oil wells and storage tanks. A more menacing act of environmental terrorism: Iraqi occupiers of Kuwait deliberately pumped huge amounts of crude oil into the gulf, setting a giant slick moving toward the water-intake systems of a Saudi desalinization plant at Jubail; allied authorities hoped to divert the oil with booms.

NAVAL ACTION

Increased fighting in the gulf. Iraqi ships sunk included minesweepers and a minelayer. Iraqi prisoners taken on Qaruh Island.

U.S. COMPARED WITH GULF AREA

TURKEY

IRAN

IRAQ

SAUDI ARABIA

200 mi.
200 km

Qaruh I.

Aircraft carriers

Midway

Ranger

Jubail

Battleships

BAHRAIN

Wisconsin

QATAR

Missouri

Dhahran

OMAN

Persian Gulf

Arabian Sea

Abu Dhabi

U.A.E.

IRAN

RAINING DEATH FROM THE SKY

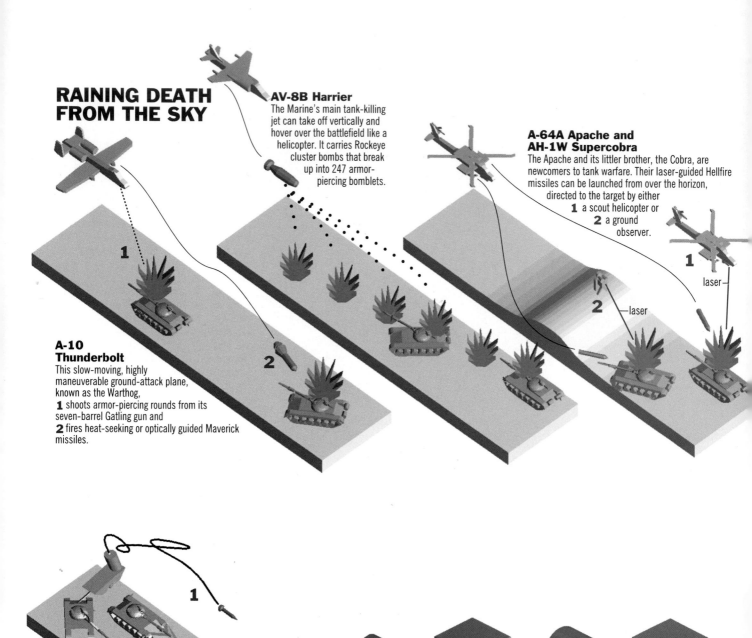

AV-8B Harrier
The Marine's main tank-killing jet can take off vertically and hover over the battlefield like a helicopter. It carries Rockeye cluster bombs that break up into 247 armor-piercing bomblets.

A-64A Apache and AH-1W Supercobra
The Apache and its littler brother, the Cobra, are newcomers to tank warfare. Their laser-guided Hellfire missiles can be launched from over the horizon, directed to the target by either **1** a scout helicopter or **2** a ground observer.

laser

2 laser

A-10 Thunderbolt
This slow-moving, highly maneuverable ground-attack plane, known as the Warthog,
1 shoots armor-piercing rounds from its seven-barrel Gatling gun and
2 fires heat-seeking or optically guided Maverick missiles.

Clearing minefields
1 Combat engineers fire rockets that drag cables filled with explosive charges across the battlefield.
2 The charges detonate, clearing an area 8 m (25 ft.) wide and 90 m (300 ft.) long.
3 Any remaining mines are plowed away by a specially equipped tank.

TIME Diagram by Joe Lertola

Piercing armor
1 Nonexplosive rounds fashioned from depleted uranium 2.5 times as dense as steel strike with sufficient force to penetrate armored plates.

2 Explosive antitank rounds detonate on contact, squirting a jet of molten metal through the armor.

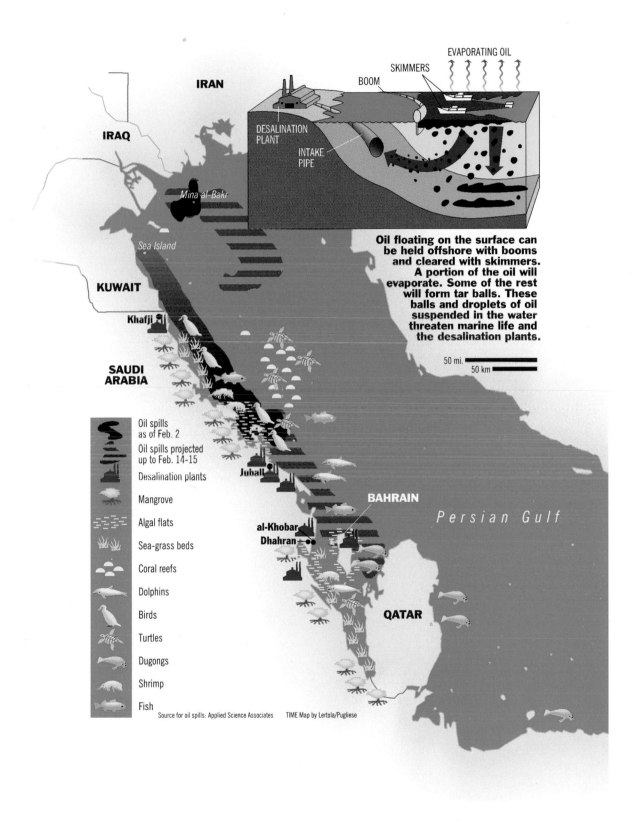

IRAN

IRAQ

Mina al-Bakr

Sea Island

KUWAIT

Khafji

SAUDI
ARABIA

Juball

al-Khobar
Dhahran

BAHRAIN

QATAR

Persian Gulf

EVAPORATING OIL

SKIMMERS

BOOM

DESALINATION
PLANT

INTAKE
PIPE

Oil floating on the surface can be held offshore with booms and cleared with skimmers. A portion of the oil will evaporate. Some of the rest will form tar balls. These balls and droplets of oil suspended in the water threaten marine life and the desalination plants.

50 mi.
50 km

Oil spills
as of Feb. 2

Oil spills projected
up to Feb. 14-15

Desalination plants

Mangrove

Algal flats

Sea-grass beds

Coral reefs

Dolphins

Birds

Turtles

Dugongs

Shrimp

Fish

Source for oil spills: Applied Science Associates   TIME Map by Lertola/Pugliese

104

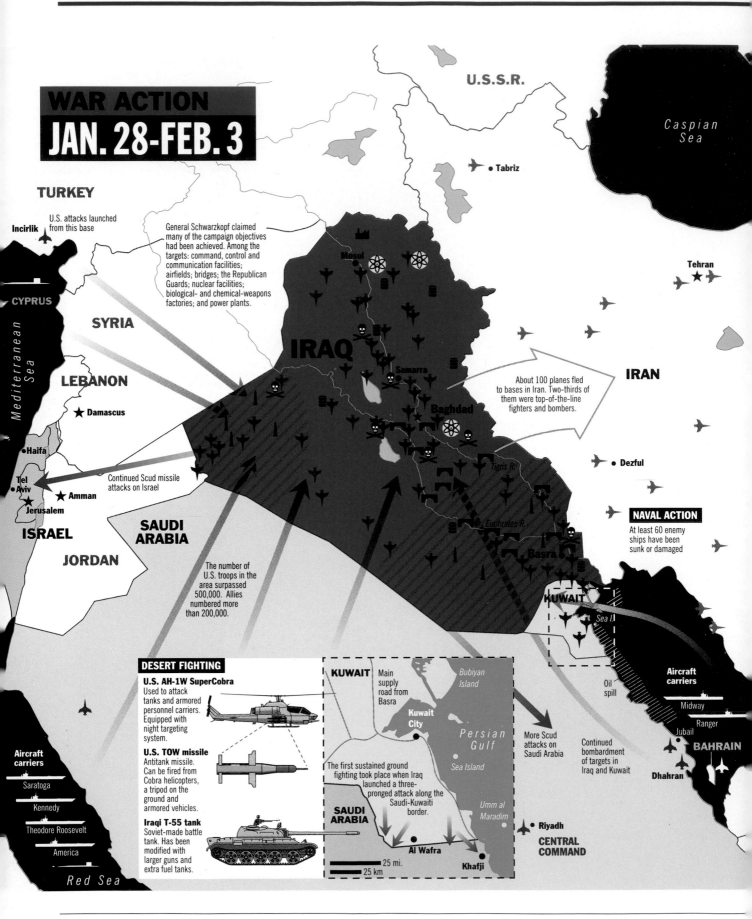

WAR ACTION
JAN. 28-FEB. 3

U.S.S.R.

Caspian Sea

TURKEY

U.S. attacks launched from this base

Incirlik

•Tabriz

General Schwarzkopf claimed many of the campaign objectives had been achieved. Among the targets: command, control and communication facilities; airfields; bridges; the Republican Guards; nuclear facilities; biological- and chemical-weapons factories; and power plants.

CYPRUS

Tehran

Mosul

SYRIA

IRAQ

Mediterranean Sea

LEBANON

Samarra

IRAN

★ **Damascus**

About 100 planes fled to bases in Iran. Two-thirds of them were top-of-the-line fighters and bombers.

•**Haifa**

Baghdad

•Dezful

Tel •Aviv

Tigris R.

★ **Amman**

Continued Scud missile attacks on Israel

•Jerusalem

ISRAEL

NAVAL ACTION

SAUDI ARABIA

JORDAN

At least 60 enemy ships have been sunk or damaged

Euphrates R.

The number of U.S. troops in the area surpassed 500,000. Allies numbered more than 200,000.

Basra

KUWAIT

Sea I

Oil spill

Aircraft carriers

DESERT FIGHTING

KUWAIT   Main supply road from Basra

Bubiyan Island

Midway

U.S. AH-1W SuperCobra
Used to attack tanks and armored personnel carriers. Equipped with night targeting system.

Kuwait City

Persian Gulf

More Scud attacks on Saudi Arabia

Continued bombardment of targets in Iraq and Kuwait

Ranger

Jubail

BAHRAIN

Aircraft carriers

U.S. TOW missile
Antitank missile. Can be fired from Cobra helicopters, a tripod on the ground and armored vehicles.

Sea Island

Dhahran

Saratoga

The first sustained ground fighting took place when Iraq launched a three-pronged attack along the Saudi-Kuwaiti border.

Kennedy

SAUDI ARABIA

Umm al Maradim

Theodore Roosevelt

Iraqi T-55 tank
Soviet-made battle tank. Has been modified with larger guns and extra fuel tanks.

•**Riyadh**

America

Al Wafra

CENTRAL COMMAND

Khafji

25 mi.

25 km

Red Sea

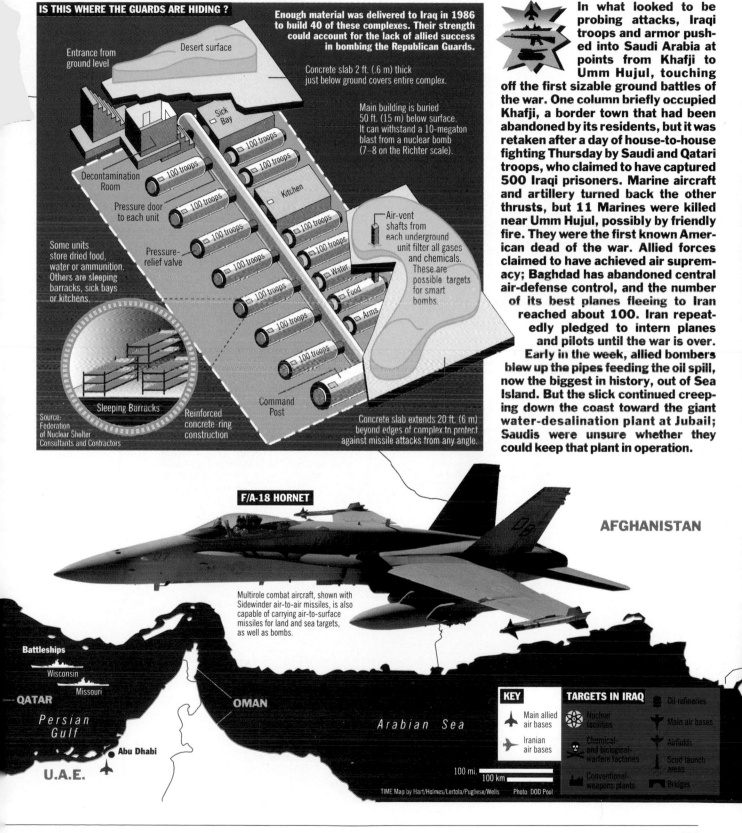

IS THIS WHERE THE GUARDS ARE HIDING ?

Enough material was delivered to Iraq in 1986 to build 40 of these complexes. Their strength could account for the lack of allied success in bombing the Republican Guards.

Entrance from ground level

Desert surface

Concrete slab 2 ft. (.6 m) thick just below ground covers entire complex.

Main building is buried 50 ft. (15 m) below surface. It can withstand a 10-megaton blast from a nuclear bomb (7–8 on the Richter scale).

Sick Bay

Decontamination Room

100 troops

Pressure door to each unit

Kitchen

100 troops

100 troops

100 troops

Air-vent shafts from each underground unit filter all gases and chemicals. These are possible targets for smart bombs.

Some units store dried food, water or ammunition. Others are sleeping barracks, sick bays or kitchens.

Pressure-relief valve

100 troops

100 troops

100 troops

Water

100 troops

Food

100 troops

Arms

Sleeping Barracks

100 troops

Reinforced concrete-ring construction

Command Post

Source: Federation of Nuclear Shelter Consultants and Contractors

Concrete slab extends 20 ft. (6 m) beyond edges of complex to protect against missile attacks from any angle.

In what looked to be probing attacks, Iraqi troops and armor pushed into Saudi Arabia at points from Khafji to Umm Hujul, touching off the first sizable ground battles of the war. One column briefly occupied Khafji, a border town that had been abandoned by its residents, but it was retaken after a day of house-to-house fighting Thursday by Saudi and Qatari troops, who claimed to have captured 500 Iraqi prisoners. Marine aircraft and artillery turned back the other thrusts, but 11 Marines were killed near Umm Hujul, possibly by friendly fire. They were the first known American dead of the war. Allied forces claimed to have achieved air supremacy; Baghdad has abandoned central air-defense control, and the number of its best planes fleeing to Iran reached about 100. Iran repeatedly pledged to intern planes and pilots until the war is over.

Early in the week, allied bombers blew up the pipes feeding the oil spill, now the biggest in history, out of Sea Island. But the slick continued creeping down the coast toward the giant water-desalination plant at Jubail; Saudis were unsure whether they could keep that plant in operation.

F/A-18 HORNET

AFGHANISTAN

Multirole combat aircraft, shown with Sidewinder air-to-air missiles, is also capable of carrying air-to-surface missiles for land and sea targets, as well as bombs.

Battleships

Wisconsin

Missouri

QATAR

OMAN

Persian Gulf

Arabian Sea

Abu Dhabi

U.A.E.

KEY

✈ Main allied air bases
✈ Iranian air bases

TARGETS IN IRAQ

⚛ Nuclear facilities
☠ Chemical- and biological-warfare factories
▮ Conventional-weapons plants

◆ Oil refineries
✈ Main air bases
✈ Airfields
▮ Scud launch areas
▮ Bridges

100 mi.
100 km

TIME Map by Hart/Holmes/Lertola/Pugliese/Wells   Photo: DOD Pool

WAR ACTION
FEB. 4-10

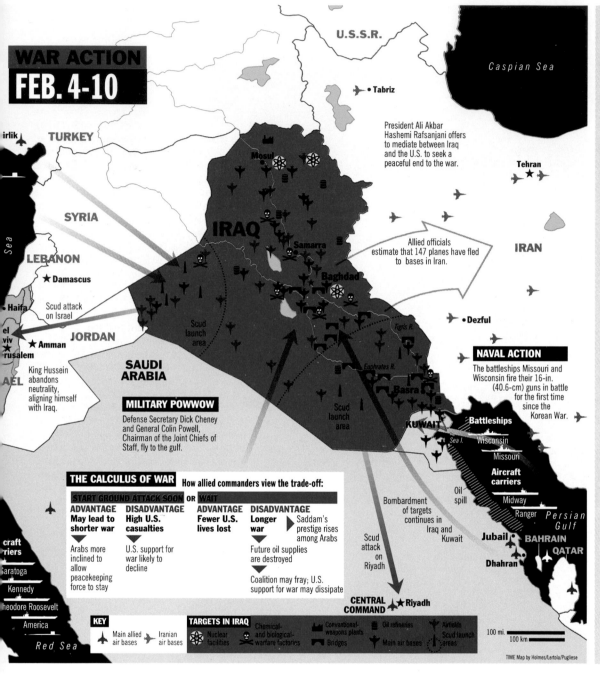

U.S.S.R.

Caspian Sea

TURKEY

SYRIA

LEBANON
★ Damascus

Scud attack
on Israel

JORDAN
★ Amman

King Hussein
abandons
neutrality,
aligning himself
with Iraq.

**SAUDI
ARABIA**

MILITARY POWWOW
Defense Secretary Dick Cheney
and General Colin Powell,
Chairman of the Joint Chiefs of
Staff, fly to the gulf.

IRAQ

Mosul

Samarra

Baghdad

Scud
launch
area

• Tabriz

Tehran ★

President Ali Akbar
Hashemi Rafsanjani offers
to mediate between Iraq
and the U.S. to seek a
peaceful end to the war.

Allied officials
estimate that 147 planes have fled
to bases in Iran.

IRAN

• Dezful

Tigris R.

Scud
launch
area

Euphrates R.

Basra

KUWAIT

NAVAL ACTION
The battleships Missouri and
Wisconsin fire their 16-in.
(40.6-cm) guns in battle
for the first time
since the
Korean War.

Battleships
Wisconsin
Missouri

**Aircraft
carriers**
Midway
Ranger

*Persian
Gulf*

Oil
spill

Bombardment
of targets
continues in
Iraq and
Kuwait

Jubail

**BAHRAIN
QATAR**

Dhahran

Scud
attack
on
Riyadh

**CENTRAL
COMMAND** ★ Riyadh

100 mi.
100 km

TIME Map by Holmes/Lertola/Pugliese

THE CALCULUS OF WAR — How allied commanders view the trade-off:

START GROUND ATTACK SOON OR **WAIT**

ADVANTAGE	DISADVANTAGE	ADVANTAGE	DISADVANTAGE
May lead to shorter war	**High U.S. casualties**	**Fewer U.S. lives lost**	**Longer war**
▼	▼		▶ Saddam's prestige rises among Arabs
Arabs more inclined to allow peacekeeping force to stay	U.S. support for war likely to decline		▼ Future oil supplies are destroyed
			▼ Coalition may fray; U.S. support for war may dissipate

KEY
▲ Main allied air bases   ➤ Iranian air bases

TARGETS IN IRAQ
⊛ Nuclear facilities   ☠ Chemical- and biological-warfare factories   ▤ Conventional-weapons plants   ▮ Oil refineries   ✈ Airfields
◼ Bridges   ✈ Main air bases   ⊙ Scud launch areas

Red Sea

irlik

Sea

• Haifa

el
viv
rusalem

AEL

craft
riers

Saratoga

Kennedy

heodore Roosevelt

America

GULF CALENDAR

MID-FEBRUARY THRU MID-JULY

Shamal winds. These hot, oppressive winds last from one to five days and, in June and early July, can continue almost without cessation. They can reduce visibility to almost zero, making navigation difficult. Shamals can also produce strange atmospheric conditions, sometimes causing fever, flu, respiratory allergies and marked changes in mood.

MARCH 17 TO APRIL 15

Ramadan. One of the most important—and demanding—months of the Islamic year. Observant Muslims will abstain from food, drink, smoking, sex and even injections, from sunrise to sunset, March 17 to April 15. The holiday will almost certainly intensify political and religious passions, though it is not perceived as a particular impediment to waging war. Allied officials say Arab governments in the alliance have assured them that Muslim troops will receive special religious dispensation to fight during this period.

JUNE

Hajj. With few exceptions, devout Muslims are required to perform the Hajj, or pilgrimage to Mecca, at least once in a lifetime. Mass travel to Saudi Arabia begins early in June, with the holiday reaching its high point June 21-22. Up to 2 million people participate each year.

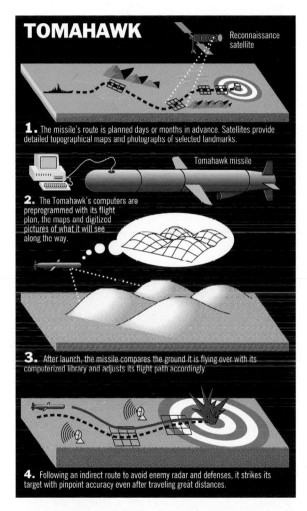

TOMAHAWK

Reconnaissance satellite

1. The missile's route is planned days or months in advance. Satellites provide detailed topographical maps and photographs of selected landmarks.

Tomahawk missile

2. The Tomahawk's computers are preprogrammed with its flight plan, the maps and digitized pictures of what it will see along the way.

3. After launch, the missile compares the ground it is flying over with its computerized library and adjusts its flight path accordingly

4. Following an indirect route to avoid enemy radar and defenses, it strikes its target with pinpoint accuracy even after traveling great distances.

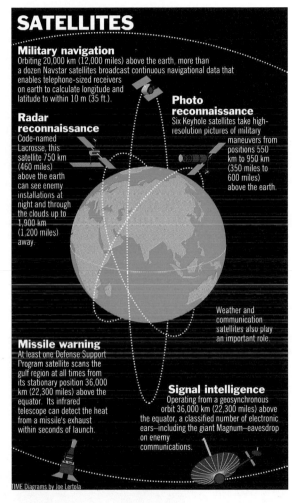

SATELLITES

Military navigation
Orbiting 20,000 km (12,000 miles) above the earth, more than a dozen Navstar satellites broadcast continuous navigational data that enables telephone-sized receivers on earth to calculate longitude and latitude to within 10 m (35 ft.).

Photo reconnaissance
Six Keyhole satellites take high-resolution pictures of military maneuvers from positions 550 km to 950 km (350 miles to 600 miles) above the earth.

Radar reconnaissance
Code-named Lacrosse, this satellite 750 km (460 miles) above the earth can see enemy installations at night and through the clouds up to 1,900 km (1,200 miles) away.

Weather and communication satellites also play an important role.

Missile warning
At least one Defense Support Program satellite scans the gulf region at all times from its stationary position 36,000 km (22,300 miles) above the equator. Its infrared telescope can detect the heat from a missile's exhaust within seconds of launch.

Signal intelligence
Operating from a geosynchronous orbit 36,000 km (22,300 miles) above the equator, a classified number of electronic ears—including the giant Magnum—eavesdrop on enemy communications.

TIME Diagrams by Joe Lertola

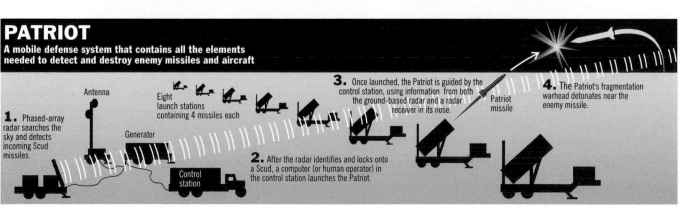

PATRIOT
A mobile defense system that contains all the elements needed to detect and destroy enemy missiles and aircraft

Antenna

Eight launch stations containing 4 missiles each

3. Once launched, the Patriot is guided by the control station, using information from both the ground-based radar and a radar receiver in its nose.

Patriot missile

4. The Patriot's fragmentation warhead detonates near the enemy missile.

1. Phased-array radar searches the sky and detects incoming Scud missiles.

Generator

Control station

2. After the radar identifies and locks onto a Scud, a computer (or human operator) in the control station launches the Patriot.

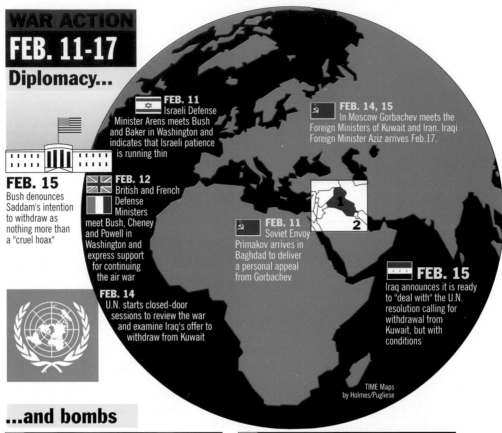

WAR ACTION
FEB. 11-17
Diplomacy...

FEB. 11
Israeli Defense Minister Arens meets Bush and Baker in Washington and indicates that Israeli patience is running thin

FEB. 15
Bush denounces Saddam's intention to withdraw as nothing more than a "cruel hoax"

FEB. 12
British and French Defense Ministers meet Bush, Cheney and Powell in Washington and express support for continuing the air war

FEB. 14
U.N. starts closed-door sessions to review the war and examine Iraq's offer to withdraw from Kuwait

FEB. 14, 15
In Moscow Gorbachev meets the Foreign Ministers of Kuwait and Iran. Iraqi Foreign Minister Aziz arrives Feb.17.

FEB. 11
Soviet Envoy Primakov arrives in Baghdad to deliver a personal appeal from Gorbachev

FEB. 15
Iraq announces it is ready to "deal with" the U.N. resolution calling for withdrawal from Kuwait, but with conditions

TIME Maps
by Holmes/Pugliese

...and bombs

1 BAGHDAD

Martyr's Bridge
Freedom Bridge
Ministry of Defense
Sinak Bridge
Republic Bridge
Al Rasheed Hotel
July 14 Bridge
Presidential Compound
Bombing site
Yarmuk Hospital
Tigris

1 mi
2 km

In the continued air assault on Baghdad a large concrete bunker was hit, killing hundreds of civilians. Three downtown bridges were destroyed.

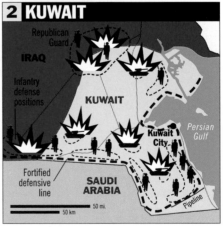

2 KUWAIT

Republican Guard
IRAQ
Infantry defense positions
KUWAIT
Persian Gulf
Kuwait City
Fortified defensive line
SAUDI ARABIA
Pipeline

50 km
50 mi.

Heavy bombing of Kuwait has increased. 1,300 of Iraq's 4,280 tanks and 1,100 of its 3,110 artillery pieces have been destroyed.

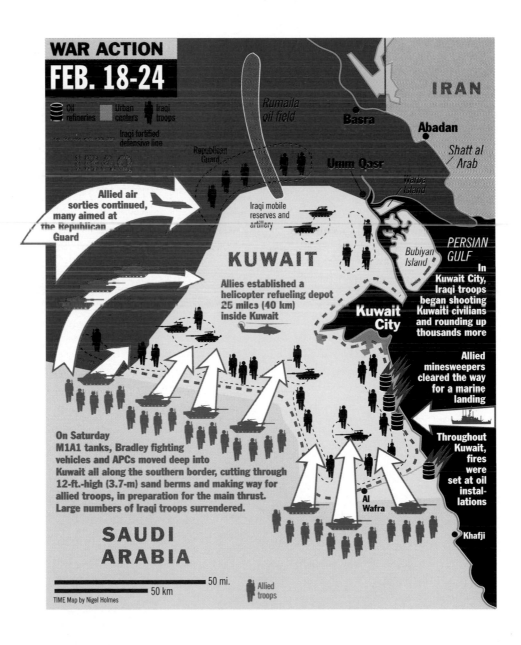

WAR ACTION
FEB. 18-24

Oil refineries | Urban centers | Iraqi troops

Iraqi fortified defensive line

IRAN

Rumaila oil field

Basra

Abadan

Shatt al Arab

IRAQ

Republican Guard

Umm Qasr

Warba Island

Allied air sorties continued, many aimed at the Republican Guard

Iraqi mobile reserves and artillery

PERSIAN GULF

Bubiyan Island

KUWAIT

Allies established a helicopter refueling depot 25 miles (40 km) inside Kuwait

Kuwait City

In Kuwait City, Iraqi troops began shooting Kuwaiti civilians and rounding up thousands more

Allied minesweepers cleared the way for a marine landing

On Saturday M1A1 tanks, Bradley fighting vehicles and APCs moved deep into Kuwait all along the southern border, cutting through 12-ft.-high (3.7-m) sand berms and making way for allied troops, in preparation for the main thrust. Large numbers of Iraqi troops surrendered.

Throughout Kuwait, fires were set at oil installations

Al Wafra

Khafji

SAUDI ARABIA

50 mi.
50 km

TIME Map by Nigel Holmes

Allied troops

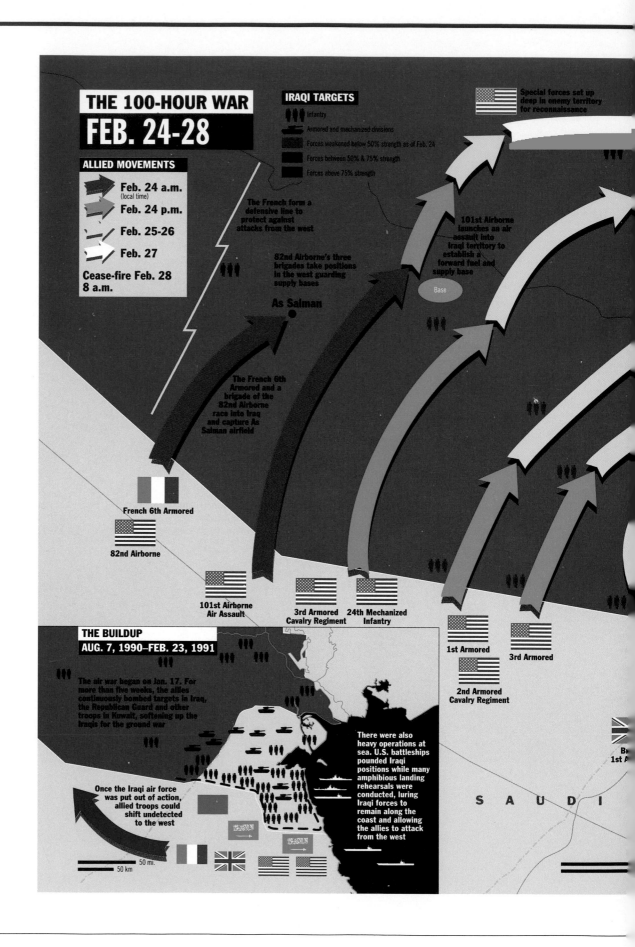

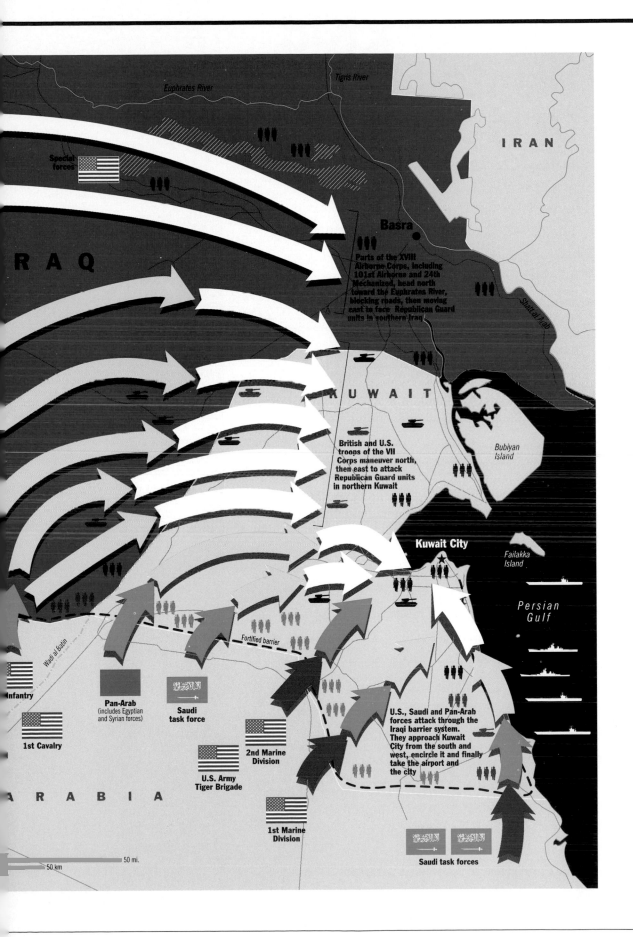

Special forces

Euphrates River

Tigris River

IRAN

I R A Q

Basra

Parts of the XVIII Airborne Corps, including 101st Airborne and 24th Mechanized, head north toward the Euphrates River, blocking roads, then moving east to face Republican Guard units in southern Iraq.

Shatt al Arab

K U W A I T

British and U.S. troops of the VII Corps maneuver north, then east to attack Republican Guard units in northern Kuwait

Bubiyan Island

Kuwait City

Failakka Island

Persian Gulf

Wadi al Batin

Fortified barrier

U.S., Saudi and Pan-Arab forces attack through the Iraqi barrier system. They approach Kuwait City from the south and west, encircle it and finally take the airport and the city

Infantry

Pan-Arab
(includes Egyptian and Syrian forces)

Saudi task force

1st Cavalry

2nd Marine Division

U.S. Army Tiger Brigade

1st Marine Division

Saudi task forces

A R A B I A

50 mi.

50 km

A South Bronx Kid Who Wanted to Be A Hero

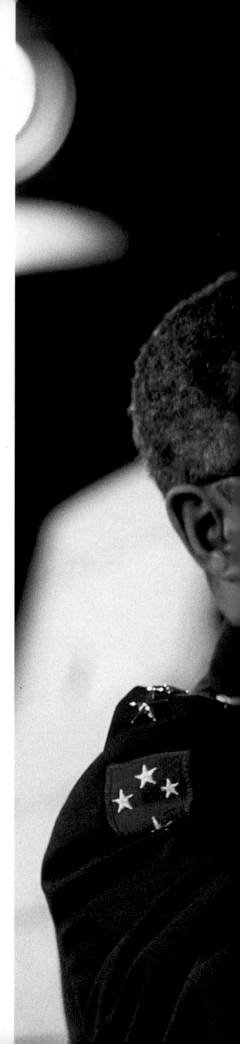

Long before Colin Powell became a four-star general in the U.S. Army—perhaps even before he began to dream about becoming one—he unilaterally changed the pronunciation of his first name. Until then, Colin had rhymed, British-style, with pollen. But when Powell learned that the first celebrated American hero of World War II, Captain Colin P. Kelly Jr., pronounced the name differently, he decided he would too. From that day forward, Colin would be pronounced colon—like the punctuation mark that promises more to come.

Whatever the symbolism, Powell has spent much of his adult life delivering on such a promise. Though not a West Pointer, he became in 1989 the first graduate of ROTC to be named Chairman of the Joint Chiefs of Staff, and in 1991 he became the first general since George Marshall to preside over a conclusive U.S. victory in war. Powell was also the first black to hold the Pentagon's top uniformed job and the first to serve as the President's National Security Adviser. Many think he could turn out to be the first general since Eisenhower—and the first black ever—to have a realistic shot at being either Vice President or President of the U.S. Says former Defense Secretary Caspar Weinberger, who played an important part in the development of Powell's career: "I don't know anybody in this town who's served so long in such sensitive jobs who's been as free of criticism as Colin."

That's not bad for a Harlem-born son of immigrants who

Colin Powell, Chairman of the Joint Chiefs of Staff, briefs the press on the campaign against Iraq.

became a soldier almost by accident. "The thing about Colin," says President Bush's press secretary Marlin Fitzwater, "is that he has an attitude of hoping for the best but preparing for the worst. He's a can-do kind of guy but without the bravado. He tells you what the military can do and what they can't do. He doesn't make any claims he can't keep. He's honest without being boorish about it."

To the dismay of more status-conscious bureaucrats, Powell democratically carried his own charts when he arrived at the White House to brief President Bush during the gulf war, but he now and then demonstrated a steelier side as well. Like that time, for example, when he was asked how the U.S. planned to defeat Saddam Hussein's army, and he unsmilingly replied, "We're going to cut it off, and then we're going to kill it."

Powell is perceived by a few perhaps envious critics as a "political general," meaning one who is more familiar with congressional sensitivities than with, say, the vital statistics of the Bradley fighting vehicle. To some extent that may be true. Smooth and relaxed, with an easy sense of humor and a broad smile, he has spent most of the past two decades in Washington, where he has performed a variety of jobs, including a rather complicated role in the Iran-*contra* scandal. During the gulf war, he not only kept the President and Secretary of Defense fully informed of the war's progress but labored to maintain congressional support as well. He is officially registered as an independent voter in his native New York, is a strong supporter of what he calls the civil rights "struggle," and has had a friendship with Jesse Jackson, who calls him "a man of integrity" and who occasionally consulted him by phone during the 1988 presidential campaign. Even so, Powell's main patrons have been in the conservative Reagan and Bush administrations.

Political or not, Powell insists he would rather be "with the troops" than hobnobbing in the Federal Triangle. He served two tours in Vietnam. The first time, in 1963, he won a Purple Heart when a hidden Viet Cong *punji* stake punctured his left foot. On his second tour, in 1968-69, he won the Soldier's Medal after a helicopter he was riding in crashed and he single-handedly rescued four others from the wreckage. In the early '70s he commanded an infantry battalion—and helped rid it of serious drug and racial problems; in the early '80s he was an assistant division commander; and in 1986 he took over the Army V Corps in Frankfurt, Germany. Like General H. Norman Schwarzkopf and others in the "never-again" generation of military leaders with bitter memories of Vietnam, Powell favors us-

ing maximum force precisely delivered in any military engagement and in giving field commanders as much leeway as possible in battle.

The gulf strategy paid off so well that the war had barely ended before members of Congress started talking about promoting both Powell and Schwarzkopf to five-star generals of the Army. Public-opinion polls indicated, moreover, that a large majority of Americans preferred Powell to Vice President Dan Quayle as a running mate for Bush on the Republican ticket in 1992. Powell's response: "I have no interest in politics at the moment. I am Chairman of the Joint Chiefs of Staff and hope to remain Chairman of the Joint Chiefs of Staff." Many saw artful meaning in the phrase "at the moment." The White House, for its part, let it be known that Powell had a good shot at serving a second two-year term as Chairman. Besides, top Bush aides pointed out that the President's own standing in the polls was at record highs and bringing in Powell would merely cast doubt on Bush's judgment in choosing Quayle in 1988.

A number of Powell's friends think he would prefer, in any case, to serve another term as Chairman. It's not a bad life. He and his wife Alma live in a large Army-provided house at Fort Myer, Va., near Arlington cemetery, with a panoramic view of Washington. Powell, who works hard but is no workaholic, managed even during the war to get home at fairly regular hours. Alma, named one of the world's best-dressed women in 1991, enjoys entertaining a good deal and has a sharp sense of humor. She not only tries to ignore his scowls when she lights an after-dinner cigarette but retaliates by letting him know when she thinks he has had too many rum and Cokes, his favorite drink.

On weekends Powell devotes much of his spare time to his hobbies: repairing old Volvos in his garage or driveway and watching old movies on his VCR. Otherwise, he'll get down on the floor and join his two-year-old grandson Jeffrey in playing with Lego blocks. Family is important to Powell. His 28-year-old son Michael (Jeffrey's father) is a law student at Georgetown University. Michael's military career ended in 1987 when, as an executive officer, he suffered severe injuries in a jeep accident. The Powells also have two daughters, Linda, 26, an actress who had a small part in the movie *Reversal of Fortune* and played a leading role in an off-off-Broadway play shortly after the gulf war ended; and Annemarie, 21 in May, a student at William and Mary in Virginia.

Colin Powell arrived where he is today through a mixture of skill, luck, good timing, good friends and good upbringing—plus, as he puts it, "the sacrifices of those black soldiers who served this great nation in war for over 200 years previously." Powell was born in Harlem on April 5, 1937, and raised, along with an older sister, in the South Bronx. Neither of his parents, natives of Jamaica, finished high school. Powell's father was a sales clerk in Manhattan's garment district, his mother a seamstress. As Powell remembers his late parents, both repeatedly urged that he and his sister, now a fourth-grade teacher in Santa Ana, Calif., "make something of your life."

Young Colin found that advice a little hard to follow in the beginning. He earned indifferent grades at public elementary schools and Morris High School and got off to a slow start at City College of New York, to which he began commuting by bus in 1954. Enrolled as an engineering major, he remained in that discipline for exactly one semester—until the day a teacher "asked me to visualize a cone intersecting a plane in space." He quickly changed his major to geology and duly earned a degree in what he describes as "mastering the rock formations under Manhattan."

Long before graduation, however, something significant happened to Powell. On a fine spring day in 1954, he saw "a bunch of fellows wandering around Amsterdam and Convent avenues in uniform." They were Reserve Officers' Training Corps cadets at CCNY. More specifically, they were members of the Pershing Rifles, who, as Powell describes them, wore a whipcord on their shoulders, "suggesting that they were a little more serious than the average ROTC cadet." At the mere sight of these uniformed dandies, Powell was hooked. He signed up in the fall for ROTC, successfully pledged the Pershing Rifles, and spent the next four years "concentrating on ROTC . . . and tolerating the academic demands of the college as best I could." Powell's final grade average "barely crept above C"—and that only because he earned straight A's in his military subjects. After college, he went directly into the Army in 1958.

Much about the military appeals to Powell. He discovered early on that he was suited to a life of "discipline." He also soon discovered that the military offered minorities "a route out, a route up." He had not really understood the need for such a route when he was growing up. As a boy, he says, he had little firsthand experience with discrimination. For one thing, the West Indian heritage passed on by his parents was more positive than that of many American blacks. For another, Powell grew up in the ultimate melting pot (even managing to pick up a little Yiddish along the way). "On Kelly Street in the South Bronx," he wrote not long ago, "everybody was a 'minority.'" Indeed, he added, "I was 21 in Fort Benning, Ga., before I ever saw what is referred to as a white Anglo-Saxon Protestant."

But Powell does recall being refused service in a Georgia diner because he was black. Also, a Southern state trooper briefly detained him for speeding in an old Volkswagen Beetle that bore an ALL THE WAY WITH LBJ bumper sticker.

Powell's awareness of racial reality was heightened during the early '60s when he met a speech therapist named Alma Vivian Johnson on a blind date while he was stationed at Fort Devens, Mass. A native of Birmingham, Alma had far more personal knowledge of Jim Crow laws than Powell did. Her father and uncle had been high school principals in segregated Southern schools and had been among the frontline troops in the battle for integration. Alma and Colin Powell were married in 1962, and when he went to Vietnam for his first tour, she returned to Birmingham, the scene of many civil rights demonstrations and much violence, to live with her parents. Being there while her husband was in Vietnam, she later told an interviewer, "was like we had two wars going on at once."

Powell tries hard—perhaps a little too hard—not to dwell on the racial implications of his career and defends the disproportionately high percentage of blacks in today's volunteer Army. But when he is being interviewed by a reporter for a black publication or is speaking to a black audience, he is more forthcoming. To the National Association of Black Journalists, Powell said two years ago, "The armed forces of the United States afford the kind of opportunity for [black] advancement that, regrettably, does not exist in every part of our society, even within your own profession." Noting the military contributions of blacks throughout U.S. history, he insisted that now "almost all barriers have dropped." His generation, Powell said, witnessed the sea change. They "saw a Chappie James come along and prove that he was as qualified as anybody to drive an airplane . . . Or General Roscoe Robinson, who became our first black Army four-star . . . And all those NCOs and soldiers who have served their nation so well." Powell continued, "So the real story is that, yes, I have climbed well, and I climbed hard, and I climbed over the cliff. But always on the backs and contributions of those who went before me."

Things began really breaking Powell's way in 1969. Having returned from his second Vietnam tour as a major, he was sent by the Army to get an MBA at George Washington University. Powell was deeply troubled by the anti–Vietnam War protests he saw on campus—and by the way Vietnam veterans were sometimes treated by the other students—but he generally found college much more rewarding the second time around. He earned excellent grades, including two A's in computer courses from Professor Marvin Wofsey, who recalls that his only problem with Powell was that "he split his infinitives." In 1972, during the Nixon Administration, Powell was chosen for a White House fellowship program, which provides well-qualified special assistants to key federal offices. NATO Ambassador William Taft IV was a member of the screening panel that year and recalls that the chairman started the final selection by asking, "Aside from Colin Powell, whom do we select?"

Powell was assigned to the Office of Management and Budget, where he worked directly under Budget Director Caspar Weinberger and his deputy, Frank Carlucci. It was, Powell says, a "dream job." Not only did he get to see the arcane federal budget process up close, but he also acquired Weinberger and Carlucci as future patrons.

During the Carter Administration, Powell won his first general's star and worked in both the Energy Department and the Pentagon. But it wasn't until Ronald Reagan became President in 1981 that Powell's career, already impressive, took on real star quality. Reagan made Weinberger his Secretary of Defense, Weinberger made Carlucci his principal deputy, and Powell came aboard two years later as Weinberger's military assistant. There were exciting things to be done, the rebuilding of the U.S. military.

But the Reagan Administration was also preoccupied with trying to overthrow the Sandinista regime in Nicaragua, at almost any price. It began providing aid to anti-Sandinista guerrillas, the *contras,* and when Congress voted to cut off that aid, key people in the Administration, including gung-ho Marine Lieut. Colonel Oliver North, began looking for covert ways to keep the *contras* in action.

The Iran-*contra* scandal was about to happen, starting with the secret sale of U.S. arms to Iran in hopes of gaining the release of American hostages, then continuing with the illegal use of arms-sale profits to finance the *contras*. According to documents and testimony compiled by the special congressional committees that investigated the scandal, Powell's involvement began in November 1985, when John Poindexter or Oliver North at the National Security Council secretly asked the Defense Department to provide HAWK antiaircraft missiles (and, later, TOW antitank

missiles) for sale to Iran. Weinberger and Powell both opposed the deal, but when the White House insisted, Powell responded by trying to find a way in which arms could be exported to Iran, via Israel, without telling Congress. When his subordinates replied that this was impossible without breaking the law, Weinberger carried their message back to the White House. At that point, it was decided to handle the arms-for-hostages deal covertly, through the CIA, transferring the weapons from the Army to the agency for direct shipment to Iran. Since President Reagan claimed he could delay indefinitely his legal obligation to inform Congress about the covert operation, the complicated scheme seemed to accomplish the White House's goal of preventing congressional scrutiny. Powell then arranged the transfer of TOW and HAWK spare parts from the Army to the CIA, instructing senior Army officials to ensure that there was no paper trail and that the Army's own review system for such transfers was bypassed. The Pentagon official Powell turned to after the NSC's November 1985 request for HAWK missiles was Noel Koch, then the principal deputy in the Office of International Security Affairs. Asked recently by TIME to explain his perception of Powell's role in Iran-*contra*, Koch said, "Colin clearly was opposed to it. [But] it was a delicate situation. All his instincts were to do what was required but to take a *de minimis* approach to it. As he saw it, he was answering the mail, and the mail was coming from the White House . . . If it was going to be done, it needed to be done in a way that would minimize the damage to the national interest. The thing was to conceal a politically devastating act."

Later, when the Secretary of the Army raised questions about whether the arms transfers to Iran through the CIA were being reported to Congress as required by law, Powell reluctantly delivered a memo from the Army to Poindexter, the President's National Security Adviser, in which it was pointedly noted that the Army expected the CIA to notify Congress about the arms transfers. It was a classic case of bureaucratic behind covering, and with it Powell's role—and the Army's—ended. Basically, Powell had been caught between strong, contradictory imperatives: Weinberger opposed the operation, and Powell initially helped him try to kill it; on the other hand, very powerful people, including President Reagan, favored the scheme, and Powell helped them carry it off in a way that circumvented normal checks and balances. In doing all this, Powell violated no laws, and no one has even suggested that he knew anything about the diversion of money to the *contras*. But if his hands were not quite as clean as he and others afterward maintained, he had clearly shown that he could walk a bureaucratic high wire with the best of them—and without a net to catch him if he fell.

Shortly after Iran-*contra* broke into the headlines, Poindexter resigned as National Security Adviser. Carlucci, who replaced Poindexter, recommended Powell as his deputy. Later, when Carlucci moved over to become Secretary of Defense, Powell became National Security Adviser. At the NSC, Powell impressed people, both inside and outside the Administration, with his intelligence and grasp of complex foreign-policy issues. Indeed, Carlucci recalls that "within a couple of weeks, Reagan was totally sold on Colin." The same went for Vice President Bush and Secretary of State George Shultz, who frequently took Powell with him on his official trips abroad. Nevertheless, when Bush was elected to succeed Reagan in 1988, he informed Powell that he would like to have his own man, Brent Scowcroft, at the NSC. Powell said he understood and was glad to accept the U.S. forces command at Fort McPherson, Ga., because it would put him back on track for the job he really wanted, Chairman of the Joint Chiefs.

A mere seven months later, with the retirement of then Chairman Admiral William Crowe, Powell had the job he wanted. He couldn't have got it at a better time: just three years earlier, Congress had passed the Goldwater-Nichols Reorganization Act. Among other things, that act transformed the Chairman of the Joint Chiefs from a committee chairman for the individual service chiefs to the unchallenged uniformed head of all the armed forces. Said Barry Goldwater of his bill: "It's the only goddamned thing I've done in the Senate that's worth a damn." The allied success in the gulf war, especially the smooth coordination of U.S. Army, Marine, Air Force, Navy and even Coast Guard forces, suggests that Goldwater may have been right.

And a beneficiary has been a soldier named Colin Powell, who remains remarkably unchanged from the South Bronx kid who fell in love with ROTC uniforms nearly 40 years ago.

Aboard the U.S.S. *Wisconsin*: Powell says he would rather be with the troops than hobnobbing in Washington.

The Very Model Of a Major Modern General

During a visit to Kuwait some years ago, H. (for nothing) Norman Schwarzkopf was given a set of Arab robes and tried them on, for the fun of it. This got him to thinking about one of his heroes, T.E. Lawrence. "It was just like the scene in *Lawrence of Arabia,*" Schwarzkopf said later, "when the British officer's clothes are taken away and replaced by robes, and he waltzes into the desert, intrigued by their feel and grace. I stood in front of the mirror and did the same dance. It was wonderful."

It may well come to pass that when the story of the gulf war is sifted and studied in military classrooms, the accomplishments of the four-star General Schwarzkopf, 56, will rank, if not with those of Lawrence, quite possibly with such World War II desert warriors as General Erwin Rommel and Field Marshal Montgomery. Schwarzkopf himself, not exactly a self-effacing man, might prefer to be lodged in the pantheon with Alexander the Great as well, but that is for the historians to decide. What no one will dispute or fail to marvel at is that Schwarzkopf is the very model of a major modern general: he conceived and executed the gulf-war battle plan with such brilliance and daring that it far outran even his own expectations. One major reason is that the man who commanded the vast armadas of the allied coalition had prepared for this role throughout his professional life.

By all accounts, Norm Schwarzkopf is a passionately engaged leader of considerable talents, and what's more, of a

General H. Norman Schwarzkopf answers press questions during wrap-up briefing on the war.

prophetic mind. As long ago as 1983, he foresaw the possibility that the U.S. might find itself fighting in the Middle East if an unfriendly nation succeeded in taking over a neighbor. More than two years ago, as chief of the U.S. Central Command (which covers the Middle East and South Asia), Schwarzkopf set out to design a full-fledged contingency plan. "He always believed the big eruption would come in the Middle East," says his sister Sally. "He took the job at Central Command with the idea that he might well have to fight."

Late last July, just five days before Saddam Hussein launched his invasion, Schwarzkopf and his staff happened to be running a computer-simulated war game predicated on the possibility that Iraq might overrun Kuwait. All that was necessary after that was for Schwarzkopf to polish his plan. It became the model for Operation Desert Shield, and when the Shield became a Storm, it was Schwarzkopf who got the job of running the campaign as commander of the allied forces.

Throughout the war, he never had to worry about second-guessing or interference, either from Washington or from other leaders in the coalition. Some past Presidents, like Lyndon Johnson and Richard Nixon, have fancied themselves cunning battlefield tacticians, and liked to direct their generals hither and thither; George Bush, Dick Cheney and Schwarzkopf's immediate boss and old friend, Colin Powell, knew better. Desert Storm, said Cheney at the outset, "is basically Norm's plan. It's fundamentally Norm's to execute."

After directing—on perilously short notice—the biggest buildup of U.S. forces since Vietnam, Schwarzkopf orchestrated a complex logistical, tactical and strategic war machine comprising forces from 28 Western and Arab nations totaling 675,000 troops, hundreds of ships and thousands of airplanes and tanks, all fully equipped, and all operating right on schedule.

At the same time, he demonstrated the talents of a first-class diplomat, achieving cohesion not only among the traditionally rivalrous U.S. military services, but among the various Arab and Western allies, with all their conflicting interests. He was especially careful in his dealings with the sensitive Saudis. When King Fahd sent word that he was worried about the possibility of an attack on Riyadh, Schwarzkopf went to the palace to reassure him, advising Fahd that his main concern was the possibility that Saddam could fire Scud missiles with chemical warheads at the capital. That was not much in the way of reassurance, but at least the King got straight talk.

That's Schwarzkopf's way: subtlety and euphemism

do not come easily to him. When Desert Shield began, he called Iraqi commanders a "bunch of thugs" and their troops "lousy." He declared, "I don't consider myself dovish, and I certainly don't consider myself hawkish. Maybe I would describe myself as owlish— wise enough to understand that you want to do everything possible to avoid war; that once you're committed to war, then be ferocious enough to do whatever is necessary to get it over with as quickly as possible in victory."

His strategy, he explained, was to "suck [Saddam] into the desert as far as I could. Then I'd pound the living heck out of him. Finally, I'd engulf him and police him up." The same straightforward approach characterized his style in the war room of his Riyadh compound. After developing his battle plans with the help of top allied commanders, Schwarzkopf delegated day-to-day operations to his four commanders. A resolute overseer, he ran his campaign 18 hours a day. "I started out with what I thought was going to be a very orderly schedule," he told a TIME reporter. "A 7 a.m. staff briefing, a 10 a.m. coalition briefing, then a 7 p.m. briefing with the component commanders. Boy, it looked like it was great. But I've got to tell you, more often than not, the 7 a.m. meeting did not come off because everybody was up so late at night."

The fault, he said, was mainly his own. "I just can't drag my body out of bed at 7 in the morning, given the lack of sleep I've had. So sometimes that first meeting was at 8 or 9. I think it was a great military leader, Norm Schwarzkopf, who once said one of the principles of war is never to miss the opportunity to take a nap. I learned that in Vietnam. There have been a couple of occasions [recently] when I arrived at the fuzzy-headed stage and literally took myself out of action because I realized I was getting a little bit punchy and shouldn't be making decisions."

His admiring colleagues found it easy to forgive him. "Initially," said a British commander, "we were somewhat taken aback by his gung-ho appearance, but in a very short time we came to realize that here was a highly intelligent soldier—a skilled planner, administrator and battlefield commander."

That judgment came as no surprise to Schwarzkopf's old friends, who seem to regard him with unalloyed admiration, if not outright idolatry. Retired Army General Ward LeHardy, who was Schwarzkopf's West Point classmate, says, with not a little hyperbole, that "Norm is this generation's Doug MacArthur. He's got the tactical brilliance of Patton, the strategic insight of Eisenhower and the modesty of Bradley."

Many people might quarrel with the modesty part. Schwarzkopf can be lighthearted and amiable, but he can also display the ego—and petulance—of a field marshal. He has been known to pore over his press clippings, underlining criticisms or perceived slights, and flogging memos about them to his subordinates. He has had epic temper tantrums. When these erupted, said a senior Joint Chiefs of Staff officer, Schwarzkopf would start "yelling and cursing and throwing things." What is most striking about him is a familiar characteristic often found in military leaders everywhere: an abiding certitude, a bristling self-assurance. Many Army brats acquire this with their first pair of long pants, and they nurture it into adulthood. Schwarzkopf's father, Herbert Norman Sr., the son of German immigrants, was also a West Pointer who became a general. In the straitened period between world wars, Norm Sr. left the Army to enter civic life. As head of the New Jersey state police, he led the investigation into the sensational kidnapping of Charles Lindbergh's baby son in 1932. For a time, Schwarzkopf even became a radio star, narrating the popular *Gangbusters,* a semi-documentary shoot-'em-up series about the FBI.

At the outbreak of World War II, he rejoined the Army and from 1942 to 1948 led a mission to Tehran, where he organized Iran's imperial police force. According to U.S. and Iranian historians, he returned to Tehran in 1953 to play a key role in the CIA operation that overthrew nationalist Prime Minister Mohammed Mossadegh and re-established the Shah on his throne.

Norm Jr., who was born in Trenton, N.J., began looking to his father's stars at an early age. When photos were taken for the yearbook at Bordentown Military Institute, near Trenton, 10-year-old cadet Norman posed for two pictures, one smiling, the other grim faced. His mother preferred the smiling version, but little Norm hung tough. "Someday, when I become a general," he said, "I want people to know that I'm serious." He wasn't kidding.

His first overseas posting, at age 12, was to Tehran, with his father, and the exposure to the exotic ways of the Middle East was to have a lasting impact on his sensibilities. After a year, he was packed off to European schools, where he developed a fluency in German and French and dreamed all the while of a military career.

At West Point, the young plebe was known variously as Norm Jr., Schwarzie, the Bear and, in deference to his short-fused temper, Stormin' Norman. Nobody ever called him Herb; Norm's father, who detested Herbert, refused to inflict the name on his son but gave him the *H.*

Looking back on the West Point years, Schwarzkopf's old friends still marvel at his single-minded, unapologetic ambition. "He read widely on war," says Retired General Leroy Suddath, a former roommate who remains no less enthralled than General LeHardy. "He saw himself as a successor to Alexander the Great, and we didn't laugh when he said it. He just assumed he would be an outstanding success."

Norm's favorite battle was Cannae, in which Hannibal crushed the forces of Rome in 216 B.C. "Cannae," says Suddath, "was the first real war of annihilation, the kind Norman wanted to fight." He desperately wanted to take his country's forces into a major battle. "We'd talk about these things in the wee hours, and Norman would predict not only that he would lead a major American army into combat, but that it would be a battle decisive to the nation."

Suddath claims that Schwarzkopf, with a reported IQ of 170, could easily have graduated first in his class of 480 instead of 43rd, "but he did a lot of other things except study." He wrestled, played a bit of soccer, tennis and football, and on weekends slipped down to New York City to see Broadway shows. He sang tenor and conducted the chapel choir and loved listening to what Suddath calls the "uplifting" martial music of Wagner and Tchaikovsky's cannonading *1812 Overture*—"the sort that makes you feel on top of the world."

After he was graduated in 1956, Schwarzkopf earned a master's degree in mechanical engineering at the University of Southern California, then began a measured training program that took him from post to post, command to command. He and Colin Powell became fast friends when both, for a period, were assigned Washington duty (their daughters appeared in the same high school play).

Schwarzkopf served two tours in Vietnam, first as an accomplished paratrooper advising Vietnamese airborne troops, then as commander of an infantry battalion. Twice he was wounded, and three times he won the Silver Star, as well as three Bronze Stars and the Distinguished Service Medal. On one occasion he tiptoed into a minefield to rescue a wounded soldier ("Scared me to death," he said later). As a result of another occasion, the family of a slain G.I. accused Schwarzkopf of negligence. Though he was exonerated, the experience was devastating. Says his sister Sally: "He went off to Vietnam as the heroic captain. He came back having lost his youth."

What he did gain was the conviction that the Vietnam debacle resulted from a failure of domestic public and political support for the military. Bitterly, he determined that the U.S. should never again engage in a limited war of ill-defined aims.

He had no such reservations about the gulf war; he wanted only to win it fast and suffer the fewest casualties possible. His chief worry was that the Iraqis would unleash their chemical weapons. "A nasty shock," he said before the ground war got under way, "would be if Saddam were somehow to launch a surprise attack against our forces, blanket them with chemical weapons and kill large numbers of Americans and our allies. We've got a strategy to defeat that. We are not letting down our guard at all. One of the biggest errors a commander can make is to assume away the capabilities of his adversaries. I think we have made that mistake in the past. I'm not going to make that mistake."

Apart from that concern, Schwarzkopf fretted because his long hours in the Riyadh war room prevented him from visiting his troops as often as he wanted. When he did venture out, he was always accompanied by a sergeant lugging a 60-lb. backpack containing the general's satellite relay hookup for instant communication to his headquarters or to the Pentagon. Also in the entourage: four military bodyguards in civilian clothes and armed with AR-15 assault rifles. On one of his infrequent tours before the unleashing of Desert Storm, Schwarzkopf gazed across the Saudi border into Kuwait and declared that it was the most peaceful moment he had had in weeks. Then, it was the general who took command: surveying the vast expanse of desert, he pronounced it perfect for tank warfare.

In the war room as in the field, noncoms and enlisted soldiers alike were as devoted to Schwarzkopf as were his officers. None seemed overly intimidated by his gruffness, his size (6 ft. 3 in., 240 lbs.), his rank, his aggressive challenges or even his tempestuous flare-ups. He was, after all, the Bear, whom some described as only part grizzly and the rest Teddy.

His wife Brenda and his three children, ages 13, 18 and 20, know him mainly as the latter. He helps the kids with their homework, entertains them with magic tricks. He is a devotee of mint chocolate-chip ice cream, and he is a cookie muncher (on hearing that he described himself as owlish, his sister sent him owl-shaped cookies). He loves fried rice, hates Brussels sprouts. Hc is a music fan who lulls himself to sleep listening to tapes of Pavarotti or the sounds of honking geese and rushing mountain streams. He is also addicted to Charles Bronson and Clint Eastwood movies. He gets grizzly only when the family sits down to play board games. In fact, says Brenda, "we really don't particularly like to play with him . . . because he is a sore loser."

Schwarzkopf also hunts, fishes, skis and shoots clay pigeons. He has camped out alone in the Alaskan wilderness for days at a time. His wife once drove out to fetch him at a prearranged meeting place after one of his Alaskan hikes. "It had rained all weekend," she recalls. "I found him sitting alongside the road with this smile on his face. His feet were bloody and his socks were wet."

The truth about the man, says Colonel Burwell B. Bell, Schwarzkopf's executive officer, is that the general "has a full range of emotions. He can get very, very angry, but it's never personal. He's extremely tough on people when it's necessary to get them to do something, but the next minute he throws his arms around their shoulders and tells them what a great job they're doing."

Asked at the end of the war to evaluate the man he had just defeated, Schwarzkopf burst out with the exclamation "Ha!" Then he went on: "He is neither a strategist, nor is he schooled in the operational arts, nor is he a tactician, nor is he a general, nor is he a soldier. Other than that, he's a great military man, I want you to know that." Taking out all those nors and nots, Schwarzkopf had just defined much of himself.

The general and his troops: "He can get very, very angry," says an aide, "but it's never personal."

Saddam Hussein: A Dreamer of Bloody Dreams

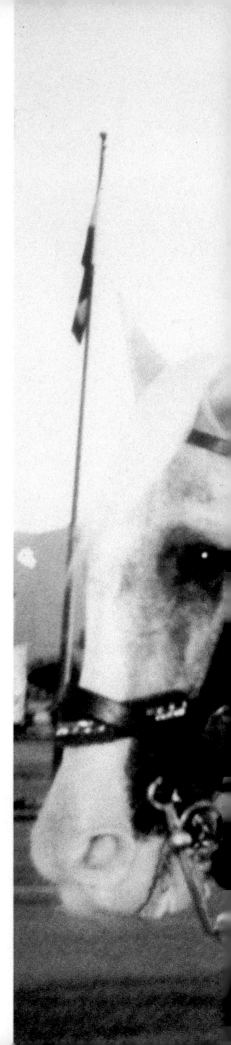

Less than two weeks into the air war over Iraq, George Bush prefaced a public statement on the hostilities with the remark, "Saddam Hussein continues to amaze the world." These words rather neatly summed up the general reaction to the Iraqi leader and to an emerging pattern of behavior that seemed to yaw between the barbaric and the bizarre. Saddam's first Scud-missile firings against civilians in Israel and Saudi Arabia, whatever their intended psychological effects, mainly confirmed the spreading impression of Saddam's brutality. So did the parading of captured allied POWs in front of television cameras and the dumping of huge quantities of oil into the Persian Gulf. Totally eerie and unsettling was the departure of more than 100 top-of-the-line Iraqi warplanes to airfields in neutral Iran; under the first shocks of attack, Saddam responded by apparently ceding the skies to his enemies. And if the world thought it had seen everything by then, it had yet to witness the panoramic destruction of oil wells in Kuwait, the prize that Saddam had risked war to obtain.

A man capable of such acts would scarcely seem to require demonizing, but the process accelerated anyhow. President Bush went out of his way to paint the Iraqi leader as a supreme villain, comparing him to Adolf Hitler. Dart boards were marketed bearing likenesses of Saddam, whose face had hardly been familiar as a target before last August. Now the roughest cartoon that included a military beret and a

A would-be Nebuchadnezzar: "I was born and grew up stubborn, independent and angry."

125

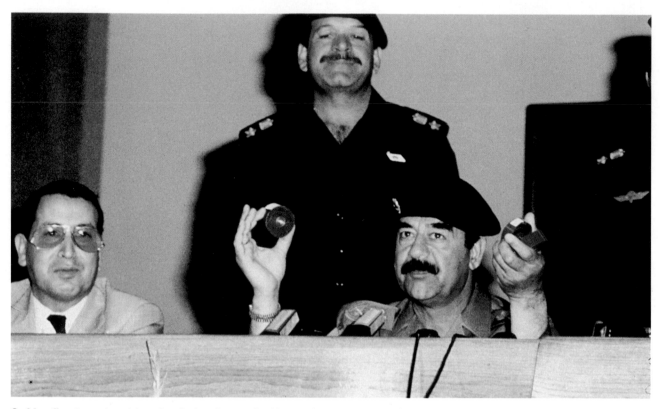

Saddam flaunts nuclear-triggering devices he acquired last spring despite U.S. efforts to prevent it.

bushy mustache was instantly recognized as the emblem of evil.

Some, not willing to call him a monster and leave it at that, began trying to put Saddam on the couch in absentia. Psychiatric professionals started throwing out terms like "malignant narcissism." The uncertain details of Saddam's childhood were sifted for signs of trauma. Even samples of his handwriting were studied; a leading graphologist, questioned by Israeli intelligence agents, claimed to see evidence of severe megalomania accompanied by paranoia. The odd thing about such diagnoses was that, even if accurate, they explained so little. Was much of the Middle East really in flames because of one man's emotional maladjustment?

What many Westerners viewed as Saddam Hussein's strangeness actually stemmed more from social than psychological factors. In truth, Saddam is not particularly complicated—in his own terms. He has played, throughout his life and political career, by rules that are perfectly well understood in his region of the Middle East. Elsewhere in the world, these rules are often seen as nasty, brutish and perhaps even psychopathic. But Saddam did not invent them; he was simply more cunning and cruel than most in following them.

Shortly before the invasion of Kuwait, Saddam ordered himself photographed in a replica of the war chariot of the Babylonian King Nebuchadnezzar. A Western leader who tried such a stunt—say, a U.S. President who dressed up in Abraham Lincoln's frock coat and top hat—would face derision for openers, almost certainly followed by mumblings about mental instability. So it was natural for observers in the West to point to the war-chariot photo as one of Saddam's delusions of grandeur.

Such a view overlooked, however, the talismanic, symbolic power that Nebuchadnezzar's image holds over the Iraqi imagination, and specifically the world view of Saddam Hussein. This fierce King, whose story is recorded in the Old Testament *Book of Daniel,* destroyed Jerusalem in 587 B.C. and drove its Hebrew inhabitants into 70 years of captivity (and the fact that he went mad, eating grass, could conveniently be overlooked). For Iraqis, here was an unequivocal triumph over an ancient foe, a high point in an imaginative terrain that has largely been blasted by more than 700 years of humiliations and defeats. This backward glance also offered an interpretation of present reality. By the subterranean logic of myth, the modern presence of Jews once again in control of Jerusalem could evoke the necessity of a new Nebuchadnezzar, and Saddam clearly wanted his people to know who that avatar would be.

But there is another, even deeper appeal in the pictorial allusion to Nebuchadnezzar: a reminder that Iraq, at the confluence of the Tigris and Euphrates rivers, was once the very center of the world. A 1988 book ostensibly written by Saddam and published in Baghdad extols the glories of the Sumerian and Babylonian epochs: "At a time our ancestors were building civilization, Americans and Europeans lived in caves."

Things had changed remarkably for the worse by the time Saddam was born, in 1937, in a village near Tikrit, some 100 miles north of Baghdad. After the dismantling of the Ottoman Empire following World War I, Iraq had finally gained independence in 1932. But a British-controlled monarch sat on its throne, and much of its population was ignorant and impoverished. Saddam, the heir of destitute peasants in a mud hut, was an all-too-typical native son.

Accounts of his early childhood—not to mention much of his life—vary considerably. Some standard hagiographies say he was orphaned at nine months; other versions claim that his father abandoned his mother shortly after Saddam's birth and that she later married a man who abused his stepson. Whatever the actual circumstances, they were not happy. Looking back on his first experiences of life, Saddam once recalled, "I was born and grew up stubborn, sad, independent and angry."

Some comfort was provided by his maternal uncle, an army officer named Khairallah Talfah, who befriended the young Saddam and treated him like one of his own children. Despite his government uniform, Talfah despised the British and their domination of his country through the puppet Iraqi King. From his uncle, Saddam imbibed at an early age the language of resentment and the intricacies of intrigue and conspiracy. This nascent education was interrupted in 1941, when Talfah was imprisoned after taking part in an unsuccessful anti-British coup. After his release five years later, Talfah saw to it that Saddam, then 10, enrolled in school for the first time. Before the boy reached adolescence, his uncle had given him a pistol.

Saddam's deferred and spotty education had an important consequence: when he later applied for admission to the élite Baghdad Military Academy, he was turned down because of poor grades. Here, psychological analysis may actually have something to contribute to an understanding of Saddam's development. Those who have studied him carefully say this rejection was devastating to the adolescent, not only fueling a well-developed sense of inferiority but also an obsession to get even with those who had snubbed him. If this analysis is accurate, Saddam's revenge was sweet, and total: he eventually acquired the power to declare himself commander in chief and design his own military uniforms.

The vehicle for his triumph was the Baath Party, which he joined as a student; this then underground organization became far and away the most important influence on Saddam's life. Baath (the name is Arabic for renaissance) was founded in Syria during the early 1940s, put together by a small group of Christian and Islamic schoolteacher-intellectuals. From the outset, Baathism's emphasis was secular and cultural rather than religious. It foresaw the difficulty of organizing and unifying the Middle East by means of sectarian appeals: some 10% of Arabs are not Muslims; Muslims are torn by the Sunni-Shi'ite schism; and millions of Muslims are not Arabs.

So Baath adopted the goal of Pan-Arabism, a mighty nation-state made up of all people whose native language is Arabic. While constructing the Baath ideology, its founders were somewhat influenced by several notions in Nazism, including state socialism and the vision of racial identity as a means of forging both unity and a presumptive destiny. But the evolving methods of Baath politics owed less to Hitler's tactics than to those employed by Josef Stalin in the Soviet Union. Early Baath theorists deplored the international aspirations of the Communist revolution; commerce with aliens, particularly from the West, struck them, in light of Arab history, as a very bad idea. At the same time, these founders saw possibilities in an ethnically purified version of Marxist-Leninist organization: absolute, invincible party control over all aspects of political and personal life. Through its slogan—"One Arab nation with an eternal mission"—the Baath Party could offer an abstract vision of the future and demand from its followers any and all sacrifices it decreed necessary to achieve that end.

That this harsh mixture of precepts from two terrible tyrannies should triumph in Iraq (and in a somewhat different form, in Syria) may seem surprising. It is not. Iraq in the late '50s and early '60s was growing increasingly chaotic. The draining away of British colonial influence created a vacuum that practically mandated bloodshed. Among the groups scrabbling for power: the Shi'ites, a slight majority of the Iraqi population; the Sunnis, to whom Saddam Hussein owed some inherited loyalty; the Kurds, a sizable Islamic but non-Arab contingent with yearnings for independence; and a confusion of splinter groups, including communists, extreme right-wing militarists and, of course, the Baath Party itself. Complicating this chaos were the old, fierce Arab loyalties to family, clan or tribe; broad alliances could explode at any time into warring factions.

Neither sweet reason nor appeals to common sense and interests would serve to unify this factious country. During the late 1950s and much of the '60s, political life in Iraq amounted to little more than a succession of coups and countercoups.

Some of this turmoil was stirred up by the Baath Party. And in Saddam Hussein, the party elders evidently saw what the rest of the world would much later recognize: a willingness to do anything, no matter how dangerous, ruthless or violent, in pursuit of a goal. In 1956, at age 19, Saddam was given a role in an attempted coup against King Faisal II. That failed, but the King was eventually toppled in a military takeover. The Baath opposed the new regime too, so in 1959 Saddam was put on a team assigned to assassinate the military leader, Abdul Karim Kassem.

Saddam and his confederates sprayed machine-gun fire at Kassem's station wagon as it sped down a Baghdad street, but they missed their target. Kassem's bodyguards killed at least one of the Baath gunmen and wounded Saddam in his left leg. His own dramatic account of his escape later became official history: he claimed to have dug the bullet out with an iodine-dipped razor blade, disguised himself as a Bedouin tribesman, swum across the Tigris, then completed his escape by stealing a donkey and making his way across the desert into Syria. For all that, he wound up in jail but was soon released and allowed passage to Cairo. On one point, legend and truth may converge: Egypt's President Gamal Abdel Nasser, then the exemplar of Pan-Arabism, had apparently heard of Saddam's exploits and took on the young man as a protégé.

Saddam spent nearly four years in the Egyptian capital. He enrolled in law school, although his studies were apparently desultory. And he found cosmopolitan Cairo daunting. A fellow Iraqi who studied with Saddam recalls, "He was very embarrassed about his poor background. Whenever we went to a party and sat down, he didn't talk at all. He just looked and listened." Not always though. Classmates spent much of their time sitting around Cairo cafés, debating the intricacies of Arab politics. On one such occasion, Saddam blurted out, "Why argue? Why don't you just take out a gun and shoot him?"

Iraqi Baathists finally succeeded in ousting Kassem in 1963, and Saddam was called home from exile to help establish a security apparatus and militia. It was an important assignment for a young man (then only 26), and Saddam handled it with relentless efficiency. He set up his base of operations in Baghdad's Qasr al-Nihayya (Palace of the End), so named because King Faisal II

and his family had been massacred there in 1958. Surrounding himself with relatives and clan members from Tikrit, Saddam constructed an interlocking system of intelligence agencies, security services and dungeons of interrogation, all designed to enforce Baath rule over unruly Iraq through the expedient of naked terror.

Despite Saddam's efforts, internal divisions persisted. Prolonged street fighting between party moderate and militant factions led to the Baathists' overthrow, after nine months, by a pro-Nasser Iraqi named Abdul Rahman Aref. This defeat only reinforced the lesson that Saddam had learned from his life thus far: power and dissent are incompatible. Argument leads to weakness, and to be weak is to invite annihilation. Working underground, Saddam strengthened his control of the party apparatus, terrorizing opponents and rewarding those bound to him by ties of blood or geography. In 1968 the Baath Party overthrew the Aref regime and regained power, under the nominal leadership of General Ahmed Hassan al-Bakr, whose younger relative, Saddam Hussein, was named Vice President. His official ascendancy to the presidency was still 11 years away, but from this time forward, Saddam ruled Iraq.

His stop-at-nothing climb to power is hardly unique, certainly not in the Middle East, and not in this century of revolutions. Also sadly commonplace is the savagery he inflicted on his enemies, real or suspected. The torture chambers of Iraq's *mukhabarat*, which Saddam had organized, resounded with the same sort of howls that echoed through the strongholds of SAVAK, the agency that kept dissent in check for the neighboring Shah of Iran.

When Saddam finally became President of Iraq in 1979, his first act, entirely predictable to students of totalitarianism, was to order the execution of 21 Cabinet ministers, including one of his closest confederates, on trumped-up charges of treason. A former minister, who had been close to one of the participants, described what happened next: "The party officials were handed machine guns. One by one, guards brought in the accused, their mouths taped shut and their hands bound. Saddam asked everyone to start shooting . . . Every victim received at least 500 bullets in his body." Shortly afterward, Saddam appeared on Iraqi television, deploring the betrayals that led to this slaughter and warning, "He who is closest to me is farthest from me when he does wrong." Now the fear that he had instilled in the population at large extended to his inner circle. Like many past despots, he claimed their loyalty through a sharing of guilt.

Other consequences were predictable as well, either from history or from a reading of George Orwell's *1984*. A personality cult made Saddam the Big Brother of Iraq.

The paterfamilias poses with his wife of a quarter-century and their five children. He favors Scotch whisky and Cuban cigars.

Huge murals of the President appeared throughout Baghdad; Saddam's expression was sometimes stern, sometimes compassionate, but those hard, dark, nearly epicanthic eyes were unmistakably watching.

For all its bloodshed and fear, Saddam's dictatorship brought a stability that struck many citizens as worth its price. Compared with a number of Arab states, Iraq became conspicuously well managed. Political turmoil subsided to a sporadic whimper. Baath ideology, as implemented by Saddam, pointed to modernization and certain elements of the welfare state; its secular stranglehold on permissible opinion squelched Islamic fundamentalists' desires to return to the past. Given the absence of nearly all basic human rights recognized in the West, life in Iraq could be described as improving under Saddam. Said Sir John Moberly, former British ambassador to Baghdad: "The Baath Party has impressive achievements to its credit, health and education, enhancing the role of women, taking electricity and water to the villages. Saddam has a vision of Iraq which is not in itself unworthy."

To be sure, Saddam's own standard of living went upscale with his power. An investigative firm hired by Kuwait told London's *Financial Times* and CBS's *60 Minutes* that Saddam and his family have skimmed some $10 billion in oil revenues and foreign contracts over the past 10 years. Beyond dispute, the mud hut of his childhood was replaced by a series of palatial presidential retreats. But the life that went on in them reflected older ways. Saddam's arranged marriage to his cousin Sajida Talfah, the daughter of his uncle and mentor Khairallah, has remained in effect for more than 25 years and produced five children; rumors of his droit-du-seigneur promiscuity have circulated for years but have been difficult to confirm.

On a normal day, which means some morning before his invasion of Kuwait, Saddam would typically arise around 5 a.m., don a Bedouin robe and wander about until breakfast at around 6. That consisted of a small bottle of camel's milk from a herd presented to him—ironically, in view of what would follow—by Saudi Arabia's King Fahd. Within an hour, he would put on a bulletproof vest and start daylong visits among his people, a tribal chief keeping in touch with his subjects. Late in the evening, back at home, he might smoke a Cuban cigar from the shipments regularly sent him by Fidel Castro. Other reported indulgences included a non-Islamic taste for Johnnie Walker Scotch and a deep fondness for the U.S. movie *The Godfather*.

All of these details could simply have added up to a typical Third World dictatorship, mildly deplored and then ignored. What catapulted Saddam onto the global stage was, of course, Iraq's oil reserves, second largest in the Middle East after Saudi Arabia's, plus the nation's strategic location vis-à-vis its mutually antagonistic neighbors, Iran, Turkey, Syria and Israel.

Shortly after becoming President, Saddam declared, "I'm a Stalinist. An iron fist at home and political flexibility abroad." As self-analyses go, that one seems fairly accurate. Given the chance, Saddam was capable of surprising accommodations in the international arena. In 1975 he negotiated a deal with the Shah of Iran: Iraq would give up its claims on the disputed Shatt al-Arab waterway in return for Iran's agreement to stop encouraging and funding Kurdish separatists in Iraq. This was a pragmatic compromise indeed, considering that Saddam was bargaining with the descendants of Persians, those ancient enemies of the Arabs. In fact, Saddam's inflammatory, expansionist rhetoric ("I struggle for the realization of Arab unity, and, if necessary, through the use of force") was rarely matched by deeds.

The two aggressions that have rendered him infamous—the attack against Iran in 1980 and the invasion of Kuwait last August—were both conceived by Saddam as essentially defensive responses. Schooled by his internal political experiences to recognize potential enemies, Saddam had scarcely assumed the presidency in 1979 before he found himself menaced by the Ayatullah Khomeini, who called on Iraq's Shi'ite majority to overthrow Saddam. The Iraqi President's response—a pre-emptive strike against Iran, based on a claim to the same waterway he had bargained away in 1975—turned out to be a costly blunder. True, Saddam could not have foreseen an eight-year war that would cost both countries an estimated 1 million casualties. Nor did he anticipate a Kurdish revolt, arising in the midst of Iraq's larger struggle against Iran, which he would feel obliged to put down with the aid of poison gas, resulting in some 5,000 civilian deaths. But the final results—a stalemate against a well-armed enemy twice Iraq's size—probably seemed worth the price.

The Iran-Iraq war led directly to the crisis in the gulf. Some $80 billion in debt, Saddam looked for thanks and

Saddam hunting with fellow dictator Nicolae Ceausescu of Romania.

financial relief from Kuwait and Saudi Arabia for having spared them, as well as himself, the reforming ardor of Khomeini's revolutionaries. He desperately needed oil revenues, but his rich neighbors increased their production, driving down prices. At the same time, he claimed to see evidence that Kuwait was slant-drilling oil from a field that stands on both sides of the disputed border between Kuwait and Iraq. To add insult to injury, the gulf sheikdoms were nagging him to repay the billions he had borrowed to fight a war that he said served Arabs' common interests. Claiming that he was being robbed, he struck.

While the West had a hard time understanding Saddam's views, Saddam himself knew almost nothing about the West. Except for a brief stay in Paris in the mid-'70s, he had no direct experience of life and affairs in Western democracies. He had heard about the protests against the Vietnam War and noted that U.S. peace-keeping forces had pulled out of Lebanon shortly after 218 Marines were killed in a 1983 bombing. According to an Iraqi-released transcript, he warned U.S. Ambassador April Glaspie last July that the U.S. could never tolerate 10,000 casualties in a single battle. (Glaspie disputed the transcript's accuracy at a congressional hearing on March 21.) As for the Iraqis, they were supposedly tougher. During the Iran-Iraq war, one senior Iraqi general informed Saddam that an attack he had ordered would lead to extremely high casualties. Saddam reportedly asked the general into an adjoining room to discuss the matter in private. Behind the closed door, the sound of a gunshot was heard. Saddam emerged, holstering his pistol.

Kill enough messengers and no bad news gets through. But the logic of force is only effective against weaker adversaries; it has no chance against superior might, and that is what Saddam Hussein had stirred up against himself. He must have thought for a time that someone as ambitious, cunning and charismatic as he could lead his people, all those Iraqis and disaffected Arabs who came to see him as a hero, toward something more than another ruinous defeat. Unfortunately, the Saddam who could have done that would probably never have come to rule Iraq in the first place. He exploited the political rules of his incendiary region, but he was also the victim of those same harsh rules.

The misled and the deluded: pro-Saddam supporters rally in Baghdad to cheer Big Brother's invasion of Kuwait.

Kuwait: A Story Of Conquest, Chaos, Revenge

When the allied armies entered Kuwait, the focal point of the Persian Gulf war, they found the country burning—physically, politically and spiritually. Kuwait City, where 80% of the prewar population of 2 million people lived, had become a sad, lonely town. The skyscrapers stood abandoned. Some had been hit with tank fire as the Iraqis retreated; all had their ground-level shops looted. Nearly everything was covered with an oily soot, a reminder of the continuing conflagration outside the capital—hundreds of oil-well fires depleting the nation's lifeblood at a rate far greater than anyone had predicted. Wherever one traveled, nerves were raw, tensions deep. Many of those who remained while Iraq pillaged and raped their land resented those who fled, and sizable numbers in both camps wanted nothing less than the wholesale expulsion of Kuwait's Palestinians, despite the evidence that many of them had opposed Iraqi oppression.

If one complaint bound all, it was anger at Kuwait's government, which had had months to plan for the nation's recovery but had done very little. When the 65-year-old Emir, Sheik Jaber al-Ahmad al-Sabah, belatedly returned to his smoking capital on March 14, his first reaction was to weep. Many of his subjects, who had long been shut out of the nation's political life, had organized themselves admirably well to survive the Iraqi occupation; understandably enough, they now wanted a say in public affairs. Less than a week after the Emir's return, Kuwait's Cabinet, recognizing its

After the liberation, an observer takes stock of the destruction in Kuwait City.

Burying the dead: Kuwaitis cannot escape the reminders of the war and the many victims of the Iraqi occupation.

inability to restore basic services to the country, re-signed, staying on as a caretaker government. Across all groups and all issues, the question, now that Kuwait had been freed, was simple: Freed for what?

A TIME *correspondent who roved through newly liberated Kuwait in early March reported these things:*

At 3:30 in the morning on Sunday, March 3, in the shadow of Kuwait City's Maryam Mosque, a Kuwaiti resistance member who calls himself "Mike" poked his French-made automatic rifle at the chest of his childhood friend, Mustafa al-Kubaisi. "This is your last night," he whispered. Then he fired a single shot. Unsatisfied by the effect, Mike used his 7.65-mm MAB pistol to put another round in Mustafa's head.

Mustafa al-Kubaisi, who was 29, was born in Kuwait to Iraqi parents. He worked as an overseas telephone operator and enjoyed the cradle-to-grave benefits of Kuwait's welfare state, but could never be sure of his status. Because of his parents' Iraqi origins, and despite

his having been born in Kuwait, he had to have a work permit to remain in the country. Naturalization, common throughout the world, is virtually impossible in Kuwait. Mike, 33, is the son of wealthy Kuwaitis. He graduated from San Francisco State University, trained to be an airline pilot, but he quit to manage his family's real estate empire. Mike's house is within shouting distance of Mustafa's, and he recalls being something of a "big brother" to Mustafa. Mike advised him about work and girls and gave him rides in his Ferrari. He also supplemented Mustafa's salary. "Nothing big," says Mike, "but on a fairly regular basis."

When Iraq invaded Kuwait, Mike lay low. But then another childhood friend, a woman named Esrar al-Ghabandi, was killed. Unlike Mike, Esrar had joined the resistance immediately. After Esrar had made four trips to Saudi Arabia to deliver information about Iraqi troop movements in Kuwait, Mike and some friends discovered her mutilated body near Mike's villa. Esrar had been axed in the head and shot seven times in her breasts and vagina. Within a few days, Mike and his friends formed their own resistance cell, which operated apart from the more organized efforts of other Kuwaitis. They met frequently to plan strategy, and Mustafa was usually present. "Why not?" says Mike. "We had known each other all our lives. I didn't think we had any secrets."

But Mustafa had one. As he once confessed to another neighbor, Mustafa had always resented his uncertain status. Whether Mustafa also had been a longtime spy for Iraq's secret police, as Mike believes, is debatable. What Mike and several other resistance members know for certain is that Kuwaiti army officers operating with Mike's cell began to disappear whenever Mustafa took part in the group's deliberations. "So we began watching his movements," says Mike. "He was informing. There was no doubt."

When the resistance was certain that Mustafa was aiding the Iraqis, Mike invited him to stay at his home. "That way I could better keep an eye on him," says Mike. "I used him to help me get through checkpoints and to move some weapons around. It was minor stuff, and it bound us more closely together. We kept the important things from him, of course, but I am sure he thought he was continuing to penetrate us." Shortly after the liberation, Mustafa was arrested by the Kuwaiti intelligence service and removed to the local jail.

"But he was mine," says Mike, "and one night I prevailed on the guards to turn him over to me. I wanted to kill him myself. I cooked him a last meal and told him that I was going to turn him in as a POW. I told him he would be traded for allied prisoners. I told him to get his things, and we walked to a wall about a hundred yards from my house, which is where I did it. And that was it. I have no regrets. He was also helping to run Palestinians who informed on Kuwaitis. How could I let him go?"

When the allies first rode into Kuwait City, on Feb. 26, they were led by Arab forces, though not by Kuwaitis. Earlier in the campaign, a Kuwaiti soldier had killed a surrendering Iraqi and shoved his body into a ditch. "From that moment," says a U.S. military officer, "we were determined to restrain the Kuwaitis." Kuwaiti patrols are now accompanied by American special-forces troops. Mike says he knows of at least 80 "proven collaborators" who have been executed. "The word has gone out to be calm for now," says a resistance leader, "to cool it until the journalists leave."

"That's right," confirms a senior Western diplomat. "The government is operating with a light hand. The country is an arsenal. Everyone has weapons. They turn some in, to be perceived as cooperating with the call to lay down arms, but everyone is keeping some—just as they are keeping the names of some collaborators to themselves when turning over their lists to the army." The problem, another Western diplomat says, is the government's poor credibility. "No one really knows if cracking down on the resistance would work, or whether they'd tell the ministers to shove it," he says. "All the government knows for sure is that at the end of the day it doesn't want Kuwait perceived as no better than Saddam. We hope that the idea of sanctioning an open season later on won't really come to pass. We're counting on the passage of time to calm emotions."

Kuwait is a tense nation at a tough time, "a place in need of therapy," says Abdul Rahman al-Awadi, a physician who long served as his country's Health Minister and subsequently as Minister of State for Cabinet Affairs. Everyone has witnessed an atrocity or has a tale to tell. Al-Awadi turns pale when he recalls the story of an Iraqi patrol that spotted some Kuwaiti children playing in the street. "They were told to stop, and all but one did," says al-Awadi. "That one was picked up by the hair by an Iraqi soldier—he was still holding his soccer ball—and shot in the head in front of the other kids." Some of Mike's friends had to cut down the bodies of seven young Kuwaiti girls who had been hanged in a schoolyard after having been raped. There are several hundred women awaiting abortions, says a doctor at Mubarak al-Kabir Hospital. All were victims of gang rape.

Even when Kuwaitis try to forget the tragedies, they cannot escape reminders of the occupation. The sky is what everyone first notices each morning. When the wind blows toward Kuwait City, the sky darkens like a storm moving across the plain. At times, night appears at noon. The oil fires are that horrendous. There is no electricity, the result of last-minute Iraqi sabotage. Few believe the repeated assurances that at least some electricity will return "tomorrow." Too many tomorrows have passed. Water and power were operating until shortly before the Iraqis withdrew, apparently to pacify the population and permit Iraqi looters to figure out which houses were unoccupied. When the Iraqis visited inhabited homes, it was mostly to make their presence felt. "We left things around, watches and some jewelry," says Tariq al-Riaz. "That usually satisfied them, and their searches were perfunctory. When we did need to hide, we did so in rooms we created behind walls."

The hardest thing to do was to teach Kuwait's children to "like" Saddam, says Salah al-Awadi, manager of credit-card sales for the Gulf Bank. "When Iraqis visited us, we would serve them soft drinks. Once, my son Youssef, who is almost four, said, 'Take this glass and put it on

Saddam's head.' We had to teach the kids to say good things about Saddam for fear they would be killed if they didn't."

People move more freely now, of course, but a favorite pastime, a walk on the beach, is impossible. The seaside fortifications built by the Iraqis—four separate lines of trenches and obstacles—"look like Normandy from the air," says a U.S. Army general. Mines are everywhere, and the minefield maps that Baghdad provided the coalition are "useless," says U.S. Ambassador Edward Gnehm. The city is rocked by explosions several times a day as U.S. Army experts detonate Iraq's abandoned ordnance. Sporadic gunfire is heard throughout the day—celebratory rounds discharged mainly by Saudi soldiers. (It is the Americans, however, who are in demand for pictures and autographs.)

Expatriates—Palestinians particularly—are subjected to time-consuming searches. In the Hawalli area, where many Palestinians live, Kuwaiti troops roam the streets, instructing the population to "turn in your weapons, Palestinian people. This is for your own security." The latest graffito reads, DEATH TO PALESTINIAN TRAITORS. WE DON'T WANT THEM. "They are hypocrites!" screams Massmoa Hassan, a Kuwaiti woman passing by. "We went to school with you. We helped you. The P.L.O. donation boxes were filled by us. And you are traitors. Get out!" Palestinians have taken to displaying Kuwaiti flags and portraits of the Emir. A Palestinian begins to argue, but the Kuwaiti army comes into view and he slinks away.

Hawalli residents tell of suspected collaborators being taken roughly away. Sarah Hamdan Salman says her three sons were blindfolded, handcuffed, beaten with machine guns and shoved into the trunks of cars by civilians who the Palestinians are convinced were resistance members. When she went to the local precinct to inquire about her children, she was told, "You're a Palestinian"—and then she was spat upon. Did it happen? "I don't doubt it," says a U.S. Army major assigned as an adviser to the Kuwaitis. "All I can say is that we're trying to hold it down."

All residents, even Kuwaitis, are subject to the three-month martial law decree and its 10 p.m.–to–4 a.m. curfew. "It's not fake," says Colonel Jesse Johnson, the commander of U.S. special-operations forces in Kuwait City. There have been several nighttime incidents "where people drive up to the checkpoints and open fire" on the Kuwaiti soldiers, says Johnson. The troops assume their attackers are Palestinians.

The clash between those who remained and those who left (more than half of the 800,000 native Kuwaitis)

is felt everywhere. Some Kuwaitis who stayed behind surrendered their automobile license plates for Iraqi tags. At a checkpoint, a Kuwaiti without plates was harassed. "So you changed your plates!" shouted a Kuwaiti soldier. "And you fled, you coward!" the driver yelled back.

Some Kuwaitis have taken to visiting the house where the Iraqis constructed an elaborate torture chamber, with electric-shock devices the most prominent feature. Pinups of half-naked women adorn the walls. The government is thinking of turning the place into a museum. "We should preserve this so we remember," says Minister of State al-Awadi, whose indoor swimming pool was used by the Iraqis to extract information from prisoners by dunking them into the water while they were tied to ropes hung from the ceiling. A more poignant scene occurs almost daily when Kuwaitis visit the Riqqa cemetery searching for the remains of loved ones. Kuwaiti authorities say 2,792 bodies of people who died unnatural deaths since Aug. 2 are buried there. Another site of interest is the ice rink, which served as a makeshift morgue for Kuwaiti dead. There are no bodies there now, only some dried blood and a persistent stench.

Ambitious travelers journey about 30 miles toward Basra to see the remains of a convoy of fleeing Iraqi vehicles destroyed by allied aircraft. Several thousand Kuwaitis were kidnapped by Iraqi soldiers in the last days of the occupation. Baghdad suddenly released about 1,175 in early March, transporting them back to Kuwait City in trucks bearing the seal of the Republican Guard. Most had been held at a military barracks near Basra, so tightly confined that they had to take turns sleeping. For the first three days, they were given no food or water. From then on, they subsisted on a single rock-hard roll a day.

Those who show up at the border are usually a bedraggled lot. At night, they look like ghostly figures, small bands of refugees suddenly illuminated by the headlights of military convoys. Mostly they are expatriates or foreigners who lived in Iraq and are fleeing from the the danger of a civil war there. Thousands of Egyptians, for example, are being deported. Mohammed el-Habal, 65, is one of about a dozen Egyptians who has camped near the border to wait for his status to be determined. "The Republican Guard told us that if Egypt had stayed with Iraq, if we had supported Iraq, we would not have been turned out," says el-Habal, who reports that some of his compatriots have been murdered by Iraqis.

The plight of those Iraqis who lived in Kuwait before

The legacy of bitterness: A newly liberated Kuwaiti youth pelts a portrait of Saddam Hussein with rocks.

Resistance fighter Mike willingly executed a childhood friend: "I have no regrets. How could I let him go?"

the war and are now trying to return to Kuwait is even more desperate. Men, women and children are encamped near the border highway. U.S. soldiers have given them rations, but they have no water. On a cold, rainy night, the Iraqis huddled around campfires. The horizon was lighted by the flames of the burning oil fields. In her tattooed hands, Fadiyah Saad held her new granddaughter, born by the roadside on March 5. The family was debating whether to name the child Hudud (borders) or Istiqlal (independence).

With Kuwait independent again, some of those who stayed behind still yearn for aspects of the occupation. Supplies were plentiful then, and those who had previously felt themselves to be mere employees of a business called Kuwait Inc. banded together as a nation. "For the first time," says Ali Salem, a resistance leader, "all barriers were breached. Shi'ite Muslims, who have long been discriminated against by the Sunni majority, were major

players, perhaps even the most significant. We were, at least for that time, truly one."

There were approximately 60 resistance groups operating at any given time, each with 40 to 50 members. The head of each cell knew his opposite number in other units, but his subordinates did not know one another. Elaborate codes were developed to fool eavesdropping Iraqis. Young girls carried bullets in their underwear. Fake identity papers were common. A sophisticated printing operation was hidden a block from the headquarters of Iraq's secret police.

In addition to the organized resistance, many Kuwaitis operated on their own. Since Iraqi soldiers examining cars at checkpoints frequently stole whatever was in sight, some Kuwaitis added rat poison to bottles of orange juice and then hid them in the trunk. Iraqi sentries would discover and seize the bottles—and presumably drink the poison later.

Salem presided over a network that distributed nearly $100 million smuggled into Kuwait from the government-in-exile in Taif, Saudi Arabia. "We used the money for bribes to get people out of jail, to pass checkpoints, to buy fruits and vegetables brought from Iraq," says Salem. "This is the Middle East, and money talked even more here because the Iraqis are so poor."

Much of Kuwait's current chaos can be blamed on its leaders. Like most governments, Kuwait's regime is sometimes savvy, sometimes incompetent. But at the top, with a few notable exceptions, Kuwait's Cabinet is decidedly mediocre—an opinion shared by most Kuwaitis. The government's primary mission for seven months has been to plan its return. The ministers began well by removing themselves from direct responsibility. A reconstruction plan was concocted in Washington by Fawzi al-Sultan, an executive director of the World Bank, who assembled a team of international experts.

But as the war of liberation neared, the ministers in Taif became jealous of an organization that threatened to supplant them. In short order, al-Sultan's team was torpedoed. Each ministry recaptured control of its own work, coordination evaporated, and the resistance movement, which knew what was needed and how to accomplish it, was effectively shut out.

The results of mismanagement are everywhere. Sup-plies of essential goods, supposedly stockpiled and ready to go in Dhahran, Saudi Arabia, were delayed at the border because Kuwait's Interior Ministry had failed to provide proper documentation. Some of the foodstuffs spoiled. When a shipment finally arrived in Kuwait City five days behind schedule, the Commerce Ministry's distribution plan had to be scrapped because it could not do the job quickly. Some of the needed food was distributed by U.S. Ambassador Gnehm. "He had the media with him," says a Kuwaiti minister admiringly. "He wanted to embarrass us into moving faster, and it worked." But the shipments still lag. "Quite literally," says Salem, "we had more in the stores when Saddam controlled Kuwait."

The oil industry, Kuwait's backbone, is in even worse shape. Rashid al-Amiri, the Oil Minister, is roundly denounced by his colleagues. A committee of other ministers recently was appointed to "assist" him. "What is unforgivable," says one of al-Amiri's associates, "is that he is in no small measure directly responsible for much of the havoc we face."

Some months ago, Kuwaiti operatives trained by Western intelligence agencies successfully sabotaged Iraq's plan to cripple Kuwait's oil-producing centers. The wires leading to explosive charges buried in the sand were snipped and reburied. Al-Amiri was so delighted

Kuwait City's once beautiful beach remains off limits because of the fortifications and mines left by the Iraqis.

Games of Cat and Mouse
A Photo Essay

Whenever one people suffers a harsh military occupation by another, the end of that occupation becomes partly a time of liberation and partly a time of retribution. There are many scores to be settled, wrongs righted—and in the course of that, new wrongs often occur. Justice is not blind, but her vision is not clear either. Rumors come to seem facts, accusations proof. This was the scene during the first days after the Iraqis fled, and the Kuwaitis regained control of the streets.

The chase is on: A Kuwaiti resistance fighter searches apartments for pro-Iraqi collaborators.

Divided loyalties: A Palestinian woman rails at resistance after her son gets arrested.

Protest: Arrested boy's father pleads for the release of his son. He gets no sympathy.

Manhunt: Kuwaiti resistance fighters scour the streets in search of Iraqi supporters.

Hot pursuit: A vigilante chases an accused Palestinian in Kuwait City.

145

Caught: A Kuwaiti suspected of collaborating with the enemy is arrested and handcuffed.

Reprisal: This arrested man—identity unknown—faces danger of summary justice.

Prisoners of War
A Photo Essay

At first there were only a few of them, hungry and exhausted, then thousands, then still more thousands, all across the desert. Feeling blessed to be alive after weeks of being bombed, the armies of surrendering Iraqis held out white flags, and many of them chanted the only English words they knew: "Thank you, thank you, thank you." Said one Marine as he handed out water and cold rations to the bedraggled prisoners: "What are we going to do with all these poor guys?"

An appeal to the Almighty: A Marine stands guard while an Iraqi prisoner of war prays.

Forward march: Iraqi prisoners trudge from Kuwait to the Saudi border, guarded by troops of the 2nd Marine Division.

Captive hands: An Iraqi displays Saudi-created leaflet on how to surrender.

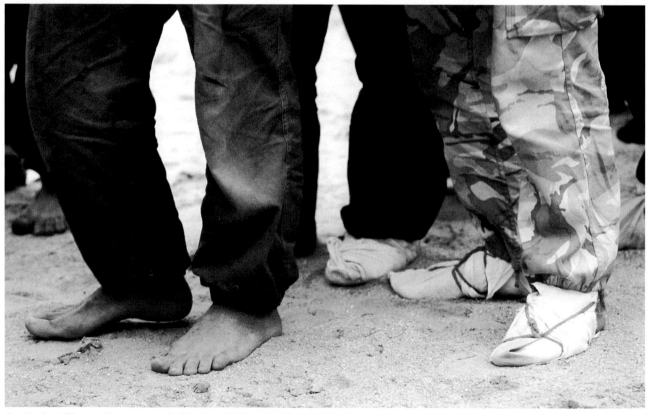

Captive feet: Disarmed, worn-out and often barefoot, Iraqi soldiers shuffle along.

149

IRAQI PRISONER OF WAR
DIED: 2200 24 FEB 91
WAFRA MINEFIELDS

An American-dug grave: Just a few days before the war ended, this Iraqi soldier was killed when he stepped on a mine while trying to surrender.

151

that he bragged about it in an interview he gave to an Arab newspaper. Whether the Iraqis would have checked the wires in any event may never be known, but Kuwait says it is now losing 6 million bbl. a day from the 600-odd wells ablaze.

What is really on the government's mind these days—and on everyone else's as well (which is why the government is consumed by it)—is the matter of democracy. The Prime Minister, a poet of noncommitment who usually deflects direct inquiries by saying "That will be discussed," is promising elections for a new parliament. The opposition wants a return to the dissolved 1986 parliament. But that is the same assembly that refused to expand suffrage to include women and "second-grade" Kuwaitis—people who cannot trace their ancestry in the country to a date earlier than 1920.

Many Kuwaitis, including those who served in the resistance, believe voting rights must be expanded. In addition, says Hamad al-Towgari, 34, a San Jose State University graduate who owns the Kuwait Plaza Hotel, the "real issue is what powers any parliament has. We want to be modern. We want something closer to a constitutional monarchy, something closer to the British system." Says Salem, a member of the ruling al-Sabah family: "The oligarchy must give way."

The person who perhaps best expresses the pervasive disgust of many Kuwaitis is Laila al-Qadhi, a Kuwait University English professor. Few say on the record what al-Qadhi says, but many agree with her. "At best," says al-Qadhi, "we have a democracy tailored for a few. It can't be real, of course, until women and the children of expatriates who are born here are entitled to vote as full citizens. Certainly those who stayed and fought for Kuwait while the cowards fled deserve to participate in their government. But I am not optimistic. Many will collaborate to restore the old order because it is so comfortable for so many. The Sabahs are smart. They have bought the loyalty of most with a system that makes all comfortably lazy. What has changed is that we who stayed no longer fear those who rule, and they fear us because we do not fear them. But if we don't change, then the answer to the question 'Is Kuwait worth dying for?' is no."

Among those in the government most disposed to change is al-Awadi, an enlightened liberal. "It is not easy to establish a democracy in this part of the world," he says, "especially when other nations will be upset if we do. But it will come, all of it, including the right of

Jubilation: Kuwaitis celebrate liberation. The Kuwaiti flag, not seen in public during the Iraqi occupation, is unfurled.

women to vote. It will just take time." To which al-Qadhi simply says, "Why should we have to wait?"

The biggest losers in Kuwait are its Palestinian residents, who numbered 400,000 before the invasion. About 180,000 stayed behind. The resistance estimates 50,000 actually collaborated with the Iraqis. But even those who helped Kuwait resist the occupation are likely to suffer. "The Palestinians were invaluable," says Hamad al-Towgari. "They got us through checkpoints and got us fake identity papers saying we were foreigners. We know who the good ones are, and we want to tell the world about them. But they say no. They are scared of P.L.O. retribution. It is a vicious circle. Maybe when things calm down, people will realize how much we need the Palestinians just to get on here."

Maybe later, but not quite yet. At the Doha power plant, a Kuwaiti army lieutenant who had spent the past seven months in exile refused to allow six Palestinian workers to enter the facility. His orders, he said, came straight from the Defense Minister: No Palestinians. Arguing with the soldier was the plant's director, who patiently explained that the whole country was waiting for electricity and that it would never be restored until the Palestinians were admitted, because they were the people who knew how to do the work. Still, the lieutenant was unmoved. Finally, and just by chance, al-Awadi arrived. For a time, even he could not budge the soldier. He succeeded finally, but as the Palestinians walked toward the plant, the lieutenant spit at them.

"The worst hatred toward the Palestinians is coming from those who left," says al-Awadi. "On the outside we heard about the atrocities, and had to listen to Yasser Arafat's support of Saddam. Perhaps after people have come back and have a chance to assess the real situation, their attitudes will change." For the time being, the Palestinians who remained in Kuwait through the occupation will be allowed to stay, but even those who did not collaborate may never be trusted again. "For a time," says Major Mohammed Hamoud, a Kuwaiti air force HAWK-missile battalion commander, "we let some Palestinians into the army, mostly the sons of longtime residents. I had 30 or so in my battalion, and they performed well on the first day of the invasion when we shot down 12 Iraqi planes and helicopters. But now you can never be sure if they will turn, and so they must go."

One goal of al-Sultan's disbanded reconstruction team has survived Kuwait's internal politics: the proposal to cut the country's preinvasion population of 2 million almost in half by shedding many of the country's non-Kuwaiti resident workers. "Demography is the key," al-Sultan says. "We want Kuwaitis to work, to have incentive, to be productive. We want a merit system in education and at work, without guaranteed government jobs. The way to make Kuwaitis not be lazy is to force them to fend for themselves. And the way to do that is to strip away the foreigners who have done most of the hard work while Kuwaitis lie about."

The process has already begun. On March 2, the Gulf Bank ran an advertisement in the daily newspaper *Voice of Kuwait* seeking Kuwaitis to be trained as bank clerks in Dubai. "That's the start," says Salah al-Awadi, who works for the bank. "What will happen in my office is that we will gradually replace foreigners with Kuwaitis. I am sure that others will follow."

Last fall those Kuwaiti officials who would hazard a guess at the optimum size of the Palestinian population put the figure at 100,000. "Now surely we can achieve that," says one Minister. "We can do it either by denying readmission to those who left and deporting some of those who stayed—or we can kick out some who stayed and replace them with some who left who we are fairly sure can be trusted."

As he drove through Kuwait City inspecting the damage inflicted by Iraq, al-Awadi could barely contain his anger. "You see what they did to the museum, to the scientific center, to art in people's houses," he said. "I know it is said that the Iraqi soldiers were just following Saddam's orders, and I am sure they were. But living in a place like Iraq, with a regime like Saddam's, makes little Saddams of everyone or brings out the Saddam in all of us. When you live in a society without principles, the rape of Kuwait is what you get. If there is a silver lining to all of this, it is that we may now understand the value of having principles as we try to build a new, more democratic and merit-driven country. If people can understand that, Saddam will have done us a great good.

"I hope that will happen," said al-Awadi as he noticed the wind shift, "but I just don't know." The dark cloud was rapidly approaching, and perhaps in anticipation of its arrival, al-Awadi began to cough the cough many suffer whenever they are near the area where Kuwait is burning.

Sporadic gunfire continues long after liberation: A Kuwaiti fires a celebratory round into the air with an AK-47.

Israel Under Fire: The Grim Need For Restraint

Viper snake were the two dreaded code words that flashed
over Israel Radio at 1:50 a.m. on Jan. 18. Soldiers based
at hundreds of observation posts across the nation
began scanning the skies. Reconnaissance planes soared
upward to join F-15 and F-16 fighters on patrol. Air-raid sirens
began wailing, and millions of men, women and children
scrambled out of bed, strapped on gas masks and dashed into
pre-equipped safety rooms, quickly sealing the
doors with tape. Within minutes, eight Iraqi Scud missiles
slammed into the densely populated coastal region, six in the
Tel Aviv area and two in Haifa.
The thunderous explosions of the 350-lb. warheads, which
shattered windows four blocks away, immediately
destroyed any hopes that Israel could remain safely on
the sidelines of the gulf war. Saddam had failed in his repeated
attempts to forge a political link between his annexation
of Kuwait and Israel's occupation of the West Bank and Gaza.
Now, barely 24 hours after the allies had launched their
bombing campaign against Iraq, he was determined to create a
military link. The Scud missiles dared Israel to strike back.
As terrified Israelis sat in their sealed rooms, Army
Chief of Staff Dan Shomron hurried to an underground
command bunker known as the Bor (which means hole in
Hebrew) beneath the Defense Ministry in downtown Tel Aviv.
There he riffled through reports from civil-defense teams
at the various explosion sites, all checking for signs of poison

U.S. Patriot missiles shoot up to intercept an incoming Iraqi Scud over Tel Aviv.

One week into the war, rescuers rummage through apartment buildings damaged by a Scud in a Tel Aviv suburb.

gas. At one site toxic chemicals were detected, but a further investigation showed that they were industrial products from a nearby textile factory.

The Iraqi warheads gouged 15-ft. deep craters, smashed cars and damaged hundreds of buildings. Miraculously, only 12 Israelis were directly injured by the explosions. Panic took a higher toll. Dozens of elderly heart-attack victims, some of them Holocaust survivors, were rushed to hospitals. Others suffered from physical reactions after prematurely injecting themselves with the nerve-gas antidote atropine, which had been distributed along with gas masks. Four Israelis suffocated to death inside their gas masks, including a three-year-old girl whose parents had neglected to open the filter of her mask.

Israelis had been living under the threat of an Iraqi missile attack since April 1990, when Saddam first vowed to scorch half the Jewish state with chemical weapons if he were attacked. When Iraqi troops stormed into Kuwait on Aug. 2, few Israeli officials expected President Bush to fight back. Prime Minister Yitzhak Shamir limited himself to a reassertion of the traditional Israeli policy: "If we are attacked, we will respond."

But when Washington began building alliances with Arab states, it also pressured Jerusalem to keep quiet and avoid any action that might jeopardize the delicate coalition. Israeli officials obeyed with uncharacteristic restraint, but they chafed when the U.S. announced plans to sell billions of dollars in advanced weapons to the Saudis, including F-15s, Patriot-missile batteries and M1A2 Abrams tanks. "They will never use these weapons in self-defense, and if they do use them, we fear it will be against us," said Shamir.

In October Congress voted to reward Egypt's role in the anti-Iraq coalition by canceling its $6.7 billion military debt; it also authorized Bush to provide Israel with $700 million worth of military supplies from existing U.S. stockpiles. That vote, Israeli officials noted, marked the first time that Egypt had won a better deal from the U.S. than Israel.

Shamir and Bush have never liked each other. Shamir doubts Bush's commitment to Israel, while Bush hasn't forgiven Shamir for rejecting U.S. efforts to launch Palestinian-Israeli peace talks. But on Dec. 11, when the two leaders sat down for a meeting in the Oval Office, they were both eager to please. Shamir hoped to repair relations and win additional aid; Bush wanted assurances that Shamir would not launch a pre-emptive attack against Iraq.

During that meeting, Bush held out the prospect of increased aid as well as intelligence sharing in return for Israel's continued military restraint. Shamir agreed that Israel would not strike first—unless it detected preparations for an Iraqi chemical missile attack. When the January talks between Secretary of State James Baker and Iraqi Foreign Minister Tariq Aziz broke down, a reporter asked Aziz whether Iraq would respond to a U.S. attack by striking Israel. His chilling reply: "Yes, absolutely, yes."

The Israelis did their best to warn Iraq against any such move. "Our pilots are in their cockpits," said Air Force Commander Brigadier General Avihu Bin Nun as he appeared on TV standing beside a fully armed F-15 equipped with external fuel tanks for the more than 500-mile trip to Baghdad.

That morning Foreign Minister David Levy had warned visiting U.S. Congressmen that "Israel is not cannon fodder . . . and cannot allow itself to be attacked without responding just to preserve some coalition, which is following the United States." Defense Minister Moshe Arens announced, "We are ready for war" and advised Israelis to stay tuned to their radios. As the government began broadcasting civil-defense advisories, residents stockpiled bottled water, food and batteries. The army had already distributed 4 million gas masks (but not to Palestinians) as part of "personal protective kits."

Bush sent Deputy Secretary of State Lawrence Eagleburger to Jerusalem as his personal envoy to try to keep Israel out of the coming war. Arriving Jan. 12, Eagleburger asked for assurances that Shamir would not respond to any Iraqi provocation. According to one high-ranking Israeli official, "Eagleburger promised that the U.S. would eliminate the missile threat to Israel within 48 hours after the start of the war." Shamir and Arens refused to rule out an Israeli counterstrike if attacked, but they agreed to consult with the U.S. before taking any action.

Back in October, Bush had announced that the U.S. would provide Israel with two advanced PAC-2 Patriot-missile batteries, and Israeli crews were sent to Texas for training. But in December the Pentagon decided that the Patriots were needed in Saudi Arabia. The U.S. offered to provide Israel with the PAC-1 version, which could shoot down planes but not missiles. Israel refused them. Now Eagleburger offered Israel two PAC-2 batteries to be manned by U.S. crews.

Israeli military intelligence estimated that Iraq had at least 65 fixed and mobile Scud missile launchers. At daybreak on Jan. 17, the U.S. conducted an intelligence evaluation of its initial bombing and quickly told Tel Aviv that most of the 36 fixed launchers in western Iraq were reported destroyed (wrongly, it would turn out). The allies launched several more waves of attacks against Iraqi missile launchers that day, but Israelis remained indoors, anxiously tuned to the news.

The first two Iraqi Scuds actually were fired at Tel Aviv at 4:30 p.m. on Jan. 17 and caught Israeli authorities by surprise. The missiles were seen plunging out of a rainy sky and splashing harmlessly into the sea about 400 yds. offshore. Unwilling to admit their vulnerability, Israeli officials at first dismissed reports of the attack, then suppressed news of it.

At 7 p.m., perhaps persuaded that the Americans had wiped out the missile threat, the Cabinet debated whether to lower the civil-defense alert. Even as they did so, Iraqi technicians were fueling and targeting eight more Scuds for the 5- to 6-min. flight to Israel.

Shortly after the first Scuds hit Tel Aviv on Jan. 18, Defense Secretary Arens got a telephone call from Dick Cheney and began to push aggressively for an Israeli air strike. He outlined two plans: the U.S. could allow Israeli forces to work exclusively in Iraqi air space, either west of the Euphrates or in a smaller area west of the 42nd meridian. He also requested that the U.S. clear an air corridor over Saudi Arabia to prevent Israeli warplanes from having to fly over Jordan and risk a clash with King Hussein, who had promised to resist any such overflights.

Cheney rejected the idea. But he did promise to send a U.S. general from Saudi Arabia to Tel Aviv to facilitate intelligence sharing, and he offered to provide real-time access to U.S. satellite photos of western Iraq. He also offered to airlift the two American-manned Patriot batteries to Israel. Arens accepted the offers but warned that Israel felt itself in an untenable position. In a Cabinet meeting later that same Friday, General Shomron said, "The great American ability doesn't alter the principle that the protection of the civilians of Israel is the responsibility of the State of Israel. This incident cannot go without response."

Privately, Shamir decided not to act, hoping that Iraq wouldn't force his hand with additional missile attacks. But on Saturday, Jan. 19, at 7:20 a.m., four more missiles were fired at Israel. One warhead landed just a few feet from a huge oil storage tank in northern Tel Aviv. Amazingly, only 16 Israelis were wounded in the attack.

Within three hours, Bush was on the phone. In a pattern that would repeat itself throughout the war, he assured the Prime Minister that the allies were doing everything possible to destroy the missile launchers and warned that any Israeli retaliation might jeopardize the coalition.

Shamir held a second emergency Cabinet meeting. During the somber debate, nearly half the ministers called for military action. It was inconceivable, they argued, for the Jewish state to sit back and absorb blows from an Arab aggressor. That same day the two Patriot-missile batteries arrived at Tel Aviv's Ben Gurion Airport aboard U.S. Air Force transports from Germany. Shamir again decided to hold his fire.

Israelis called it *Ha Milchama Ha Muzara* (the strange war). For the first time since 1948, when the nation was born in war, the front lines were in the rear and civilians were in greater danger than soldiers. In 19 separate attacks over a 40-day period, Iraq fired 41 Scuds at Israel, killing four civilians, wounding nearly 200, damaging 4,100 buildings and leaving 1,600 families homeless. "We've had short wars, long wars and wars of attrition, but we haven't had a war like this," said Brigadier General Nachman Shai, the army spokesman who became known as Mr. Valium for his soothing briefings after every attack. "Each Israeli family has become a military unit."

After the first missiles hit Tel Aviv, Shai advised citizens to "stay in your apartments, eat, drink, enjoy yourselves, drink coffee, watch television, listen to the radio and have your protective kit next to you." But gradually the claustrophobia and an unwillingness to let Saddam paralyze the nation emboldened Israelis to return to work.

The bizarre quickly became the routine. In Tel Aviv and Haifa, the cities that suffered the worst destruction, restaurants closed at night and the streets were deserted. Discos and movie theaters opened only during daylight hours. At least 30,000 Tel Avivians left the city each day just before nightfall, causing tremendous traffic jams as they headed for safer ground. Tel Aviv Mayor Shlomo Lahat provoked an uproar when he labeled these commuters "deserters." Those who remained proudly displayed bumper stickers declaring, "I stayed in Tel Aviv."

When the air-raid warnings sounded, even women in labor were forced to don masks, and newborns were quickly placed inside protective tents. One attack interrupted a concert in Jerusalem by Zubin Mehta, Isaac Stern and the Israel Philharmonic. The audience, which included Defense Minister Arens, was instructed to remain seated and put on gas masks. After a few moments of confusion, Stern returned to the stage without a gas mask and resumed playing.

Civil-defense authorities banned large gatherings in Tel Aviv, so the Maccabi Tel Aviv basketball team played its European Championship home games in Brussels. For security reasons, no weather reports were broadcast during the war. Many citizens tuned in to a special radio station that remained silent at night, sounding only during missile attacks for the benefit of those who couldn't hear their neighborhood sirens.

After several missile explosions, Israelis hiding in their antigas chambers began wondering whether they wouldn't be safer in bomb shelters, but officials conceded that there were not enough public shelters available. Former Defense Minister Yitzhak Rabin caused a small scandal when he publicly admitted that he headed for a bomb shelter at the sound of an alert. When an Israeli was crushed to death in his apartment while others were saved by fleeing to bomb shelters, Chief of Civil Defense Uri Manos conceded that bomb shelters were safer if properly sealed. But General Shai insisted that people should run for their sealed rooms, warning that few would have time to reach their bomb shelters.

Despite the missile threat, 14,267 Soviet Jewish immigrants arrived at Ben Gurion Airport during the war. One planeload disembarked just as the sirens started to wail. As the stunned newcomers entered the terminal, officials handed out gas masks and rushed the immigrants into a sealed room. Even prostitutes in Tel Aviv carried gas masks on the job. Police arrested several "Scud bandits" for robbing homes while the occupants were sealed in their safe rooms.

Adults suffered from insomnia, children from nightmares. Counselors at the Ministry of Education handled 1,500 calls a day from frightened youngsters. Said Dr. Bilha Noy, who ran the hot-line service: "Many children vomited inside the masks, found it difficult to breathe and wanted solutions. They complained of fear, anxiety and sweating."

The 1.7 million Palestinians living in the West Bank

Rabbis pray outside a Tel Aviv building wrecked by a Scud. In all, Iraq fired 41 of the missiles at Israel.

and Gaza spent the war under military curfew, allowed out only occasionally to buy food. The army said the drastic measures were intended to prevent Palestinians, who strongly supported Iraq, from opening a second front. Despite the threat of being shot on sight, some Arabs ran to their rooftops during attacks to applaud the incoming Scud missiles. Some even carried signs saying, "Gas the Zionists."

The army at first refused to provide Palestinians with gas masks, arguing that the West Bank was not on Saddam's target list. Officials also were worried that Palestinians would use the masks to protect themselves against tear gas during demonstrations. But the Supreme Court, noting that Jewish settlers in the West Bank were provided with masks, ordered the army to distribute masks to Palestinians as well. By the end of the war, fewer than 120,000 masks had been given to Palestinians, however, even though four missiles did land in the West Bank.

At 8:30 p.m. on Jan. 22, a Scud missile was nicked but not disabled by a Patriot, and the warhead slammed into a densely populated residential neighborhood in Ramat Gan, near Tel Aviv. Ninety-six people were wounded in the explosion, and three died of heart attacks. More than 900 people were forced to evacuate their damaged homes. "We experienced this sort of thing back in Poland," said an elderly Israeli sitting on a curb in the rain beside the ruins of his apartment.

That attack, the most devastating to date, severely tested Jerusalem's policy of restraint. During a heated Knesset debate, National Religious Party member Hanan Porat insisted, "We must not turn the other cheek. We must act immediately but with the courage and originality for which we are known." Major General Ehud Barak, Deputy Chief of Staff, said the military's "fingers itch" to counterattack. Defense Minister Arens appeared on Israel television to warn, "We shall retaliate. We shall retaliate. We shall retaliate."

Arens feared that further restraint would weaken Israel's deterrence against future Arab aggression. But Arens knew that any Israeli strike would require operational coordination with Washington to prevent an accidental clash between Israeli and allied planes. More important, Israel wanted Bush's political backing for retaliation, lest Jerusalem be blamed if something went wrong. During the war, Arens spoke by phone with Cheney at least 60 times, according to aides, and constantly pressured the Americans to approve an Israeli

Prime Minister Shamir welcomes the arrival of U.S. Apaches. "If we are attacked, we will respond," he said. But he held his fire.

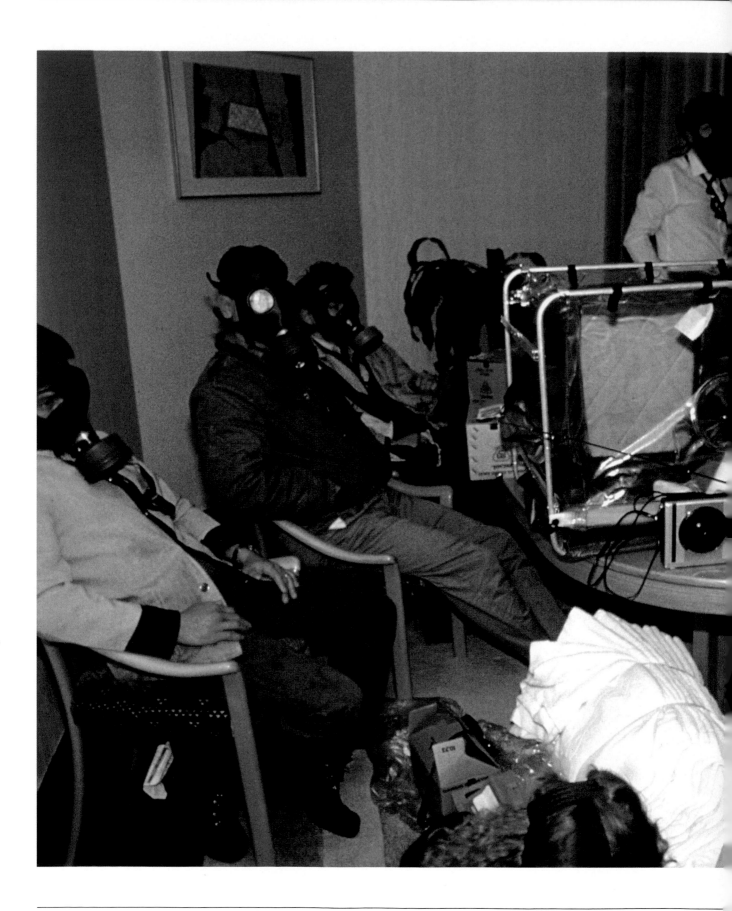

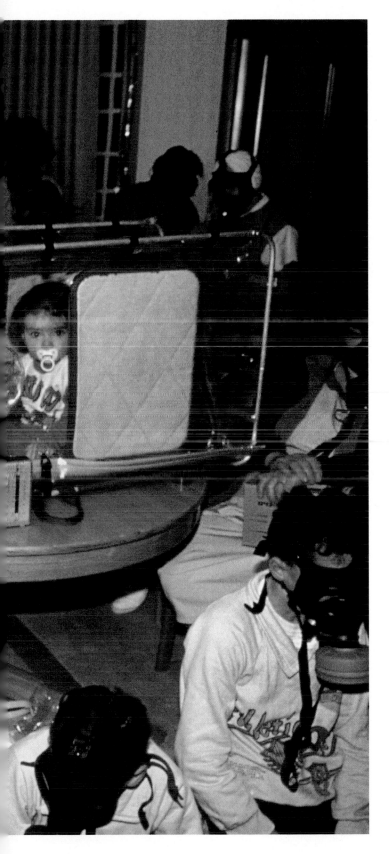

strike. Arens argued that allied tactics were insufficient and recommended that if Israel were not allowed to act, the Americans should launch a ground operation using special forces in western Iraq to ferret out and destroy the missile launchers.

Shamir was more cautious than Arens. If given the green light by the U.S., aides say, Shamir would have ordered a strike. But without Washington's backing, Shamir concluded, the political fallout from a retaliation would exceed the military benefits. Shamir also had his eye on the future. His policy of restraint was earning important credit in both Congress and the White House, which he hoped would lead to more favorable treatment in any postwar negotiations on the Arab-Israeli conflict. He also intended to transform the surge in sympathy for Israel into billions of dollars in additional U.S. aid to help absorb Soviet-Jewish immigrants. He did finally win Washington's promise of $400 million for housing those immigrants.

Though Israel never believed its involvement would completely destroy the coalition, it feared that a possible clash with Jordan could develop into war. There was another critical consideration: Israel was worried that if it hit back at Iraq before the ground war started, Saddam would use the attack as an excuse to pull out from Kuwait and redeploy his troops in western Iraq, thus perhaps saving his army from complete destruction at the hands of the allies.

Nonetheless, the military was still pushing for action, confident that it could do a better job than the allies in abolishing the missile threat. At a Cabinet meeting on Jan. 26, General Shomron praised the allies' persistence but told the ministers that the methodical U.S. tactics against the missile launchers were inadequate. He complained that instead of aggressively pinpointing their targets, the allies were firing from higher and safer altitudes, where they were unable to distinguish between real and decoy launchers. (In a closed-door meeting after the war, Chief of Intelligence Amnon Shahak said he could only confirm that half of Iraq's fixed launchers had been destroyed.) Shomron and Air Force Commander Bin-Nun then outlined various military options, ranging from an air strike to a combined air-land operation deploying commandos to attack the launcher sites.

The government dispatched David Ivri, director-general of the Defense Ministry, and General Barak to Washington on Jan. 28 to brief Pentagon officials and

In fear of poison gas, Israelis don protective gas masks, seek the safety of sealed rooms and wait for the all clear on radio and TV.

request additional military aid, including spare parts for Israeli fighters, which were forced to remain on constant patrol. They found the Americans adamant in their opposition to any Israeli strike and reluctant to provide more military aid. But Pentagon officials did agree to adopt several Israeli recommendations for more aggressive allied bombing tactics.

When Arens arrived in Washington on Feb. 11, Israel had withstood 11 attacks by Iraqi Scuds. Though the restless Israelis had acceded to Washington's pleas not to retaliate, the continuing threat of Scud attacks and fear of chemical warheads had stretched Jerusalem's patience to the limit. Said a high-ranking military official: "The probability that Saddam will use his chemical weapons increases tremendously as he becomes more desperate."

The Oval Office meeting between Arens and Bush was interrupted when Arens received word of another Scud attack. This time a missile landed near his home in Savyon, and Arens excused himself briefly to phone his wife. Then he unveiled his plan for an Israeli air and ground operation in Iraq that could take place after the allied ground war had begun. Bush was sympathetic but refused to go along with the plan and again cautioned Israel against taking any action on its own.

When the final U.S. ultimatum to Iraq expired on Feb. 23, Israelis were sitting in their sealed rooms and wearing gas masks. Minutes earlier, Saddam had answered the ultimatum—his last chance to avoid a ground war—by firing a Scud missile at Israel's Dimona nuclear complex. It missed, landing harmlessly in the Negev Desert. On Feb. 25, Israelis were awakened at 3:30 a.m. and 5:30 a.m. by two more missiles, which also landed in the Negev Desert. Each time, civil-defense units clothed in chemical-protection suits raced to the impact site to examine the contents of the warhead. To their relief, the first warhead contained a conventional explosive. But the second warhead was different. After performing a series of tests, the Israeli team began to laugh. The warhead was filled with concrete, which is used as ballast for test missiles. Saddam's last Scud was a dud.

School reopens for the first time in February since the war starts, with gas masks as part of every child's classroom equipment.

Stealth and Smart Bombs: Will Star Wars Work?

A new age of high-technology military weapons opened in the first seconds of the gulf war. CNN reporters complained that they couldn't see any aircraft dropping the bombs that were making Baghdad erupt in flames. But then neither could Iraqi radar operators, for the initial attack was the first real operational test of America's new F-117A "stealth" fighters, which proved virtually invisible to the Iraqi equipment. Saddam Hussein was soon to bear the brunt of a whole range of previously unknown weapons. The F-117As had barely departed when Tomahawk cruise missiles, launched from ships in the Persian Gulf, zoomed in on Baghdad. In the six-week air campaign that followed, precision-guided weapons, both missiles and shells, flattened Iraqi targets. When the ground war began, American technology soon proved overwhelming. U.S. forces destroyed or captured 3,850 Iraqi tanks while losing only three. Looking back, Brigadier General Thomas Kelly, the avuncular Pentagon briefer, concluded, "High tech made the difference between slow success and a quick victory."

The war brought to Americans at home a whole new lexicon of technical terms: stealth, laser-designated, infrared range-finding, light amplification. Most of the new weapons had in common a reliance on miniaturized computer technology. Just as they have changed modern civilian life in VCRs, high-fidelity sound and color television, these microprocessors have transformed the face of the battlefield.

A Tomahawk cruise missile is launched from a ship in the Persian Gulf.

Little wonder that some pundits labeled this the Microchip War.

The success—and in some cases, failure—of these weapons will become the focus of the upcoming debates over not only how to spend defense dollars but also how to define effective strategy and doctrine worthy of the new technology. Critics, or at least cautious observers, warn that considerable analysis is still required to define with any precision the performance of the weapons and, even more, their cost effectiveness.

Nevertheless, Air Force advocates have already rushed to make the F-117A's performance over Iraq serve as a rationale for the B-2 Stealth bomber. Air Force Secretary Donald Rice went to Capitol Hill to argue that eight F-117As armed with smart bombs and accompanied by a small number of support aircraft could devastate as many targets as a 75-plane squadron of conventional F-16Cs. The F-117As, said Rice, attacked 31% of all the targets bombed in the first 24 hours of combat.

The technology, or rather the physics, of both aircraft is similar. Stealth technology—more properly "low observable," for the plane is still detectable under certain conditions—depends on several basic phenomena. There are two ways to defeat radar: either absorb the radar signal or reflect it away from the enemy's receiver. Certain construction materials like graphite epoxy absorb radar signals and turn their energy to heat. And the aircraft can be designed to reflect signals away from rather than back to enemy receivers. Infrared detection can be reduced by burying the heat-generating engines inside the fuselage.

In these terms, the F-117A, which Lockheed built and first flew in 1981, is only a first step. Engineers basically fitted stealth technology to a standard aerodynamic shape. The aircraft was designed with boxy, wedgelike wings, awkward fuselage angles and elongated pyramids, all fine for directing radar signals away from the receivers, but not so great for aerodynamic stability. Pilots called the F-117A the "Wobbly Goblin," tough to fly and even tougher to maneuver effectively.

The B-2 Stealth bomber now in the test phase is an entirely new, radical design. It resembles a flying manta ray and designed from the beginning as a stealth aircraft. Consequently, its flying-wing silhouette is presumed to have markedly better stealth characteristics. And it carries a much bigger bombload than the relatively tiny F-117A. Compared with the $106 million cost of an F-117A, the B-2's price tag is also revolutionary: $860 million and climbing, more than the plane would cost if made entirely of gold. Still, the apparent success of the F-117A (though admittedly against an ineffective Iraqi air defense) is certain to encourage support for the $4.6 billion now proposed in the 1992 budget for building four more B-2s in a total projected purchase of 19.

The impact of the war on the prospects for the Tomahawk cruise missile is more uncertain. The Tomahawk is essentially an unmanned aircraft. It flies at low levels (500 ft.) at aircraft speeds (600 m.p.h.) and is visible to both human eyes and radar.

On the plus side is the Tomahawk's presumed accuracy—within 20 yards after a flight of 400 miles. The Tomahawk is guided initially by an internal memory map of the route to its target. The weapon's radar altimeter plays a big role in identifying terrain features against which course corrections are made. Nearer to the target, the system's terrain contour (TERCOM) system takes over, comparing pictures of the target stored in its memory with what the missile sees optically through a sensor in its nose.

Despite the demonstrated capabilities of the Tomahawk in the gulf, its use posed as many questions as it answered. For one thing, the Tomahawk proved less reliable than planned. There were 20 failures in the first-day launching of 104 Tomahawks; the missiles did not ignite properly or crashed en route. The Pentagon seemed to sense a problem. Although 216 were fired in the first 36 hours of the war, only 68 were fired after that and apparently none in the last half of the war. Initial Pentagon claims of great successes were later disputed by independent military observers, creating an as-yet-unresolved credibility gap.

Another problem is that the Tomahawk is a rigid tactical system that, once launched, cannot change course or switch to alternative targets. No less serious is the extremely demanding and time-consuming preparation of the "road map" to the target. These maps rely on extensive digital mapping from satellites and require weeks to perfect.

Another major shortcoming is the Tomahawk's relatively small payload, only 1,000 lbs. of explosives, in contrast to the 24,500 lbs. carried by an F-15 fighter plane or the 18,000 lbs. on the Navy's A-6. As always, destructive force is a product of explosive yield times accuracy, so on this basis the Tomahawk—at $1 million apiece—is not always cost ef-

Loading an F-117A Stealth fighter: its boxy shape helps deflect radar but makes the "Wobbly Goblin" hard to maneuver.

fective. Compared with the B-2, on the other hand, the Tomahawk is cheap: for the price of one B-2, some 860 Tomahawks could be purchased. "The Tomahawk is a useful but limited weapon," says naval expert Norman Polmar. "It will not replace attack aircraft."

The biggest technical breakthrough in the gulf war, however, was not so much in "platforms"—ships or aircraft—as in ordnance, missiles and bombs. According to one estimate, the U.S. fired 12,500 tons of ordnance in the first five days alone. Nobody will easily forget the televised views taken through cameras in the noses of weapons, the crosshairs fixed on the target for several seconds before everything, camera and target, disappeared.

Laser-designated, precision-guided bombs were used at the end of the Vietnam war and involve little more than a laser source (which can be on the bombing aircraft itself, on a nearby plane or on the ground) and a laser monitor on board the bomb. The laser beam source is aimed at the target; the

bomb's laser sensor fixes on the reflected laser ray from the target; and the bomb, guided by tiny fins, travels a path directly down to its goal, adjusting the flight path to maintain the strongest possible brightness and color in the reflected laser. Among the most successful of this series was the GBU-10, a 2,000-lb. bomb carrying 945 lbs. of high explosive.

Some ordnance, like the 2,000-lb. GBU-15, uses either infrared or electro-optical (video camera) homing devices. With the infrared system, the bomb aims at heat sources identified by the bombardier and computer-programmed into the guidance package. With the electro-optical method, the image detected by the TV camera in the nose of the bomb is transmitted to the bombardier, who "steers" the bomb to target with a joystick. Such a bomb can blast a hole the size of a typical suburban swimming pool.

This technology is used in the stand-off land attack missile (SLAM) and the Israeli-developed Have Nap AGM-142, both of which are directed to targets by pilots watching on a cockpit screen the image picked up by a camera in the nose of the weapon. The technology is not foolproof; initial reports from the battleground suggest that the AGM-65 Maverick air-to-ground missile's guidance system proved something of a disappointment, since many of them missed their targets. For the most part, however, smart bombs proved revolutionary.

One veteran bomb damage assessment officer noted a curious feature of satellite BDA photos of the gulf war: the absence of nearby "miss" craters that traditionally surround targets. One bomb, it seems, was all it took. Furthermore, unlike past photos showing building walls caved in by near misses, BDA photos after smart bomb attacks showed walls knocked outward from direct-hit internal explosions. Precision-guided munitions simply hit their targets more accurately and often do so with less collateral damage to nearby civilians. Even in Vietnam, the general bombing accuracy was about 800 yards; in the gulf (not counting the B-52s, whose accuracy is still as faulty as it was in Vietnam) many of the strikes were direct hits, accurate within a couple of yards.

The precision-guided bombs had an impressive accuracy rate of 90%, officials said. However, because of their limited supply and high cost, they made up only 7% of the 88,500 tons of bombs dropped by U.S. aircraft. And the 81,980 tons of old-fashioned dumb bombs missed their target 75% of the time. Each type of bomb clearly has its applications, but for pinpoint accuracy the smart bombs proved invaluable in hitting such key targets as command and control centers.

Infrared sensors for bombs explained one remarkable shift during the war. Pilots at first lost considerable air time in "trolling" for targets, looking for tanks and armored vehicles moving in the desert. But most vehicles were dug into sand ditches and covered with sandbags. Only late in the war did the U.S. discover that the tanks had to be started daily to remain operable, and that this heat, along with the way the tanks' chassis absorbed the sun's rays, made them glow on infrared sensors in the early evening hours. By switching attack times, U.S. airplanes increased their daily kill rate from 75 vehicles to as many as 200.

Perhaps the most basic advances in high-tech

American technology proved overwhelming throughout the war. Here radar operators keep close watch on the gulf from the *Valley Forge*.

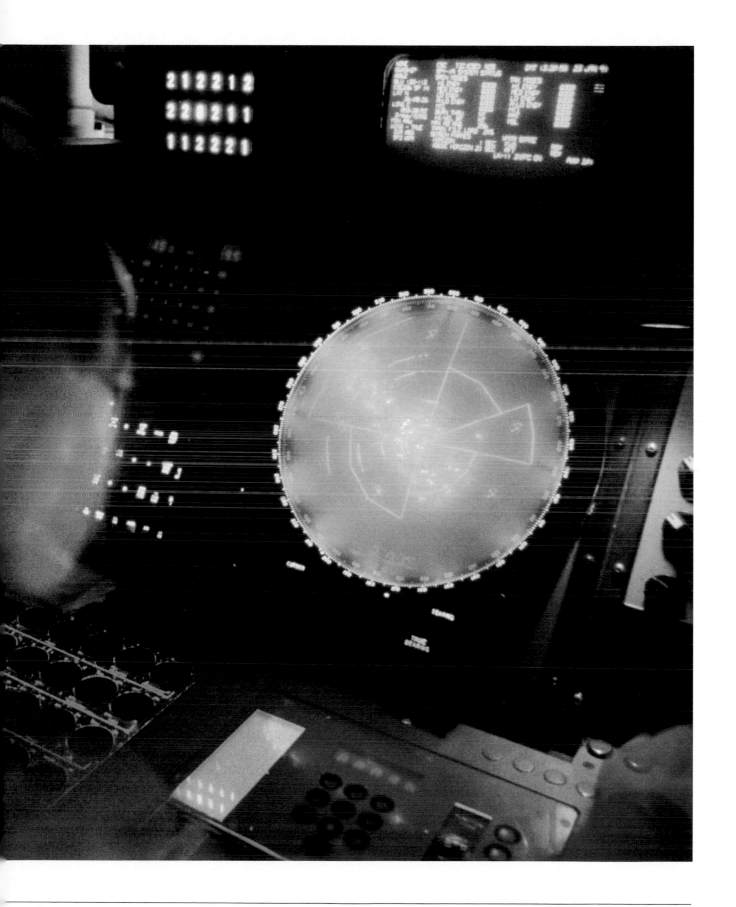

warfare have come in navigational systems—how to get where you want to go. Radar, infrared and light amplification are all essential elements in reaching a target. Every type of modern attack aircraft carries some sort of basic radar, while many carry forward-looking infrared (FLIR) or the more modern low altitude navigation and targeting infrared system for night (LANTIRN), which enables attacking F-15E fighters to identify an individual building in a crowded city or even a vehicle in a forest. Most of these same systems are installed in attack helicopters like the Apache and Cobra, as well as combat planes like the F-15E and F-16. Both in the air and on the ground, light-amplification night-vision goggles that allow visibility for up to seven miles even on dark nights were routinely used. The goggles, although limited by a narrow 40° field of vision and a susceptibility to "white out" in the presence of a bright light, proved enormously effective.

A pilot sees not only his own immediate battlefield. The gulf war proved anew the utility of the Boeing E-3 airborne warning and control (AWACS) aircraft. These electronics-laden Boeing 707s, cruising in lazy eights, not only directed attack aircraft but provided early warning of Iraqi aircraft and Scud missiles. One big surprise in the gulf war, however, was the successful introduction of a partner to AWACS known as joint surveillance target attack radar system. JSTARS was still in the testing stage, and the introduction of its two prototype models without adequate repair parts or maintenance was a gamble that paid off handsomely. While AWACS is designed to track aircraft, the JSTARS airplane performs the much more difficult task of monitoring action on the ground, blocking out the enormous background "chatter" from TV and radio while it keeps track of enemy tanks, trucks and armored personnel carriers. With 17 consoles and 34 crewmen aboard, JSTARS can spot a tank at a distance of more than 60 miles.

The gulf war was the first in history fought with direct support from space systems. The U.S. equipment included three KH-11 satellites carrying high-resolution optical and infrared cameras, both of which are enormously effective at night. The photo-multipliers of those cameras enhance available moonlight, while infrared actually "sees" in the dark. So sensitive are these sensors that, using computer enhancement, U.S. agencies can differentiate between 120 shades of gray and instantly spot any changes from previous images.

The gulf war also witnessed the first combat use

of the Lacrosse radar-imaging satellite, capable of penetrating clouds, fog and smoke. In higher orbits are the 15 satellites of the NAVSTAR global positioning system, which could tell troops their own position within 10 yards.

The emphasis on high-tech weapons dominated the ground war as well. Gone were the days of the motto, "The best anti-tank weapon is another tank." The U.S. was prepared for just such a battle, and it delayed the invasion of Kuwait largely to bring in more of its M1A1 model Abrams tanks, a 65-ton behemoth with a much-improved 120-mm smoothbore cannon, a computer-controlled stabilization system, laser rangefinder and infrared thermal imaging. All of this technology is designed to give it a 95% first-shot kill capability even while moving at 40 m.p.h. over rough terrain. The best the Iraqis could muster against the Abrams was the Soviet T-72, much lighter at 45 tons but armed with a 125-mm cannon that could devastate the Abrams with a direct hit. Most Iraqi tanks were the older T-62, T-55 and T-54 models.

In two instances, the Abrams fought *mano-a-mano* against T-72s and in one battle scored 40 kills without a loss, but American strategy called for a high-tech solution here too. Although the Abrams is better than the Soviet models, the superiority of U.S. missiles is even greater. U.S. warplanes and helicopters equipped with Hellfire missiles dominated the battlefield. The Hellfire is available in either the laser-designated or electro-optical version targeted by the pilot through a television screen in the cockpit.

The high-tech performance of U.S. weaponry was not flawless, however. One major shortcoming was the lack of an effective portable antitank missile. Although such weapons date back to World War II, the U.S. has failed to keep up with progress. One such system carried into battle, the Dragon, was widely judged inadequate against modern armor. One expert, retired Army Colonel Harry Summers, dismissed the old-fashioned Dragon as a "disgrace." Not only can't it penetrate modern armor, but it is also difficult to aim and requires the soldier to stay exposed to enemy fire while aiming.

The tube-launched, optically-tracked, wire-guided missile (TOW), carried either by infantrymen or aboard the Humvee utility vehicles, is effective

U.S. warship carries an impressive array of missiles and high-tech bombs. It was here that breakthroughs came.

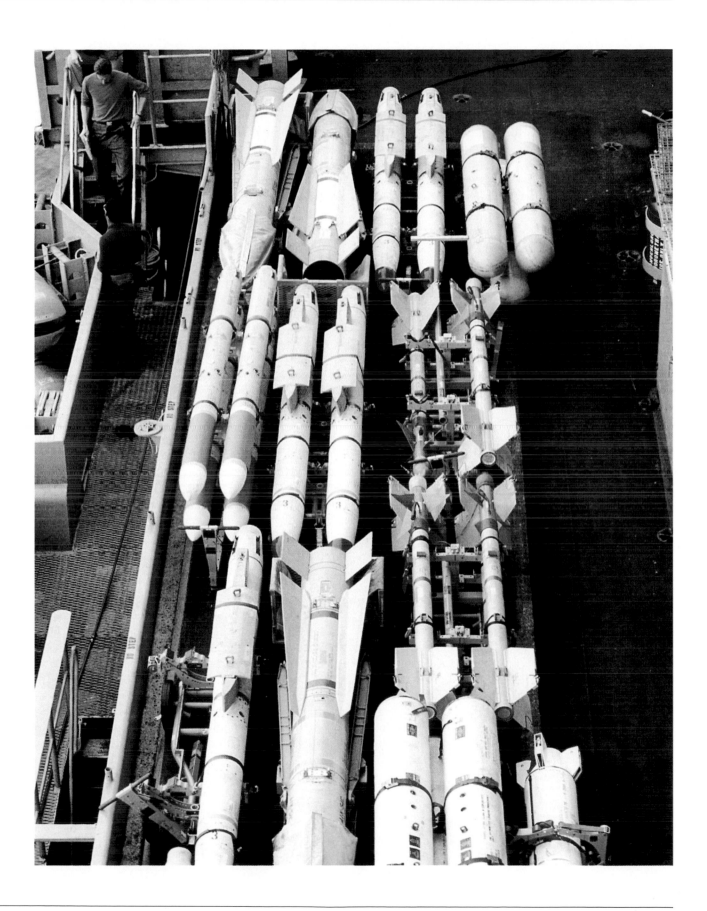

enough, but it too requires the gunner to remain motionless and exposed, keeping the crosshairs on the target during the missile's flight time, which may be 16 seconds over 2,000 yards.

The final verdict on one of the most ballyhooed new weapons, the Patriot missile, is not yet in, and it will long be evaluated. The Patriot was originally designed to defend military targets in isolated areas— an airfield, for example— rather than to act as a protective shield for cities. Its purpose was to intercept aircraft; only later was it adapted to target ballistic missiles. Fired from boxy mobile launchers, the 17-ft.-long missile will fly about 40 miles, and costs $1 million. U.S. officers claimed that Patriots had intercepted 45 of the 47 Scuds launched by the Iraqis against Saudi Arabia and Israel that were considered a threat. (An additional 39 Scuds headed for open water or desert were judged not dangerous, and Patriots were not sent against them.) President Bush was so enthusiastic that he personally visited the Raytheon plant in Andover, Mass., to hail the workers who had made the missile. "Not every intercept results in total destruction." said Bush, "but Patriot is proof positive that missile defense works."

Upon closer inspection, though, the Patriot's performance seemed less dazzling. Hints of this seeped through official briefings, where it was admitted that some damage on the ground appeared to have been caused by undestroyed Scud warheads, not "debris" as initially reported. Then officials conceded that better software was necessary to ensure that the Patriots destroyed the Scud warheads and not just the fuselages behind them. General Colin Powell, Chairman of the Joint Chiefs of Staff, said in a congressional briefing in February that Patriots had not always achieved a "catastrophic kill." A few days later, a Scud crashed into a U.S. barracks near Dhahran, killing 28 soldiers. Pentagon insiders said after the war that the data on the Patriot were still under study and that a definitive answer was a long way off.

Whatever the lingering questions, the nightly TV spectacles of the Patriots attacking incoming missiles over Tel Aviv and Riyadh unquestionably awakened a renewed public interest in antimissile defense. Not surprisingly, although the Patriot had nothing to do with President Ronald Reagan's 1983 Strategic Defense Initiative, or SDI, program, known as Star Wars, supporters seized on the Patriot's supposed success as evidence that technology was available to provide a real defense for the U.S. against

ballistic missiles. The Patriot success, said retired Army Lieut. General Daniel Graham, head of a pro-SDI group called High Frontier, proves "you can hit a bullet with a bullet."

That wasn't the point. A nuclear ICBM would have to be intercepted in space, beyond the reach of earthbound defensive systems and this brings with it all the problems of deploying and defending a system in space. Unlike the aged, lumbering Scud, which flies at Mach 3 to 4 (roughly 2,200 to 3,000 m.p.h), a modern ICBM comes in at Mach 15 to 20. Also, none of the Scuds carried nuclear or chemical warheads, both of which would have to be destroyed by a direct hit high in space to diffuse the effects. Said John Pike, chief space expert for the Federation of American Scientists: "All Patriot proves is that a ground-based system may work. It completely ignores the complexity of putting such a system into space." Former Defense Secretary Harold Brown was even more blunt: "The people who say the Patriot's success shows that SDI works don't know what they're talking about."

Nonetheless, Star Wars partisans moved into high gear. And they found new evidence for their case in the successful testing of an extremely advanced defensive system named ERIS, which recently intercepted an ICBM 100 miles high traveling four times the speed of a Scud. Secretary Dick Cheney's budget message received a last-minute insert speaking of a new program for Global Protection Against Limited Strikes, and President Bush mentioned SDI to considerable applause in his State of the Union message to Congress. The GPALS program would provide some space-based "brilliant pebbles," satellites that include sensors to track missiles and the rockets with which to attack them. SDI Director Henry Cooper immediately held a press conference in which he promised that, if adequately funded, part of GPALS could be working within five years. Critics have pointed out, however, that the 1972 Antiballistic Missile Treaty forbids the development of a nationwide missile defense, a problem that might delay development of the program. Partisan controversy aside, there's no question that the idea of missile defense has been rejuvenated. As SDI's Cooper put it, "Why should we develop systems to protect people only in Tel Aviv? Why not New York? Indianapolis? The only difference is the distance, and it's just a matter of time before the Third World has long-range capability." That argument may find even more adherents, but it remains to be seen whether it will also raise the $4.6 billion that President Bush has requested for SDI in his latest budget.

"Nervos belli, pecuniam infinitam," wrote Cicero. "The sinews of war, unlimited money." Cicero had it right. The high cost of high technology will be at the center of the continuing post-gulf debate over defense budgets. Contemporary high technology is expensive enough, but most of the technology in the gulf war was actually a decade or more old, and there's another generation of far more extensive weaponry ahead.

Critics of rushing ahead point out that many of the weapons in the gulf war, though not quite state of the art, were sufficient for the purpose. The Air Force's standard F-15E and F-16 aircraft, the Navy's F-14 and F/A-18, literally wiped the sky clean of Iraqi aircraft. And yet the Air Force has halted production of the F-15E in favor of an as-yet untried Advanced Tactical Fighter (ATF). Despite the demonstrated superiority of the M1A1 tank, the Army has halted further production in favor of an entirely new, and certainly more expensive, future model. Although both the Apache and Cobra helicopters

acquitted themselves well in battle, the Army is dropping both in favor of the new Light Helicopter Experimental (LHX) still on the drawing boards.

Now that the U.S. has dealt decisively with Iraq, its strategists must determine what lessons should be drawn regarding U.S. capabilities either in another Third World crisis or against some superpower. Iraq was a special case. U.S. transports sailed or flew unhindered to bases in Saudi Arabia, and the desert proved particularly vulnerable to high-tech sensors. Weapons that worked wonderfully well under those circumstances might yet prove of little value in fighting Philippine insurgents in the jungles or Shining Path guerrillas in Peru's mountains.

Stills from a video camera in the nose of a smart bomb (see arrow top left) hitting and destroying an Iraqi target.

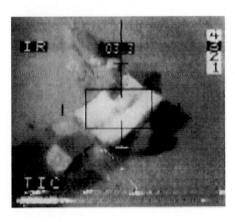
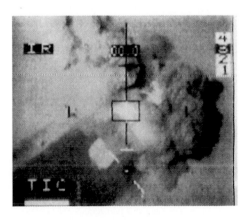
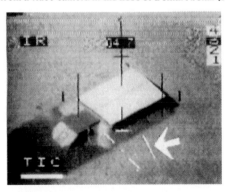
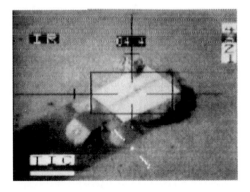

The Civilians Often Suffer A Cruel Fate

Slaughter and pillage are as old as warfare itself, but in times gone by, battles were most often fought mainly by soldiers against other soldiers. They met in open fields or trenches away from towns. They did not think of the very old and the very young as combatants. Modern battle puts whole populations in jeopardy. As the Persian Gulf war demonstrated in a painful variety of ways, the structure of modern life, the force of modern technology and the relentlessness of modern ideology all increase the vulnerability of defenseless civilians. Iraqi children incinerated in a bomb shelter, Israelis huddled in gas-proofed rooms, Pakistani and Bangladeshi refugees pleading for food, Americans held hostage as "human shields" in Baghdad—all these and thousands more fell victim to the pervasiveness of modern war.

The first civilian casualties in the traditional sense were those many Kuwaitis—nobody knows exactly how many—who succumbed to Saddam's initial blitzkrieg. Some residents fled to safety; some died in the desert, trying; some were shot; some imprisoned. Saddam's army seemed to follow a random policy, or none at all, about whether to allow Kuwaitis to leave. Sometimes their flight would be permitted, even encouraged. At other times, departing Kuwaitis were turned back by force or imprisoned for their attempt.

The 3,000 Americans living in Kuwait behaved like most other Westerners there. About 500 fled by any means they could find; the rest, ordered to stay put, stayed put. Most of

Iraqi refugees in Jordan plead for water, sometimes spilling what they manage to get.

The Civilians Often Suffer a Cruel Fate

those who took headlong flight were like Benny Whitaker, an oil-drilling supervisor from Abilene, Texas, and his wife Marjorie. Seasoned to the vagaries of international work, they grabbed just their cocker spaniel and whatever they could stuff into two suitcases and drove to the Saudi border. Steve Betts, a coach of the Kuwaiti national swimming team, whose family was back in the U.S. on vacation, joined two American neighbors (with three poodles) in driving out through a sandstorm. He took a bag of belongings and eight cans of Diet Pepsi—one of which he used to bribe an Iraqi soldier at a checkpoint 20 strategic miles short of the Saudi Arabian border.

For those who couldn't get out, life soon grew inconvenient, primitive and sometimes dangerous. Robert Morris, who taught dentistry in Kuwait City, stayed hidden for 120 days until Saddam issued a general amnesty for hostages and hideaways. With his own eyes, Morris saw Iraqi soldiers looting and beating people. He learned of Iraqi assaults on women in his building, and of the Iraqis' leaving a man hanging dead for three days in a nearby square. He and eight other foreigners resident in the building formed a security system based on coded phone calls and knocks. To discourage intruders, they disabled all but one of the seven elevators in the 450-apartment complex and carried the doorknobs for the fire doors in their pockets.

An additional 500 U.S. citizens found themselves trapped in Iraq when President Bush condemned Saddam's invasion, and Saddam responded by forbidding their departure. Few thought there was any effective way either to escape from Baghdad or to hide there. Among those who felt the greatest anxiety were foreigners of Arab descent. That was the tricky position of Ghazi Shaba, a naturalized American physician from San Diego, and his wife Edna, a schoolteacher, who were visiting relatives in Baghdad.

When they saw Iraqi soldiers going from house to house to round up teenage boys for military service—and began to fear that Ghazi might be drafted to help treat troops—the Shabas decided to take their sons Namir, 12, and Steven, 10, back to the safety of Southern California. "Things were changing from hour to hour," Edna recalled. "There was no sense in talking anymore. We decided to get rolling." They figured the best exit route was to Amman, Jordan, and the best method by bus, which seemed to offer safety in numbers. For the 600-mile journey, they brought a few slices of

An air-raid victim is buried in Baghdad. The distinction between civilian and military targets proved hard to maintain.

bread, a piece of beef, some chocolate and just two liters of water for all of them. The purported luxury vehicle they boarded (at $5 each) had no air conditioning, no toilet and few working windows. But discomfort changed to fear with the arrival of the first of what would eventually be 10 separate groups of Iraqi military investigators. They forced about 20 Kuwaitis off in the middle of the desert, without transport or resources, and threatened to do the same to an American who was denounced as stupid because he spoke no Arabic. When the Iraqi troops reached the Shaba clan, they called the parents traitors and imperialists and said, "Tell Bush we have a better army and will melt your soldiers down before they can throw anything at us." Ghazi and Edna feigned admiration for Saddam and thereby the family escaped, undergoing a 16-hour journey inside Iraq, a five-hour wait at the Jordanian border, another five-hour trek to reach Amman, and a flight home, at the end of which the sons literally kissed the California soil.

For "guest workers" from Third World countries, life inside Iraq and Kuwait rapidly grew scary, and the effort to escape was often much rougher. Both nations, especially Kuwait, had relied heavily on foreign workers to provide everything from engineering skills to menial services. On the eve of the invasion, the total number of Indians, Pakistanis and Bangladeshis in Iraq and Kuwait was estimated at 430,000. Egypt alone had supplied some 1.3 million workers—compared with a total of just 9,000 from the U.S., Britain, France and Germany. There were also substantial numbers of Sri Lankans (150,000), Filipinos (93,000), Lebanese (60,000), Vietnamese (17,000), and even Yugoslavs (7,000) and Turks (4,000). During the first three weeks after the invasion, more than 200,000 refugees went streaming into Jordan, some forced out by the Iraqis, others running in fear. Some headed straight on to Egypt or elsewhere. But many were penniless and physically broken by the long, hot journey, and they often felt they had nowhere to go.

In the filthy Shaalan One refugee camp, on ground infested with snakes and scorpions, Melia Tabono, a Filipino seamstress who had worked in Kuwait City until the invasion, lay semiconscious on a cot, her face gleaming with sweat and sand. Her countrywoman Thelma Nonatura tried to combat the 95°F heat by fanning a piece of cardboard. In the next cot an elderly Sri Lankan woman shook uncontrollably with thirst, hunger and heat. Not far away babies were dying.

Mashama Nawaz, a Pakistani, tried to feed himself, his wife and three children on one piece of bread and three tomatoes. When water trucks came by, the camp inmates were so desperate, so quick to jostle and threaten one another, that they often spilled most of the precious water onto the ground. Mohammed Tahir, a former restaurant worker who had fled Kuwait, kept wondering what he had done to deserve all this. "I have come," he said, "to a place that is even worse than what I left behind."

Among the other refugees were Mohammed Aftab, an Egyptian whom the Iraqi invaders had stripped of everything, even his prayer beads. And Khaled Atieh, who had been sales manager in a factory that was now burned down. And Mambo Hosni, who had been robbed by Iraqi soldiers of his hard-won Toyota sedan.

These people's plight only briefly commanded the world's attention. The U.S. and the European Community sent a few scant millions to help. The United Nations delayed for weeks in providing any of its experienced refugee apparatus, limiting help to its disaster-relief organization, on the tortured bureaucratic reasoning that these were not true refugees threatened by persecution. India and Pakistan did eventually manage to fly their refugees home. Sri Lankans said they could not afford to do so, but others joined in chartering Aeroflot planes for them. In all, at least 700,000 non-Westerners fled through Jordan to be evacuated. But long before they settled in new jobs and shelter in some other land, they had largely faded from the world's view.

The next highly publicized category of civilian victims were the foreigners who had stayed on in Iraq, the "guests of the Iraqi people," as Saddam's government now called them. At the time of the invasion, there were more than 1.5 million foreigners in Iraq, but at most a few thousand from the U.S. and its close Western allies. On Aug. 14 the Iraqi Foreign Ministry announced that these Westerners were henceforth forbidden to leave until the crisis ended. Similar constraints applied to the somewhat larger number of Westerners who remained in Kuwait, now under Iraqi military control. Some of these "restrictees" were installed in comfortable hotels, but others found themselves little better than prisoners. Some were dispersed to various military sites to serve as "human shields," an open violation of international law. Like Saddam, but for obviously different reasons, President Bush initially balked at calling these detainees hostages. He didn't want his Administration to become a political prisoner of the situation, as had befallen Jimmy Carter because of the hostages in Tehran; he wanted to deny Saddam any leverage based on his captives. But finally Bush

Saudi rescue workers carry an injured civilian out of a Riyadh building hit by an Iraqi Scud missile.

turned blunt. "When Saddam Hussein specifically of-fers to trade the freedom of those citizens of many na-tions he holds against their will in return for conces-sions," Bush said, "there can be little doubt that whatever these innocent people are called, they are in fact hostages."

Saddam seemed eager to convince the world that he was not mistreating his "guests." Hence on Aug. 23 he staged a macabre scene in which he visited a group of British hostages and chatted in an unctuously avuncular way with a five-year-old named Stuart Lockwood. In an official Iraqi videotape aired to appalled audiences in the West, Saddam fondled the round-cheeked boy and asked if he was getting enough cornflakes and milk. Stu-art rather grimly nodded. The dictator asked if there was enough space for exercise; Stuart replied with a few words about volleyball and soccer. Saddam ruffled Stu-art's hair, and a military aide stroked the boy's neck; Stu-art, his arms crossed and his manner impassive, delicate-ly inched away. Saddam, seeming to recognize that the boy was proving the better man, quickly moved on.

Perhaps realizing that his holding of hostages aroused not fear but disgust, Saddam announced that he would release all women and children. And so, with-in 10 days, young Stuart came home. By a couple of weeks later, about 2,000 Westerners, particularly de-pendents, had got away. But for many of their nations' menfolk—plus a few women in special circum-stances—the wait was much longer and more unnerv-ing. They were, as President Bush emphasized, being used as bargaining chips. When the display of the chips brought no bargains, just a lot of negative publicity, Saddam began releasing them anyway, a few at a time. Nine French hostages, out of 350, left Iraq on Oct. 1. About 360 people, mostly American men of Arab de-scent, were allowed out of Kuwait Oct. 10. Some who were released said they had been treated so badly that they had rioted against sadistic guards and starvation diets. So it went, in dribs and drabs, until most of the fi-nal 2,000-plus Westerners (and most of the 3,000-plus remaining Soviets) departed between Dec. 8 and 13. Saddam's Foreign Minister Tariq Aziz voiced on ABC-

TV's *Nightline* a merry seasonal wish: "I certainly hope they will all be out by Christmas."

While few returned to quite the hero's salute that Stuart got from Britain's Duchess of York, nearly all eventually escaped with the bulk of their possessions and in better physical shape than the Third World refugees. The hostages had benefited from some potent advantages: powerful governments demanding their release, global news media waiting to talk to them. The world cared and showed that it cared.

Soon after the hostages were gone, the bombing began. Thousands of allied sorties every day dumped thousands of tons of explosives on crowded Baghdad and Iraq's other cities, turning night into hellish day. U.S. officials repeatedly said they were making every effort to avoid injuring civilians—"collateral damage," as some military spokesmen called it. To that end, allied pilots sometimes canceled attacks because of poor visibility, or took extra risks in how they approached their targets. But as in almost every war, the distinction between civilian and military targets proved hard to achieve in practice and hard to define in theory. Many targets—bridges, electric power stations—have both military and civilian functions. Soldiers and civilians live and work closely together. And there are inevitable accidents and miscalculations.

As early as Jan. 22, less than a week after the air war began, refugees from Iraq reported that the bombings were killing civilians, particularly in Baghdad, a city of nearly 5 million. "Food and water are no longer available," said B. Singh, head of an Indian construction company. "Everybody is afraid. The people have no morale." Hamed Sayeed, 31, an Egyptian, recalled, "We ran to the bomb shelter, but there was no room at the shelter, so we sat beside the door. All the raids were concentrated on military targets, but there were civilian casualties. There were ambulances all day long."

Outside the capital, the raids were also punishing. "They bombed without mercy," said Saeed Ahmed Mohammed, the Egyptian manager of Al Yarmuk Hotel in Diwaniyah, 110 miles south of Baghdad. "They hit the hotel, full of families, and then they came back to hit it again." A nearby telecommunications center was apparently the main target, but 11 residents of the hotel were killed and 49 wounded. "Four turned insane because of fright," Mohammed said, "because of the loud voices of the bombs."

After the first attack on Baghdad, Hadi Sultan, 56, moved with his three children to Al Hillah, about 60 miles to the south, "thinking it was safe because there are no installations of military value here. Next day, bang! The house next door was obliterated. There's no safe place in Iraq, no place to run."

No matter how good the intentions of U.S. pilots, they were often unable to tell whether a target was military. Pilots could not know, for example, whether some vehicle on a highway was serving a military purpose. When several truck drivers were killed by U.S. aircraft strafing civilian oil trucks on the often raided highway from Iraq to Jordan, U.S. officials said that those trucks could have been carrying Iraqi military fuel.

A Jordanian named Chehadeh Ibrahim, 50, was fleeing from Kuwait on a bus with his 22-year-old son when the allied planes came. A bomb landed in the road ahead, and the windshield shattered. "We started running out, and then another missile struck the middle of the bus," Ibrahim said. By his account, 30 passengers burned to death, including four small children; 25 escaped. Ibrahim suffered cuts on the head. He spent the night in Basra. "In the morning they hit al-Amara market in Basra, and people started running like flies," he said.

The worst mingling of military targets and civilian victims occurred on Feb. 13, when two Stealth fighter-bombers delivered two laser-directed 2,000-lb. GBU-27 bombs at a concrete building in a residential neighborhood of Baghdad. The smart bombs smashed through a 10-ft.-thick concrete roof, sealed off the exit and incinerated about 400 civilians who had taken shelter there, mostly women, children and old people. U.S. officials said that this was a military command-and-control center and that they had known nothing of the civilians hiding there; CNN's Peter Arnett inspected the site and concluded that "there was no sign of any usage of the shelter other than for civilian use." For the occupants of the shelter, the 4 a.m. explosion was pure hell. "I was sleeping, and suddenly I felt heat and the blanket burning," said Omar Adnan, 17, whose parents and three younger sisters died in the holocaust. "Moments later, I was suffocating. I turned to try to touch my mother, who was next to me, but grabbed nothing but a piece of flesh."

In the last days of the war, when U.S. aircraft showered cluster bombs on Iraqi troops retreating from Kuwait, fleeing civilians also got caught in the rout—and suffered the consequences. Amid the thousands of stalled trucks, loot-filled cars and other vehicles, artillery shells were delivered and explosives dropped,

And still more refugees: An Iraqi in Nassiriyah carries his daughter as thousands search for food and safety.

The Civilians Often Suffer a Cruel Fate

some killing Kuwaitis who had survived the long invasion and were at last on the verge of being free. One British reporter later described packs of wild dogs ripping flesh from the corpses in one Iraqi truck and carrying it into the desert. "It's very sad to bury civilians," said Lieut. Andrew Nye of the 1st Battalion, Staffordshire Regiment. "There were women and children here. They were hit by the air strikes, or by Iraqi artillery." The bodies were so charred that the British often couldn't tell the difference between soldiers and civilians, or even men and women.

Even after the war had officially ended, the suffering of the noncombatants was far from over. In another horrifying turn of the wheel, the defeated Iraqi army went ferociously into action against various dissident groups—Shi'ite Muslims in the south and Kurds in the north—and indulged in a new round of slaughtering civilians. That in turn sent tens of thousands of new refugees fleeing toward the borders of Turkey and Iran. Officials in those countries took in some of the refugees but said they did not know how to deal with a major migration without international assistance.

Looking ahead, a United Nations team inspected Iraq from March 10 to 17 and reported that the destruction was "near apocalyptic," that Iraq's economy had been reduced to that of a "pre-industrial age." Some 9,000 Iraqi homes had been destroyed and 72,000 people left homeless; 90% of the nation's industrial work force had been "reduced to inactivity." The Iraqi people, deprived of water, food, fuel and electricity, the U.N. investigators said, "may soon face a further imminent catastrophe, which could include epidemic and famine . . . Time is short."

Saddam's latest victims: Hundreds of thousands of Kurdish refugees seek hope of sanctuary across the Turkish border.

The Media War:
"This Is
Peter Arnett . . ."

"Absolutely nothing happening here," ABC's Baghdad correspondent Gary Shepard told Peter Jennings at headquarters in New York just a few moments before he heard the first bombs exploding overhead. Shepard managed to get his first bulletin on the air, then found his telephone connection cut off. NBC had worse trouble. *Nightly News* anchor Tom Brokaw was hearing about the air raid sirens from Baghdad correspondent Tom Aspell, but Aspell added, "We have not heard any incoming yet, so perhaps this is a false alarm." Then his phone line also broke down, and NBC's live coverage of the war's first bombs ended. CBS never even got that far. Moments before the bombing began, the network lost telephone contact with correspondent Allen Pizzey, and it was unable to reach him for the rest of the night. Thus, with bombs still falling in Baghdad, the mighty U.S. television news organizations were out of the action. Except for one. At 6:40 p.m. (2:40 a.m. in Baghdad), viewers of the Cable News Network encountered the voice of correspondent John Holliman. He could not hear CNN headquarters in Atlanta telling him that he was in fact on the air live, so he just started talking. "Hello, Atlanta, Atlanta, this is Holliman," he said over the phone. "The skies of Baghdad have just been filled up with the sound of gunfire tonight." For the next 16 hours, CNN had the war to itself. Technology has a way of shaping not only the outcome of wars but also the manner in which noncombatants experience

Briefing in Riyadh: "I'm not a great fan of the press, and I want you to know where we stand."

Peter Arnett shows CNN viewers a damaged bridge in Baghdad; for a time, he had the war all to himself.

them. Before the development of the telegraph, news of distant battles could take weeks, sometimes months, to reach the home front. The Spanish-American War was the first in which masses of people could read news of the fighting almost as soon as a journalist could get to a telegraph office. World War II was a radio war, the first conflict to be heard by millions of people in their homes more or less as it was happening. American listeners were stirred by the voice of CBS's Edward R. Murrow describing in almost poetic detail the German air attacks on London, with the sound of air-raid sirens and bombs bursting in the background. Vietnam was the "living room war," in critic Michael Arlen's durable phrase, the first time Americans could see grisly scenes of actual combat on the networks' newly launched newscasts every evening around dinnertime; those images are credited with weakening public support for the war.

The conflict in the gulf was something new. For want of a better phrase, it could probably be called the satellite war. With the spread of commercial telecommunica-tions satellites and the miniaturization of microwave technology in the 1970s and '80s, it became relatively inexpensive for news organizations to obtain live video images from any part of the world. Thus, combat scenes like those from Vietnam (which used to be seen on the evening newscast at least a day later, after the footage had been air-freighted to Hong Kong or New York) could now be shown live, as they were happening.

That was bad news to U.S. military officials. With the traumas of Vietnam etched indelibly in their minds, they were worried that gory reports transmitted live from the battlefield might undermine the U.S. war effort. This time, the officials decided, Americans would see only authorized versions of the fighting. To accomplish that goal, the Pentagon imposed an unprecedented regime of restrictions on the press. War correspondents were denied access to the front, except as members of "pools" led by U.S. officers who took them only where the military wanted them to go. For the first time since World War II, all reports from the theater of operations were subject to censorship. Those restrictions, together with subtler forms of persuasion, veiled threats and selective disclosure, touched off a storm of protest from journalists, civil libertarians and sympathetic politicians. The moves also raised disturbing questions about the rights of citizens in a democracy to know how their war is being conducted. Curiously, not many of the citizens themselves seemed bothered by such issues. In fact, most Americans thought they were receiving tons of timely information about the war. That impression was created at least in part by the heavy use of live, satellite-transmitted reports by the U.S. television networks.

The most successful among them, at least in the opening phase of the war, was the brash upstart, CNN, a service launched in 1980 by Atlanta entrepreneur and yachtsman Ted Turner as the first 24-hour, all-news cable network. In its early years, CNN was considered a second-rate operation, staffed with network retreads and inexperienced nonentities. But what CNN may have lacked in expertise, it eventually made up for in tenacity and its unique around-the-clock availability. CNN's gripping, on-the-spot coverage of the 1989 Tiananmen Square massacre in Beijing won widespread praise. On the eve of the gulf war, CNN was ready: it had approximately 100 staff members in the region, more than half again as many as each of the other three networks.

CNN had another advantage over the majors. In the 1980s, the cable network undertook a major program of expansion outside the U.S. It was an uphill climb. Few foreign countries were wired for cable, and some officials had never heard of CNN. Britain's Margaret Thatcher, for instance, balked at the network's application for a license in Britain because she mistakenly thought it showed blue movies. Nonetheless, by the time the gulf war began, CNN could be seen in more than 105 countries—including Iraq. Americans traveling to exotic foreign locales were sometimes surprised to turn on their hotel television sets and find a CNN anchor speaking English to them, live from Atlanta.

That ubiquity gave CNN a special status among diplomats and heads of state: they could use the network to send messages and signals to officials in other countries without going through the usual channels of diplomacy; they could watch CNN to find out, sometimes with more accuracy than their own intelligence services and the local controlled press provided, what was going on around the world; and they could see what the world thought of them in return.

CNN's global character gave it a political edge over the major U.S. networks after the gulf war began. For the crucial first weeks of hostilities, CNN was the only for-

eign news operation allowed to broadcast from Baghdad. The other networks quickly recovered, and by war's end were turning in distinguished performances. In fact, the conflict in the gulf was also a battle of considerable magnitude among the networks for prestige and ratings. It was the first war with its own theme music and its own "logos," snappy graphic devices that networks flashed on the screen to introduce their war coverage.

Despite all the glitz that technology made possible, CNN's exclusive marathon broadcast of the bombing of Baghdad sometimes sounded as if Edward R. Murrow were reporting the blitz from London again: since they could not send video signals over their phone connection, Holliman and his two CNN colleagues in Baghdad, Peter Arnett and Bernard Shaw, simply described what they saw out their ninth-floor window in al-Rasheed Hotel—and occasionally held up a microphone to catch the sounds of battle. Back in Atlanta, CNN producers could do nothing but keep a map of Iraq on the screen. "You can feel the building, which is a very well-built hotel, shaking underneath us as the attack apparently continues," Holliman said, moments after the first bombs fell. "It looks like a Fourth of July display at the Washington Monument. The sky is brightly lit." A few seconds later he exclaimed, "Holy cow!"

At this point, Arnett took over. "If you're still with us, you're going to hear the bombs now hitting the center of this city," he said. Over the phone connection came the sounds of explosions, this time louder than before. Said Arnett: "I guess the planes are circling and coming back for more targets . . . The bombing has intensified now, and the explosions are coming closer to this part of town."

Said Shaw: "This feels like we're in the center of hell."

For the next 16 hours, Arnett, Holliman and Shaw crouched at the center of hell and described the scene outside their windows. They were bereft of electricity and water, unable to flush the toilet (though, for reasons they never understood, they were provided with regular maid service). They subsisted largely on canned tuna. Whenever the air-raid sirens sounded, they would jump under tables and into closets to elude Iraqi authorities, who tried to pack all the foreign journalists staying at the hotel into the basement bomb shelter.

At one point Holliman was escorted to the bomb shelter. After three hours of incarceration, he convinced one of the guards that he had a heart condition (he did not) and had to return to his room to retrieve medication. Once out of the shelter, he sprinted up nine flights of stairs to CNN's offices. Finally, after 16 hours on the air, the CNN staffers were confronted in their suite by Iraqi officials, who ordered them to stop broadcasting. They argued with the officials to no avail. "Well, that's that," said Holliman. Added Arnett: "I hope we can resume our communication with you in the very near future." Then there was silence.

How was CNN able to stay on the air so long after the other networks were cut off? One factor was familiarity: Iraqi officials knew CNN, and Saddam Hussein himself was reported to watch the network to see how he came across to the world at large. Another factor was technology. The CNN crew used backup batteries and a small generator that they had kept in the hotel. The most important piece of hardware was a "four-wire," a highly reliable two-way overseas telephone connection that requires no operators or switching connections and can continue working even when local phone and power lines are cut. After lobbying Iraqi authorities for months before the war began, CNN was allowed to use the connection. It cost $16,000 a month to maintain the four-wire and its satellite relay from Amman, Jordan, to Atlanta. That was a bargain, considering that the link allowed CNN to continue broadcasting when its competitors could not. During the war's first day NBC asked if it could share the line; CNN declined, though it did allow anchor Tom Brokaw to use it—to interview CNN's Bernard Shaw.

More than 200 U.S. television stations, including dozens of network affiliates, carried CNN feed. In some U.S. cities, viewers could pick up CNN not only on its usual cable channel, but also on a number of other over-the-air channels simultaneously. WCCO-TV, the CBS affiliate in Minneapolis, substituted CNN's dramatic first-night footage for its own network's reports and drew the highest ratings of any CBS affiliate in the top 25 markets.

All that exposure pushed CNN's Nielsen ratings into the stratosphere. On the war's first night, 10.8 million of America's 93.1 million households were tuned to CNN. The audience was the biggest in the network's history. Perhaps the highest accolade came from Defense Secretary Dick Cheney and Colin Powell, Chairman of the Joint Chiefs of Staff, who both referred to CNN in their first press conferences following the air strikes on Baghdad. When Powell contended that U.S. bombing had seriously damaged Iraqi communications, he added, "at least according to what Bernie Shaw tells me."

The other networks were quick to catch up. An ABC cameraman filmed tracer bullets lighting up the night sky over Baghdad. ABC's Forrest Sawyer and NBC's Arthur Kent reported the first Scud missile attack on Dhahran seconds after it happened. Kent, with his dark good looks, became something of a media superstar, dubbed the "Scud stud" by the American popular press and the fan clubs formed in his name. Meanwhile, CNN's lack of depth—its shortage of eminent military experts and experienced correspondents—began to show. In Saudi Arabia, CNN correspondent Charles Jaco lost his cool during a report and hastily donned a gas mask. He later explained that he had mistaken the odor of a jet plane's exhaust for an Iraqi chemical attack.

When the Scuds began falling, rumors flourished, and U.S. military briefings began to appear vague and contradictory—as did press coverage. Colin Powell's assertion that Iraqi communications had been crippled was partially retracted. There were reports that the Iraqis were using nerve gas against Israel (untrue), and that Tel Aviv was under Scud attack (untrue then, true later). CBS reported that Israel had retaliated against the Scud attacks (also untrue). Nobody seemed to know what was really happening in the war. The Los Angeles *Times'* Howard Rosenberg wrote this mock paragraph in summing up the first week's broadcast foibles: "Iraq's chemical attack on Israel will surely prompt retaliation by Israel, which won't retaliate because the Iraqi missiles did not have chemical warheads, although they did, unless they didn't, in which case the Israelis will not retaliate, unless they do. Meanwhile, Dhahran, Saudi Arabia, is being hit by Iraqi missiles, unless it's an attack by Iraqi terrorists who have been spotted where they haven't been spotted, but may soon be spotted before we go off the air."

Covering the war was an especially tough assignment for print journalists, who struggled to keep up with the live-broadcast capability of their television colleagues. With limited access to the front, newspaper and magazine reporters found it difficult to come up with the masses of telling detail and colorful description that helps set print journalism apart from the electronic variety. To attract audiences conditioned by TV, newspapers found themselves running more maps, charts, boxes and other graphic devices. But newspapers were also able to offer more analysis of the war than could TV, with its limited capacity for spoken words. Newspapers were thus better able to examine the more skeptical, nonofficial views of the war, and to place some of the more positive visual images in a fuller context. Thus, early in the war when General H. Norman Schwarzkopf delivered an upbeat televised briefing on the air campaign—complete with astonishing videotapes of laser-

Slim pickings: Pool reporters in Saudi Arabia besiege a Kuwaiti soldier to hear him tell his story of escaping after Iraq's invasion.

guided smart bombs hitting their targets squarely—the New York *Times* was able to offer a more cautious appraisal. "Although [Schwarzkopf] presented a picture of a devastatingly effective allied air war against Iraq," the *Times* said in a front-page analysis, "the kind of destruction he described is a slow process, and the extent of its success in incapacitating Iraqi ground forces may not be known for weeks."

Shortly after CNN was ordered to stop broadcasting from Baghdad, Iraqi authorities commanded all of the 40 or so remaining journalists to leave the country. Because air service out of Baghdad had been halted, leaving meant a long, grueling trip over the desert to Amman. Bernard Shaw and John Holliman packed up some leftover cheese and crackers and joined a four-car caravan of American reporters for the journey.

Peter Arnett, however, chose to stay behind. A New Zealand–born veteran who had covered more than a dozen wars for the Associated Press before joining CNN in 1981, Arnett had won a Pulitzer Prize in 1966 for his reporting from Vietnam. In that war too he elected to be in the city of the enemy: Saigon after it was overrun by North Vietnamese troops in 1975.

Arnett was not, as it turned out, the only Western journalist in Baghdad. Jon Alpert, a longtime contributor to NBC News, roamed the city capturing hours of uncensored footage of Iraqis burrowed into encampments, lines of cars carrying coffins of Iraqi soldiers, and smudge pots burning around factories to fool attacking pilots into thinking the buildings had already been bombed. Yet NBC executives, troubled that Alpert had gained entry to Iraq with peace activist and former U.S. Attorney General Ramsey Clark shortly before the war began, decided not to run the footage. Alpert's images eventually appeared on MTV and on the public broadcasting station in New York City.

Though CNN's Arnett was not alone in Baghdad, he was for nearly two weeks the world's eyes and ears in Iraq's capital. Arnett described the relentless coalition air attacks on Baghdad, occasionally visiting bomb-damaged neighborhoods to do stand-up reports. He was punctilious about noting that his reports were censored and that interviews with ordinary Iraqis were conducted in the presence of government officials.

Arnett was also on hand to record the carnage at the shelter struck by allied bombs on Feb. 13. Though he merely described what he saw and heard, as he should have, many viewers were moved by his graphic video images and his matter-of-fact observations that the victims were "mainly women and children" and that "the clothes had been burned off."

Such reporting soon made Arnett's presence in Baghdad a topic of national controversy. More than 55,000 letters, phone calls and faxes (along with at least one bomb threat) poured in to CNN while Arnett was broadcasting from Iraq. Most of them denounced him harshly. Perhaps the most malevolent criticism came from Senator Alan Simpson, a Wyoming Republican and a close friend of George Bush's. Simpson accused Arnett of being an Iraqi "sympathizer" who was "being coddled by an enemy government." As evidence, Simpson noted that Arnett had remained in Vietnam for a time after the fall of Saigon and that the journalist "is married to a Vietnamese whose brother was active in the Viet Cong."

Arnett's fellow journalists rose to his defense, pointing out that he had been separated from his wife for years, that none of his in-laws had ever been linked to the Viet Cong and that his reputation for fairness and integrity was unimpeachable. (Simpson later apologized, but only for the slur on Arnett's family.) CNN also had some defending to do. The other networks alleged that the Atlanta-based upstart had become too cozy with the Iraqi government. Behind the network complaints, of course, was a certain amount of jealousy at CNN's slam-dunk performance in Iraq. Acknowledging that the knives were out, CNN President Tom Johnson on Feb. 1 sent his employees a memo. "Expect intense scrutiny, much of it critical," it said in part. "Therefore, remember this: Don't let up. Don't brag. Handle critics with this killer weapon: your best work and professionalism."

The anger directed at Arnett and CNN was symptomatic of a growing unease among Americans in general over the role of the press. For some years, ever since Vietnam and Watergate, there had been an increasingly widespread view that the press is arrogant when it challenges official opinion. War sharpens such controversies. One U.S. Air Force briefing officer in Saudi Arabia summed up the official view when he told reporters, "I'm not a great fan of the press, and I want you to know where we stand with each other. I suppose the press has its purpose. But one thing is certain: You can't do me any good, and you sure as hell can do me harm." Many agreed. Press secretary Marlin Fitzwater gloated that calls to the White House about coverage of the war were running 100% negative. *Radio & Records,* a radio-industry weekly based in Washington, rated wartime media behavior No. 2 on its Top Ten list of subjects raised on radio talk shows (the war was No. 1). "It's a hot subject," said Don Wade, a talk-show host on Chicago's WLS. "The one word to describe the reaction of many listeners is outrage, especially about Peter

Arnett." Said Thomas Plate, editorial-page editor of the Los Angeles *Times:* "They hate us. They wish we would go away."

That was not mere speculation. In a Times Mirror poll conducted in the war's second week, 78% of respondents were satisfied that the military was not hiding bad news, and 57% said the Pentagon should exert even more control over war coverage. In a similar TIME/CNN poll, 88% of those asked said they supported some censorship of the press under the circumstances.

It was not surprising that resentment toward the press resurfaced during a war that enjoyed widespread popular support. The public evidently wanted to believe that the war was going well. Any reporting that supported Iraqi claims or threw doubt on optimistic U.S. pronouncements cast the press in the role of unwanted messenger. Even asking questions seemed to show lack of support. No responsible journalist would deny that certain information—sensitive intelligence data, secret battle plans—cannot be published without posing a serious risk to U.S. troops. And the press willingly accepted censorship during World War II. But within the limits of military security, most reporters have always seen their job as finding out what is actually going on—not just what officials say is going on—and that is a view solidly supported by the U.S. Constitution and the federal courts. "If combat boots are wearing out, as they did in Vietnam, or weapons are not working, somebody has to be there to report it," said ABC correspondent Morton Dean. "If we're not there, who is going to do it?" Said David Halberstam, who won a Pulitzer for his critical reporting from Vietnam: "It isn't a popularity contest for us, and we shouldn't seek [for] it to be one. The people of this country wouldn't like it very much afterwards if it turns out that [the war] doesn't go well. Then they'll say, 'Well, where was the press?' "

Answer: Too far from the action. Part of the press's problem was that the U.S. military made this particular war especially difficult to cover. The main instrument in the Pentagon's news-management strategy was the so-called pool system, which was born after the 1983 U.S. invasion of Grenada. In that conflict, for the first time in modern memory, journalists were prevented from accompanying American troops into action. After U.S. news organizations objected strenuously to the lack of access in Grenada, the Pentagon appointed a committee to look into the matter. The panel, headed by Major General Winant Sidle, a retired chief of Army information, was composed mainly of military and government public affairs officials. It recommended, not surprisingly, that future wars be covered by pools of reporters under strict military supervision. Though many journalists objected to that proposal, it was accepted by the major news organizations as the only way the Pentagon would allow early access to a U.S. troop deployment.

When the Iraqis invaded Kuwait, journalists found themselves saddled not only with the pool system established as a result of the Sidle commission but also with a few unexpected new restrictions. On the ground—false, as it turned out—that the Saudis were reluctant to admit American reporters, defense officials were slow to activate the press pool, so there was no media coverage at all when the first U.S. military units landed in August. Once reporters were allowed into the country, their contact with frontline troops was severely limited. Of the more than 1,600 newspeople who eventually arrived in Saudi Arabia, fewer than 200 were ever allowed to join a pool. Most of the pool spots were reserved for the major news organizations—the television networks, a few radio groups, the leading daily newspapers, the newsmagazines and the wire services. And many of those spots were taken by photographers, camera operators and broadcast technicians, leaving relatively few for reporters. Because there were never more than 10 or so pools in the field at one time, the activities of many military units deployed in the gulf theater went totally unreported.

The pools consisted of seven to 18 newspeople each. The larger groups were generally sent into the field with ground, sea or air units for periods as long as two weeks, and the other groups were "rapid reaction" pools, taken from place to place as news broke. Interviews could be conducted only in the presence of the pools' military escorts, and names and hometowns of individual soldiers could not be reported. (The latter restriction was lifted after vigorous protest from news organizations.)

Perhaps the most effective technique used to control information from the gulf was the requirement that all reports be submitted to military censors. Even in Vietnam, reporters were allowed to send their dispatches home directly, and no harm to U.S. military operations was ever reported.

No direct harm, at least. In the minds of some Americans, however, the U.S. "lost" the Vietnam war because of overly candid news reporting. "The guys who are generals today were the majors and colonels in Vietnam, and they were the ones who hated the press the most," said Sidle. Marine Lieut. General Bernard Trainor described the new (and in his view irrational) military code: "Duty, honor, country—and hate the press."

The military had other reasons for restrictions. "What should we do," asked U.S. Army Colonel William Mulvey, who was in charge of coalition press operations in Dhahran. "Let 500 reporters take four-wheel drive vehicles up to Khafji and appear on the battlefield? That's not very practical from a military point of view, and it would be physically very dangerous for the journalists."

Nonetheless, reporters in Saudi Arabia generally found the controls a major frustration, especially in the war's early days. Overworked military censors sat on time-sensitive copy until it was too old to send home, or else they demanded changes that appeared to have little bearing on security. "In effect, each pool member is an unpaid employee of the Defense Department," groused New York *Times* correspondent Malcolm W. Browne. He and Frank Bruni of the Detroit *Free Press* were part of a pool that visited an F-117A Stealth base early in the war and interviewed pilots returning from a successful bombing mission. Their stories about the visit were approved without change by the escort officer accompanying the pool, but the wing commander made some subtle alterations. In Bruni's story the word "giddy," used to describe the pilots after their bombing run, was changed to "proud." In Browne's story the word "fighter-bomber," to describe the F-117A, had become "fighter." As Browne later wrote: "I can only guess why this phrase was censored. The Air Force is currently waging a campaign to save the costly B-2 Stealth bomber project. Could it be that if the F-117A is also called a 'bomber,' congressional critics might argue that a second Stealth bomber—the B-2—is unnecessary?" Though both Browne and Bruni agreed to the changes, officials in Dhahran delayed their copy another day. By then, wrote Browne, "the war has moved on and our perishable dispatches are hopelessly stale."

Many journalists grew frustrated with the pool system and decided to head for the front on their own. The San Francisco *Chronicle's* Carl Nolte, for instance, simply climbed into his rented Chevrolet Caprice one day and headed north. He got lost several times on the poorly marked roads but eventually hooked up with U.S. troops, who complained to him about everything from inadequate supplies to late paychecks. Nolte duly sent the news home. "If you sit around waiting for the scraps to be fed to you," he said, "you're going to get the kind of things a dog gets: leftovers."

Other "unilaterals," as the military called these non-pool wanderers, were not so fortunate. A CBS News crew led by correspondent Bob Simon was captured by Iraqi troops while driving near the Saudi-Iraq border. The four men were taken to Baghdad, where they were interrogated and beaten. They were finally released, after intervention by Soviet President Mikhail Gorbachev, at the war's end.

A number of journalists were detained by U.S. and Saudi troops while traveling without military escorts. A French TV producer said U.S. Marines forced his crew at gunpoint to give up its videotape of a wounded American soldier. Wesley Bocxe, a photographer on assignment for TIME, was seized by members of the Alabama National Guard near the Saudi-Kuwait border. He was shoved around, blindfolded, interrogated and held for 30 hours by the troops, who suspected him of being an Iraqi spy. "Since I heard about the CBS crew, I've been worried about being captured by Iraqis," he said. "I never thought about being captured by my own country's forces."

For journalists who couldn't get into a pool, official information consisted mostly of periodic briefings from U.S. and allied military officers in Riyadh. The briefings were heavy on statistics (1,000 sorties a day, 80% of them successful), but not on enlightenment. It took a while for many reporters to figure out that a sortie was not necessarily a bombing mission, and that "success" meant only that bombs had been dropped, not that they had hit their target.

Military officials repeatedly emphasized that journalists were denied free access to the Iraqi side of the front, and that censorship in Baghdad was fully as restrictive as that imposed by coalition forces. If U.S. military briefers sometimes did not tell the whole truth, the Iraqis were no better. When the corpse-filled ruins of a Baghdad bomb shelter were shown on American TV, Lieut. General Thomas W. Kelly complained that "everything that we're seeing relative to this facility is coming out of a controlled press in Baghdad . . . We don't have a free press there asking hard questions like you all do here."

The pool system began to break down when the coalition ground assault began. Defense Secretary Cheney first announced that regular briefings in Washington and in Riyadh would all be suspended until further notice. That policy was reversed a day later, however, when Cheney authorized General Schwarzkopf to deliver what turned out to be a very upbeat briefing to reporters in Riyadh. Encouraged by Schwarzkopf's example, many field commanders began speaking to reporters again. Over the next few days, accounts of the fighting began to dribble out from both pool reporters and unilaterals who had managed to get near the front. "Good news defeats a blackout," said Associated Press Washington bureau chief Jonathan Wolman. "The military apparently has a good story to tell, and

The satellite war: U.S. television networks transmit many reports from this Dhahran hotel.

they are abandoning their blackout to let it be told."

CBS also had good news. Rebounding from the critical and ratings drubbing it took in the war's opening days, the network dominated ground-assault coverage. Anchor Dan Rather showed up at the front. (So did NBC's Tom Brokaw, though ABC's magisterial Peter Jennings stayed home and did what anchors do best: give coherence to a fast-breaking, multilocation story.) CBS correspondent Bob McKeown sent the first live broadcasts from Kuwait City. He and his crew managed that feat by mounting a satellite dish on the back of a truck and broadcasting directly to New York via satellite (thus circumventing U.S. censors). ABC's Forrest Sawyer, traveling with Egyptian forces, was also able to broadcast early reports of the fighting via a truck-mounted dish. Before the week was out, a total of 28 network film crews were in the field.

Such efforts were expensive. Ther networks each said they were spending about $1.5 million a week beyond their usual news budgets. When lost revenue was included (many commercials were canceled because advertisers did not want them to appear amid potentially grim war reports), NBC estimated that the war cost it

nearly $50 million. Despite all the frenzied spending, the network news operations came out of the war in roughly the same competitive positions they entered: ABC dominated the ratings and the critical acclaim from start to finish, with NBC and CBS battling for second place. CNN, holding on to some of its early ratings gains, nonetheless remained a distant challenger.

As the war ended, tension between the press and the military seemed to be easing. The unilaterals were moving into newly liberated Kuwait and even into southern Iraq with little interference from U.S. authorities. Yet the issues that had been raised by the Pentagon's new-look news management, and the anger that had been roiled on both sides of the debate, remained unresolved. The Defense Department was clearly pleased with its new press restrictions. Journalists had filed at least two lawsuits to have the limits overturned, and their lawyers vowed to pursue the cases even after the war ended. Two consequences of the gulf experience seemed likely: a widened split between the military and the press, and another between the press and the public. Unlike the gulf war itself, those conflicts were destined to drag on for years.

And the Cost? $200 Billion? Maybe Even More

How does one measure the cost of war and destruction? At an average of $1 billion a day for U.S. troops and their high-tech weaponry, the price of the gulf war mounted more swiftly than in any other conflict in history, bringing the bill for liberating Kuwait to some $40 billion. Yet the cost of the combat was dwarfed by the devastation wrought by Saddam Hussein's army of occupation and the allies' retaliatory bombing. From Kuwait's flaming oil fields and shattered refineries to the vast petroleum slick that threatened to turn the Persian Gulf into a dead sea, the overall cost of the war could surpass $200 billion and keep a phalanx of corporations busy rebuilding the region for the rest of the century. Even that sum could fall short of the amount needed to repair the long-term damage as toxic black rain fouls farmland as far off as India. But there is more, much more, to the economic cost of the gulf war. Saddam's march into Kuwait helped push the already weak U.S. economy into a recession by raising oil prices and battering consumer confidence. The rising cost of gasoline reduced American spending power for other goods and services. The airline industry suffered not only higher fuel prices but also a loss of passengers because of reduced economic activity and fears of terrorism. Third World nations saw their oil bills soar even as more than a million of their overseas workers fled the gulf region, abandoning their savings and the wages they had been sending back to relatives in their home countries.

Fires in some 600 Kuwaiti oil wells threaten to cause damage as far away as India.

How much of all these war costs the U.S. taxpayers would have to bear remained a matter of conjecture when the fighting ended. Besides the $40 billion that it spent on the war, Washington contributed some $8 billion in foreign aid to Middle Eastern countries hurt by the conflict, raising total U.S. outlays to at least $48 billion. But Washington took the unprecedented step of passing the hat among its allies in the hope that they would absorb the cost of the fighting. This burden-sharing strategy worked well enough on paper as superrich countries like Saudi Arabia and Japan pledged a total of $53 billion to defray American combat costs. But the actual contributions trickled in slowly, amounting to roughly half the pledges almost a month after peace arrived.

Unlike previous wars, the brief gulf conflict scarcely boosted the U.S. economy. At the start of World War II, for example, orders for military equipment pulled the country out of the Great Depression. But Americans fought the gulf war mainly with the arsenal produced by Ronald Reagan's $2 trillion military buildup in the 1980s. Aside from new orders for the Scud-fighting Patriot missile, which cost $1 million each, the Pentagon spent little to acquire weapons during the fighting. That enabled Washington to keep the cost of high-tech equipment such as the F-117A Stealth fighter (price: $106 million each) and the F-16 Fighting Falcon fighter-bomber ($26.5 million) off the war books—though some aircraft will become part of the bill if and when the government decides to replace the 28 planes lost in combat.

While U.S. troops fought the war out of Reagan's stockpile, they fired so many missiles and dropped so many bombs that they ran up a $3.5 billion charge for munitions. That sum will be needed to restore the inventories to their prewar level. On the first day of air combat alone, Americans launched 104 computerized Tomahawk cruise missiles, worth $1 million each, at Baghdad and environs. In all, U.S. troops fired 284 Tomahawks, and launched 158 Patriots to intercept Scuds, during the six week campaign. A single GBU-15 smart bomb, which can lock onto targets as small as a chimney flue, costs more than $100,000; U.S. pilots rained thousands of the laser-guided weapons on everything from trucks to nuclear reactors. Just keeping planes airborne took staggering sums. One hour of flight time for an A-10 Thunderbolt fighter-bomber cost $1,275 for jet fuel and maintenance. Flying the giant B-52 bomber cost $6,000 an hour.

The largest part of the war bill, though, was for noncombat costs. The Pentagon spent more than $20 billion to call up the reserves and transport some 500,000 troops with all their equipment to the gulf and prepare them for battle. The cost of dismantling Iraqi minefields and re-turning the troops and equipment home ran into more billions. If the U.S. deploys a large garrison to keep peace in the region, that could add even more to the final cost of the conflict.

Until now, the Bush Administration had planned to trim the Pentagon budget. Because of runaway federal deficits and a diminished Soviet threat, defense planners proposed in February a 25% reduction in military personnel by 1995 and a 4% cut in overall spending. To reach those levels, Pentagon chiefs Dick Cheney and Colin Powell sought to phase out such expensive workhorses as the Apache attack helicopter ($12.2 million each) and the M1A1 Abrams tank ($3.5 million). But conservative politicians now argued that such cutbacks would damage America's ability to deter aggression. In the same way, backers of the moribund Strategic Defense Initiative called for its revival in light of the Patriot's performance—even though many experts argue that the two defensive missile systems have almost nothing in common.

Other nations also bore heavy military costs. For Britain, the gulf conflict marked the largest and most expensive engagement since the Falklands war of 1982. The British sent 45,000 troops to the gulf, together with more than 100 warplanes and a 25-ship armada, at a cost of $3.15 billion. But London had pledges from the gulf states and Germany for $2.6 billion of that amount. The French spent $1.8 billion to send 12,000 troops, 48 jets and a dozen ships. France received pledges for $1.2 billion, including $1 billion from Kuwait.

Washington earmarked $15 billion to pay military bills while waiting for the allies to make good on their pledges. To pressure them into paying, the Senate barred sales of U.S. arms to all countries that failed to meet their pledges. Still, the Pentagon wanted more weapons as soon as possible, and congressional Democrats resisted. They foreshadowed the coming battle over U.S. defense spending by paring back an Administration request for $324 million for 500 Patriot missiles—more than three times the number used in the war. The critics, who approved outlays for just 158 new missiles, argued that the Pentagon had more than 3,000 Patriots on hand when the fighting stopped.

The U.S. needed the Japanese, Germans and other allies to finance much of the war because it had few other options for raising the money. With the federal deficit running at $318 billion a year, Washington badly wanted to avoid more red ink. At the same time, politicians were loath to propose new taxes while the country was in a recession. Many—not least George Bush—were still smarting from hostile reactions to the $23.2 billion tax in-

Ecological calamity: cleaning up the oil spill, which spreads over 60 miles, could cost as much as $5 billion.

crease that Washington decreed in 1990 as part of the budget deal between the White House and Congress.

Nor did the Administration dare raise funds by cutting already cash-hungry social programs. That could have been politically disastrous at a time when 29 deficit-ridden states were unable to provide adequate financing for such vital needs as education, housing and police protection. The cost of a single day of gulf fighting easily surpassed the $937 million that Congress voted for aid to the homeless in all of 1991. Two days of the war exceeded the $1.9 billion earmarked for a year of Head Start. Three days totaled more than the combined federal spending to fight cancer ($1.6 billion) and AIDS ($1.1 billion).

The major contributors among U.S. allies were oil-rich Kuwait and Saudi Arabia, for whom, after all, the war was fought. Each pledged more than $14 billion to the

U.S. for 1991. In addition, the Saudis provided American troops with food, water and gasoline at a monthly cost of $1.2 billion. Despite its vast wealth, the burden of financing the war forced Saudi Arabia to borrow more than $10 billion on world credit markets to help pay for its contributions. Kuwait raised cash by selling part of its gold hoard and some of its interests in British and Spanish companies.

Washington's demands for cash focused harsh attention on Japan and Germany, which kept their troops home from the fighting. Critics in Congress accused the two wealthy countries, both of which depend heavily on Persian Gulf oil, of failing to contribute their fair share of support. Stung by the charges, Japanese Prime Minister Toshiki Kaifu staked his political future on securing $9 billion in additional pledges on top of $4 billion that Japan had already promised. Kaifu got his money, but only after a divided Japanese Diet kept haggling throughout the closing days of the war. In Bonn, after much American prodding, Chancellor Helmut Kohl increased German pledges from $3.5 billion to a total of $11 billion. The Germans also pressed Washington for a full accounting of gulf war costs to be sure they weren't overpaying.

Even as it sought funds to fight the war, the U.S. heaped aid on countries that supported its gulf policies. High on the help list were so-called frontline states, such as Egypt and Turkey, which lost billions of dollars in export sales as a result of U.S.-led trade sanctions against Iraq. Both nations sold agricultural and industrial goods to Iraq before the crisis. To help with these countries' losses—and, not incidentally, to reward their participation in the coalition—Washington rushed financial assistance. In one sweeping gesture, the U.S. forgave $7 billion of loans that it had extended to Cairo in the 1980s to finance the purchase of U.S. military hardware. The Administration earmarked $82 million of special military aid for Turkey because of the war and agreed to throw open the door to Turkish textiles. Washington also approved $650 million of emergency funds for Israel after the Jewish state accepted U.S. requests not to strike back against Iraqi for its Scud attacks.

The U.S. even provided rewards to Beijing for its help in the crisis. China merely abstained from voting on a crucial U.N. resolution that authorized the use of force against Iraq, but that was enough for a grateful Administration to invite a high-level Chinese delegation to the White House. Bush also vowed to fight to retain China's most-favored-nation trade status, which lets the country export to the U.S. with few barriers, despite congressional opposition because of Chinese human-rights violations.

The war created an outpouring of financial aid for developing countries hurt by the crisis. Members of the allied coalition pledged $15.7 billion in emergency loans, grants and debt relief. The bulk of the pledges came from Saudi Arabia and other gulf states, which agreed to provide $9.8 billion in assistance in addition to their contributions to the U.S. war effort. Japan and the European Community added a total of $5.4 billion to the humanitarian fund.

With the shooting war ended, the big task will be to rebuild the Persian Gulf region. The Kuwaitis who returned to their once prosperous homeland discovered a ravaged country, the restoration of which could cost anywhere from $50 billion to $100 billion. That would rival or surpass the Marshall Plan, which restored Western Eu-

rope after World War II at a cost of $70 billion in today's dollars. In scenes evocative of Dante's *Inferno,* the Kuwaitis found the charred hulks of office towers and refineries rising from a landscape of bomb craters, land mines and shallow graves scraped in sand. Sulfurous clouds billowed high into the air from burning oil fields before returning as greasy black rain. In the gulf, sheets of oil from one of the world's largest slicks washed up along a polluted shore.

Iraq too lay in ruins when the guns fell silent, its roads, bridges and power stations destroyed. Six weeks of the most intensive aerial bombardment in history smashed Iraq's oil industry, reducing pipelines and pumping stations to twisted wreckage. A U.N. report declared that the "near apocalyptic" destruction of this once modern economy had reduced it to a "pre-industrial" state. Iraq is much larger than Kuwait and about eight times as populous, so rebuilding it could cost even more. But while Western companies clamored for contracts with Kuwait, they avoided Iraq like the plague. Few firms trusted the bankrupt country's leadership or its ability to pay for massive reconstruction projects. And the U.S. also insisted that Iraq must pledge reparations to Kuwait—which is asking at least $60 billion—before the coalition would formally agree to a cease-fire.

Iraq's financial problems had inspired it to invade Kuwait in the first place. The eight year Iran-Iraqi war drained Saddam's coffers and left him with nearly $100 billion in foreign debt, which he sought to repay in part by seizing Kuwait's oil industry and financial wealth. Creditors now had little enthusiasm for lending more funds to Saddam or his successors. Iraq could remain broke until its oil began flowing to world markets, something that had to await the lifting of the U.N. trade embargo.

In contrast to Iraq, Kuwait seemed like the promised land to Western companies bidding on lucrative contracts. Though immediate postwar conditions were rough, Kuwait's treasury bulged with $100 billion in foreign assets, and the country could easily finance a gigantic reconstruction program. Long before the shooting stopped, Kuwait promised U.S. companies the lion's share of its business as a reward for America's leading role in the war. Sure enough, U.S. firms won 70% of the first $800 million of contracts to restore the country's infrastructure. Kuwait ordered, among other items, generators from Caterpillar, mobile phones from Motorola and computers from IBM. Kuwaitis chose the U.S. Army Corps of Engineers to assess the country's damage and award some $46 million of contracts to restore water, power and other basic services. The first contract went to Raytheon, maker of the Patriot, which received $5.7 million to build an air-traffic-control system to help get the Kuwait City airport running again.

Kuwait will probably have to borrow heavily to finance its reconstruction until it can begin selling oil again. The country's huge demand for funds could drive up interest rates around the world and worsen a credit crunch that began last year. Money has grown tight since cash-rich Germany, normally a big lender, began allocating sums that could reach $100 billion to rebuild the economic wreckage in what was once East Germany. At the same time, an economic slowdown in Japan led banks and other institutions there to become stingier with credit.

No matter how Kuwait finances its reconstruction, the real money will go to the giant oil-service companies that will rebuild the country's petroleum industry. Bechtel Group, based in San Francisco, signed a $150 million letter of intent to manage the first phase of the mammoth task, which could bring the company $6 billion in revenues during the next few years. No sooner did it get the contract than Bechtel geared up to hire 4,300 workers for the project.

The most pressing problem was to snuff out the fires that raged in about 600 of Kuwait's 1,000 oil wells as noxious reminders of the Iraqi army's scorched-earth tactics. The flames spewed poisonous fumes across the region while they consumed Kuwait's vast oil reserves. Fire fighters led by a clutch of Texas firms had to wait weeks for the Army to clear away Iraqi mines before they could start work. Putting out the flames will require tons of dynamite and millions of gallons of water. It could take $15 billion over the next five years to complete the job and restore the damaged fields to full production.

The economic damage from the fires was compounded by their impact on the environment. Thick, sooty black clouds ranged from Turkey to the Strait of Hormuz, a distance of more than 1,000 miles. For Kuwaitis living directly beneath the pall, day seemed like night and temperatures were about 20° F cooler than in areas where the sky was clearer. The clouds were rich in sulfur dioxide, a prime component of acid rain, which threatened crops and grazing lands wherever it fell.

Yet the long-term impact on the region—and the planet as a whole—could be far less severe than early reports had suggested. Even before the fires were set, scientists foretold widespread catastrophe if Saddam ignited the oil fields. The black clouds, they predicted, would rise as high as six miles into the atmosphere, interfering with India's monsoon rains and creating a drought that would threaten millions of people with starvation. Although some experts still consider that nightmare possible, most

others came to view the scenario as implausible. Their computer models showed the clouds leveling off a mile or so above the earth, too low to influence the Indian monsoon.

That is scarcely to deny that the environment suffered grievous harm. Case in point: the oil that the Iraqis released in the gulf by opening spigots at Kuwait's main supertanker-loading pier at Sea Island. Estimated at 460 million gal. by panicky first reports, the slick was later figured to contain closer to 126 million gal. That was nearly 10 times as much as the *Exxon Valdez* spill into Alaska's Prince William Sound in 1989, where the effects are still visible on tarry beaches despite a two-year cleanup campaign that cost Exxon more than $2 billion.

Damage from the gulf spill was greatest along the coast of Kuwait and northern Saudi Arabia, where the sludge killed thousands of seabirds, devastated the Saudi shrimp industry and threatened plants and other animals. The extent of the disaster will depend on the vagaries of the wind, which kept the oil north of the rich marine ecosystems in the Bay of Bahrain in the first months of the spill.

Cleaning up the worst of the spill could cost as much as $5 billion, according to Saudi and Western estimates. The slick spread along a 60-mile stretch of coastline while Saudi ministries, which were coordinating the cleanup, bickered over how to attack the problem. Although the Saudis and Kuwaitis will pay most of the cost, the cleanup has become an international cause célèbre. Japan sent floating booms to contain the oil; Norway sent oil-skimming ships to recover it. Exxon contributed booms, skimmers and technical advice to government agencies at work in the gulf. But cleanup crews can do little once the oil forms tarry clumps and sinks to the bottom. The gulf will ultimately have to cleanse itself through tidal action, something that could take as long as a century for the nearly land-locked region to achieve.

The invasion of Kuwait spread economic hardship all across the Third World. A group of Asian nations that included Bangladesh, Pakistan and the Philippines paid $5 billion more for oil last year than in 1989 because of the jump in prices. Developing countries saw their incomes plunge as exports dwindled and workers who fled the gulf stopped sending wages home to their families. Ethiopia and Sudan, already ravaged by famine and civil war, lost nearly $1 billion. British aid groups that surveyed the damage found that 40 developing countries, from Mozambique to Paraguay, suffered losses amounting to more than 1% of their GNP, the equivalent of a major natural disaster.

The war specifically dealt a devastating blow to Jordan, which more or less backed Iraq in the conflict. Some 300,000 Jordanian workers, mostly Palestinians, fled Kuwait when Saddam's tanks rolled in, and were unlikely to be welcomed back. The crisis halted imports of the Iraqi oil that fueled Jordan's economy. Without the oil, factories producing everything from paint to potash ran at only 10% of capacity. The economic impact of the war could cost Jordan nearly $2 billion, or more than 25% of its GNP. In an anguished speech, Jordan's King Hussein cataloged his country's plight. "After Iraq and Kuwait," he declared, "Jordan suffered most from this crisis. We were isolated economically till our exports shrank. We were placed unwillingly in the war zone till our tourism ceased and our airspace was closed. We were obliged to shoulder the responsibility of hosting Jordanian refugees who worked in Kuwait."

Hussein's pro-Iraqi stance could cost Jordan dearly for years. Saudi Arabia, Kuwait and other rich gulf states halted $400 million of regular annual aid to Jordan for refusing to join the allied coalition. The Saudis closed their borders to Jordanian oranges, bananas and refrigerators, helping cut in half the country's $1 billion in annual exports. In Washington the State Department showed its anger over Jordan's maverick position. After Hussein offered a "salute to Iraq" and "its heroic army" in the war, the U.S. vowed to review its aid to Jordan. Congress later froze $57 million in military and economic assistance but authorized Bush to release the funds if Jordan contributes to the search for a Middle East peace settlement.

Palestinians too paid heavily for their leaders' ties to Iraq. The 200,000 Palestinian workers who fled jobs in the gulf have little chance of returning, thanks to the support that Yasser Arafat, chairman of the Palestine Liberation Organization, gave Saddam Hussein. Nor are the Kuwaitis, Saudis and other oil-rich Arabs likely to restore much of their nearly $250 million of annual aid to the P.L.O., which funneled it to Palestinians in the occupied West Bank and Gaza Strip. The fund cutoff came at the worst possible time for the 1.7 million Palestinian inhabitants of the occupied territories, who lost many jobs in the three-year-old uprising against Israeli rule and are losing more to Jewish immigrants who have flocked to Israel from the Soviet Union.

The gulf crisis also pushed Egypt into its worst slump in years. While the country received debt relief for joining the allied coalition, the aid provided little benefit for Egyptian workers. Cairo estimated that lost tourist income alone cost it $1 billion, as fascination with the pyramids gave way to fears of terrorism. Meanwhile, construction workers, who could normally count on jobs three or four days a week, found it hard to get even a sin-

Red Adair team tries to put out fire at Greater Burgan oil field.

gle day's work. Cairo shopkeepers saw their revenues fall to half of their pre-crisis levels. Despite government figures that put the jobless rate at a little under 9% during the war, private economists pegged the real rate at nearly 20%.

Developing countries that supported the allied war effort rushed to cash in on the reconstruction of Kuwait. Pakistan, which sent 11,000 troops to the gulf, sped its Labor Minister to Kuwait to seek jobs for the 60,000 Pakistani workers who had fled the crisis. Though many Pakistanis demonstrated for Saddam during the war, Pakistan argued that such outbursts were less important than its aid to the coalition. Bangladesh, which supported the coalition with 2,300 troops, also hoped that Kuwait would overlook the fact that many Bangladeshis bitterly opposed their government's pro-U.S. stance. New jobs would be a tonic for Bangladesh, which had 70,000 nationals working in Kuwait before the war and lost some $400 million as a result of the crisis.

India, which lost nearly $2 billion, had a harder time trying to make up for it. Having declared neutrality, New Delhi refused to send troops and even curtailed refueling rights for U.S. military transports headed for the fighting.

In response, Kuwait vowed to review its contracts with Indian firms and take a hard look at job requests from any of the 150,000 Indian workers who fled when Iraq invaded.

In all, the war created an army of more than 1 million Third World refugees from the Persian Gulf who settled in often squalid camps as far east as India, putting new strain on some of the world's most impoverished regions. While rebuilding Kuwait may create jobs for Egyptians and others whose countries joined Desert Storm, many unskilled workers could be lucky to find jobs of any sort. Their misery threatened to stir political unrest.

The war created economic winners too, of course. The 13 members of the Organization of Petroleum Exporting Countries raked in some $45 billion of extra income when oil prices climbed after Iraq's invasion. Giant oil companies also reaped windfall profits. Earnings at Chevron surged nearly threefold in the fourth quarter of 1990, to more than $630 million. Firms that win contracts to rebuild Kuwait could enjoy a big increase in business. So could many defense contractors, particularly those whose high-tech weapons became media stars in the war and are now on every country's wish list.

The allies' swift victory replaced the prevailing economic gloom in the U.S. with a burst of euphoria. Oil and gasoline prices dropped sharply when the air war started and sank below pre-crisis levels after Iraqi troops surrendered by the tens of thousands. Surveys of consumer confidence showed their first gains in months. On Wall Street the Dow Jones industrial average kept up a bull rampage that began when the allies started bombing. After the triumph, the index came near to closing above 3000 for the first time ever before falling back when investors dumped stocks to cash in on their profits. Even Alan Greenspan, the dour chairman of the Federal Reserve Board, conceded that the end of the war had removed a "troublesome uncertainty" from the economy.

With the threat of a protracted war reduced to a memory, most economists predicted that the recession would end sometime during the summer. The approach of spring brought some signs of recovery. Long-dormant real estate markets began to shake off their torpor, benefiting from falling interest rates and the gradual release of pent-up demand. Even homeowners in New England, the epicenter of the recession, started taking down For Sale signs and putting up ones that read Sold. Americans lost their fear of flying as carriers resumed flights that had been suspended during the crisis, and travel agencies reported increased bookings.

The U.S. economy stood to benefit from low and stable oil prices as Saudi Arabia (and eventually Kuwait) produced at high levels to pay for the war. Even with Kuwait on the sidelines during the seven-month gulf crisis, OPEC increased its output over pre-invasion levels and reaped political and economic rewards. On the one hand, the tactic let OPEC cash in on the run-up in prices by pumping and selling more oil. On the other, the added production kept price increases from getting completely out of hand, pleasing the U.S.-led coalition that defended Saudi Arabia and forced Iraq from Kuwait. Thanks largely to OPEC's feverish production, the world remained awash in oil throughout the gulf war.

OPEC then seemed willing to live with the oil glut instead of cutting production sharply enough to cause a big jump in prices. Despite pressure from some members for just such a cut, OPEC agreed in March to trim output by no more than 5% to nudge prices back up to $21 per bbl.—the level that economists had been forecasting before the gulf crisis. The agreement reflected the leadership of Saudi Arabia, OPEC's largest producer, which resisted pleas from Iran and Algeria for larger reductions in output.

But while cheap oil could boost the U.S. economy in the short run, it could hurt in the long run by discouraging Americans from conserving gasoline and moving to develop alternative energy sources such as wind and solar power. That would lead to increased dependence on OPEC, whose share of the U.S. oil market had slid from 30% in 1979 to 24% in 1989, and could virtually guarantee another big increase in oil prices during the next supply shortage. Such developments would represent an ironic aftermath to the war, which was partly aimed at keeping Saddam from seizing control of the Middle East's oil. With Saddam gone from the picture, America's unbridled demand for oil could itself lead to higher prices.

Although the military triumph strengthened U.S. pride and self-confidence, it held out little hope that an economic recovery would have much vitality once it got under way. Americans remained too mired in troubles ranging from high unemployment (the jobless rate reached 6.8% in March) to the savings and loan crisis for the debt-laden economy to regain its strength anytime soon. Even if the recession were to end in the summer, the rebound would probably mean a return to the same weak U.S. growth rate of less than 1% that prevailed before the war. Just as the gulf crisis alone did not cause the recession, so victory by itself would not solve the country's economic troubles.

The End Game: Problems Solved And Unsolved

If Saddam Hussein's generalship left a lot to be desired, so did his political and diplomatic acumen. Time and again he misread George Bush, miscalculated the coalition's staying power and blew opportunities to exploit possibilities for recovery. Invariably, up to the very last moment, he stalled too long by haggling too much.

To be fair, once the coalition armies were arrayed for attack, even a Talleyrand might have failed to head off the Persian Gulf war. Two diametrically opposed imperatives were at work: Saddam's obsession with salvaging something— anything—of his military machine, his grip on Iraq and his image as the new hero of the Arab world; and President Bush's determination not only to force the Iraqi strongman to disgorge Kuwait but also to strip him of everything that would enable him to make trouble after the war. Still, even after hostilities began, Saddam had his chances to salvage a political, if not a military, victory. He muffed every one of them.

During the 5½-month road to war, Saddam seemed convinced that he had three things going for him in his refusal to yield anything in negotiations:

1) The American-led coalition would either fall apart or quail in the face of his powerful army, his missiles and his chemical weapons.

2) If the allies did launch hostilities, they would soon lose heart in the face of heavy casualties and growing dissent at home.

3) Even if the allies actually fought and won, he would still

Kurdish rebels eye the corpse of a slain security agent in Erbil. Insurgents were soon routed.

emerge a hero for having defended Arab honor against a powerful enemy, as Gamal Abdel Nasser did despite a disastrous military defeat in the Six-Day War of 1967.

After four weeks of incessant pounding by allied aircraft, Saddam could see that his military prospects were very poor, but he suddenly got some important diplomatic help from Soviet President Mikhail Gorbachev. Soviet support had been a major factor in the creation of Bush's anti-Iraq coalition, but in the winter of 1991 Gorbachev found himself besieged from all sides at home. Reformers were turning against him for moving too slowly toward democracy and a market economy. Reactionaries were attacking him for giving away Eastern Europe and scaling back the military and security apparatus that had kept a lid on Soviet society for seven decades. And independence movements in at least half a dozen of the Soviet Union's 15 republics were threatening to tear the country apart. Particularly worrisome to Gorbachev was the influence Saddam might have on the 50 million Muslims in Soviet Central Asia.

So when Gorbachev's own military adviser, Marshal Sergei Akhromeyev, and other top brass began grumbling about the punishment that the coalition was administering to Iraq, the Soviet President had to pay attention. The military was appalled by what was happening in Iraq. For at least 30 years, Baghdad had been a Soviet client and a principal means of projecting the Kremlin's influence throughout the Middle East. Even after the invasion of Kuwait, nearly 8,000 Soviet military and industrial advisers were still operating across the country, serving with Iraqi military units and factories. Not least, Baghdad was the biggest customer for Soviet arms and a proving ground for Moscow's most up-to-date weaponry. The Soviet generals wanted all that back.

On Feb. 9, the Soviets' nightly television news broadcast a statement by Gorbachev in which he complained that by devastating Iraq so relentlessly, the allies were in danger of overstepping their U.N. mandate to liberate Kuwait. He also announced that he was dispatching his personal adviser, Yevgeni Primakov, to Baghdad. An old Middle East hand who had traveled extensively through the area in the 1960s as a *Pravda* correspondent, Primakov had already met Saddam Hussein a number of times.

At Gorbachev's behest, Primakov had visited Iraq as recently as October to urge Saddam to pull out of Kuwait. Though the mission failed, the Soviet President said at the time that he still considered a military solution "unacceptable." Less than two weeks later,

however, Bush ordered that the number of U.S. troops in the area be doubled to 400,000, turning the defensive Desert Shield into a powerful offensive force. Now, with an invasion of Kuwait imminent, Primakov was seeking to save Saddam from an overwhelming military disaster. After his Feb. 12 conversation with Saddam, Primakov cabled Moscow that there had been "certain promising signs."

Three days later, on Feb. 15, Iraq's rubber-stamp Revolutionary Command Council offered for the first time to pull Iraq's troops out of Kuwait "in appreciation of the Soviet initiative." Had the council's proposed settlement stopped there, it might have delayed or even derailed the onrush of the ground war. But as Primakov wrote afterward, Saddam "may have thought he had a lot of time for maneuvering and should start from the harshest position possible." Saddam did just that. He festooned the offer with conditions that instantly doomed it: complete withdrawal of all allied land and sea forces, including the U.S. naval units that have patrolled the gulf for years; total Israeli withdrawal from the West Bank, the Gaza Strip, the Golan Heights and southern Lebanon; cancellation of all of Iraq's debt; and, the ultimate in chutzpah, payment of war reparations by the allies to compensate Iraq for all damage wreaked by their forces.

The allied reaction was swift and unambiguous. Bush branded the plan a "cruel hoax." British Prime Minister John Major called it a "bogus sham."

But the Soviet efforts to stop the war and save Saddam were far from over. After the Primakov mission, Iraqi Foreign Minister Tariq Aziz headed for Moscow, and on Feb. 18 Gorbachev gave him a Soviet plan for ending the conflict. Aziz carried the proposals back to Saddam—by air from Moscow to Tehran, by helicopter to the Iraq border, by car to Baghdad, because the allies refused to guarantee his safety if he were to fly. Basically, the Soviet plan would have pushed Saddam a long way toward meeting allied demands. It called for an immediate cease-fire and then a complete Iraqi withdrawal from Kuwait, over an unspecified period. In return Moscow would help keep Saddam in power, work to get economic sanctions lifted, and promote a Middle East peace conference that would address Arab-Israeli disputes.

Bush was not about to give the Iraqis an unlimited amount of time to move their tanks, artillery and other heavy equipment back home to be used another day. He was also adamant against any linkage of a gulf settlement to an Arab-Israeli conference. The whole plan, he said, "falls well short of what would be required for peace." But he and the other allies were apprehensive about international reaction. If Saddam had quickly accepted the Soviet proposals, the oft-discussed "nightmare scenario" might have unfolded: yes, Saddam would lose his "19th province" of Kuwait, but he would be left in power with enough of a military machine to continue threatening his neighbors.

Though the Soviets had asked Saddam for a swift response to the Gorbachev plan, he dithered, and Tariq Aziz did not get back to Moscow until Thursday, Feb. 21. Arriving late that night, he was rushed to the Kremlin and sat down with Gorbachev shortly after midnight. Two-and-a-half hours later, Gorbachev's spokesman, Vitali Ignatenko, outlined at a press conference what he called an eight-point plan to end the war. He concluded his briefing by saying, "I do think we can give some applause here."

The revised plan had some encouraging provisions. It called for a prompt exchange of prisoners, dropped the demand for a complete allied pullout from the gulf area and no longer tried to link Iraq's pullout with Israeli withdrawal from the occupied territories or an international peace conference on the Middle East. Saddam, who had made considerable capital since Aug. 2 by posing as the champion of the Palestinian people, coolly jettisoned them when his own survival seemed threatened.

What remained in the plan, however, was a witches' brew of problems. The chief proposal—a cease-fire preceding Iraq's withdrawal—particularly troubled U.S. officials. They remembered all too vividly how enemy forces in Korea and Vietnam used cease-fires and bombing pauses to regroup, resupply and reinforce their units. Besides, what if Saddam simply decided to renege on the withdrawal agreement and, with his army rested, fed and re-equipped, to resume the war? Later, after the ground war began, a Soviet official said such a double cross had been a real possibility. According to the official—whose story remains unconfirmed—Tariq Aziz had confided that if a cease-fire were proclaimed, Saddam would pull his forces two-thirds of the way out of Kuwait and then simply stop and refuse to budge.

The Soviet plan called for Iraq to begin its withdrawal two days after the cease-fire and to complete it within a period vaguely defined as "several weeks." That would have given the Iraqis more than enough time to move their tanks and howitzers north to safety. Moreover, Saddam's troops were already carrying out a scorched-earth policy, executing a still-unknown number of Kuwaitis and taking thousands of others back to Iraq as hostages. In light of that, said a senior

White House official, such a protracted pullout would be tantamount to saying, "Give me a couple more weeks so I can kill some more Kuwaitis."

Gorbachev phoned Bush to fill him in on the plan Thursday evening. Shortly afterward the U.S. President left to see a play at Ford's Theater in Washington, but not before assembling top aides and instructing them to figure out what the allies, poised for a ground war, should do. Meanwhile, White House press secretary Marlin Fitzwater held newsmen at bay by telling them that Bush had thanked Gorbachev "for his intensive and useful efforts" but adding, "There could well be difficulties here."

In fact, White House officials were more than a little irritated with Gorbachev for what one described as his "mischievous meddling." British diplomats were no less exercised. "We resent Gorbachev trying to help Saddam escape from the box," said one. Said a U.S. diplomat, fretting: "If Saddam is still at the helm when the smoke clears as the result of a Gorbachev initiative, Soviet influence among the Arab masses in the region will soar."

When Bush announced on Friday morning that he was giving Saddam only until noon Saturday to do what he must do—begin his immediate and unconditional withdrawal from Kuwait, he deliberately made the terms very tough and inflexible. "We must hear publicly and authoritatively his acceptance of these terms." As a White House official said, "It's vital not only that Saddam withdraw from Kuwait but that he do so without any sort of fig-leaf or face-saver. He could have had that before Jan. 15, but not now. Now it has to be clear that he has been defeated and humiliated."

Only 40 minutes after the ultimatum had been delivered, Gorbachev was on the phone again. He spoke with Bush and Baker for an extraordinary 72 minutes, informing them that he intended to continue pursuing his peace plan. "I understand," said Bush. "We're going to proceed with ours." Said a U.S. official: "The Soviets can work their side of the street for whatever mileage they can get, but in the final analysis they'll be with us. Gorbachev knows his future is with the West, not with Iraq."

At 4 a.m. Saturday, Feb. 23—just eight hours before the deadline—the Soviets and Iraqis unveiled what Ignatenko described as a "seriously adjusted" six-point plan giving the Iraqis three weeks to withdraw from Kuwait instead of the one week demanded by the allies. That still gave Saddam too much time to rescue his military hardware and was quickly rejected.

The usual last-minute peacemaking efforts fluttered on into Saturday. Gorbachev phoned Bush and spoke with him until 17 minutes before the deadline, urging a Security Council meeting for one last effort at heading off the bloodshed. The Iraqis said nothing—but almost precisely at noon they lofted yet another Scud missile at Israel. Time had run out for Saddam, and eight hours after the deadline the ground war was under way.

Once the offensive had begun, diplomacy had little chance of getting anywhere. Still, Saddam made a few stabs at persuading the allies to call a halt while he still had a chance to salvage something. On Feb. 26, with his troops in headlong flight or surrendering by the tens of thousands, he took to the air to announce that his forces were completing their "withdrawal." Said Saddam, with a characteristic mixture of gall and menace: "The harvest in the mother of battles has succeeded. The greater harvest and its yield will be in the time to come."

Bush, bent on completing the destruction of Iraq's offensive potential, was furious. Saddam's speech, he said, "is an outrage. He is not withdrawing. He is trying to claim victory in the midst of a rout. Saddam is not interested in peace but only to regroup and fight another day."

On Feb. 27 a letter from Tariq Aziz was relayed by the Soviets to the U.S. It said Iraq was withdrawing and would accept U.N. resolutions requiring Baghdad to acknowledge Kuwait's sovereignty and pay reparations to the emirate.

When hostilities ended, George Bush waxed uncharacteristically lyrical. "Our uncommon coalition," he said, "must now work in common purpose to forge a future that should never again be held hostage to the darker side of human nature." But how, exactly, was this to be done?

Saddam was still in power, although rebellion flickered across his mangled country. Kuwait, under a pall of smoke from 600-odd blazing oil wells, faced at least a $50 billion reconstruction bill. Even attempting to settle the Israeli-Arab conflict would mean wrenching and quite possibly futile negotiations. Syria's dictator Hafez Assad had been a loyal enough member of the anti-Saddam coalition but celebrated the end of the war by buying Scud missiles from North Korea; would he become the next Saddam? Syria's chief rival for power in the gulf region was the fundamentalist Islamic republic of Iran, which sat out the war but then began maneuvering to subvert Saddam. Loyal coalition partners like Turkey, Egypt and Saudi Arabia figured to benefit from American gratitude, and possibly American arms as

well. (Jordan's King Hussein, having supported Saddam to appease the Palestinians who represent more than half of his population, would need some exceptionally fancy footwork to get back into the allies' good graces.) Where in all this was a "common purpose"?

France's President François Mitterrand thought he had an answer to this cauldron of problems, but it was merely a variation on the solution he had been offering for years: an international conference. This time Mitterrand proposed that the heads of government of all 15 members of the U.N. Security Council get together to "prepare the way" for a comprehensive Middle East peace. The goals of this extraordinary summit: "secure and recognized" borders for Israel; creation of a Palestinian state; genuine sovereignty for Lebanon; guarantees that Iraq would not be dismembered by its neighbors.

George Bush's goals are no less ambitious. Addressing Congress a week after the cessation of hostilities, he called for talks on the Arab-Israeli conflict based on "the principle of territory for peace"; arms-control agreements to halt the spread of weapons of mass destruction; economic measures to reduce the huge gap between haves and have-nots; and measures to insure the region's security, including an expanded U.S. naval presence as well as regular participation by American air and ground units in military exercises by the gulf countries. But there was no hint of a U.S. effort to take the lead in creating a NATO-style security system for the region. Early in the confrontation with Iraq, when Secretary of State Baker suggested setting up just such a GULFO, Arab members of the coalition wanted no part of it, and Congress shot down the idea almost instantly.

To pursue his objectives, Bush sent his Secretary of State on a seven-nation, 10-day tour of the region less than two weeks after the cease-fire was proclaimed. Though the dust of battle had not even settled, Baker was convinced that a "window of opportunity" had opened to peace, and Bush seemed determined to use the momentum of victory to address problems that have long plagued the region. Among them:

The arms bazaar. Only hours before the cease-fire, a reporter asked General Schwarzkopf whether he thought Saddam and the Iraqis remained a regional threat. "He doesn't have enough left," replied the General, but then he added pointedly, "unless someone chooses to rearm them in the future." Count on it, someone probably will: the Chinese, who were shopping their weapons around even before the cease-fire; the Soviets, hungry for hard

The Kremlin tries to play intermediary. Here President Mikhail Gorbachev offers Iraqi Foreign Minister Tariq Aziz a peace plan.

currency and a role in the region; the Iranians, who had the cream of Iraq's air force, some 140 fugitive fighters and long-range bombers, parked on their tarmacs and could use them as bargaining chips. And eventually—who knows?—maybe the Germans, French and Americans as well, all of them past suppliers of Saddam's arsenal. Washington was already considering more than $10 billion in new weapons sales to the Saudis alone, plus another $8 billion to Egypt, Israel, several of the gulf states and Turkey.

As the war rushed toward an allied triumph, there was considerable talk about renewed efforts to banish weapons of mass destruction from the area. Don't bet on their success. Allied bombing seems to have devastated the Iraqi facilities for producing nuclear, chemical and biological weapons. To ensure that they would not be rebuilt, the U.N. was pressing to abolish Iraq's ability to produce such arms as a condition for a permanent cease-fire. Still, speculation persists that before the bombing began, Saddam whisked enough weapons-grade uranium out of his targeted factories to build a

crude nuclear device. And Israel, after six weeks of Scudding, is likely to resist more fiercely than ever any effort to strip it of its nuclear weapons, never acknowledged but widely assumed to exist.

The Palestinian conflict. No problem in the region—probably in the world—is so intractable as this one. After Aug. 2, Saddam tried to make himself a hero to Arabs from Pakistan to the Magreb by claiming to be the champion of the dispossessed Palestinians, shrewdly linking his invasion of Kuwait with the Israeli occupation of the West Bank and Gaza.

Bush and Baker hoped that the troubling ease with which Saddam was able to exploit the issue would persuade Israel that the time had finally come to budge on it. The Israelis saw things differently. Hadn't Yasser Arafat, leader of the Palestine Liberation Organization, enthusiastically embraced Saddam? Hadn't West Bank Palestinians applauded whenever a Scud slammed into Tel Aviv? And wasn't Israel owed some favors after its restraint in the face of Scud attacks?

But Bush, initially at least, put settlement of the Palestinian problem high on his agenda, and the government of Prime Minister Yitzhak Shamir reacted by resisting. Aware that Israel might be urged to return the Golan Heights to Syria as a prelude to discussions about the status of the West Bank and Gaza, Economics Minister David Magen emerged from a long and argumentative Cabinet meeting to insist sternly, "The Golan Heights is not on the discussion table." Yet in the weeks that followed, some fissures began to appear in Jerusalem's seemingly monolithic position. Chief of Staff Dan Shomron, on the eve of retirement, uttered the heretical thought that once agreement had been reached on issues like demilitarization and arms control, "one can speak about risk vs. territory." And Health Minister Ehud Olmert, a moderate member of the Likud Party and a Shamir confidant, suggested that Israel was ready to discuss "the territorial demands of the Syrians." Shamir, however, strongly rejected both suggestions.

Though Baker's efforts to nudge the Israeli government toward talks on trading land for peace could eventually prove fruitful, they began under a cloud. On the eve of his visit, a deranged Palestinian from Gaza's Jabalyia refugee camp stabbed four Israeli women to death at a Jerusalem bus stop. The killings only underlined two long-held Israeli contentions: they live in a dangerous neighborhood, and they cannot afford to yield an inch on their security.

What next in Iraq? "Anarchy, pockets of resistance, prolonged civil war—these are all possibilities." So said a Western diplomat in Riyadh as the war came to an end, and all of these seemed to be materializing. In the south, Shi'ites represent 55% of Iraq's 19 million people but wield little power; Saddam and his Sunni co-religionists, only 20% of the country's population, control the ruling Baath Party, the army and the secret police. In Basra and more than a dozen other cities in the south, some troops deserted and sided with the Shi'ites, turning their arms against the better-equipped Republican Guard. Though the rebels initially did well, Saddam's forces seemed to have regained the upper hand a month after the temporary cease-fire. The Republican Guard may have been no match for the coalition's air and ground forces, but it was far from finished as a fighting force and proved effective enough against the Shi'ite insurgents.

The uprising in the south alarmed not only Saddam but also the U.S., since many of the Shi'ites are loyal to Mohammed Bakr Hakim, a cleric who lives in exile in Iran. When Iran's Ayatullah Khomeini thought he was on the verge of defeating Saddam in the early stages of their eight-year war, he personally tapped Hakim to rule Iraq. Was another Khomeini now hoping to impose a pro-Tehran fundamentalist regime? Bush was sufficiently concerned to warn Iran against making any move to dismember its battered neighbor. Earlier, Washington and London felt it also necessary to warn Saddam, with what one British diplomat described as "absolute clarity," that if his forces used chemical weapons to crush the rebellion, allied planes would attack those units responsible.

In the north, the ever restive Kurds seized large swatches of territory—but for how long? Most of Iraq's 3.9 million Kurds live in the mountainous region straddling Turkey, Iraq and Iran, and all three countries are constantly on guard against any moves to carve a new land, Kurdistan, out of their territory. The last time the Kurds acted up, in 1988, Saddam's lieutenants showered them with poison gas, killing an estimated 5,000.

With turmoil in the north, the south and even parts of Baghdad, with Iraq's economy and infrastructure in ruins, its military devastated and its leadership discredited, it was difficult to see how long Saddam could hang on. But the allies made no move to intervene on the rebels' side to help oust him. One problem was that a successor might not be much of an improvement, particularly if the new ruler were a pro-Iranian Shi'ite mullah or a Sunni schooled in Saddam's murderous ways.

The day after the cease-fire that ended the gulf war, George Bush held a news conference in the White House. A reporter asked the President why, in that moment of complete triumph, he looked so downcast. "Well, to be honest with you, I haven't yet felt this wonderful euphoric feeling that many of the American people feel," said Bush. "I think it's that I want to see an end. Now we have Saddam Hussein still there, the man who wreaked this havoc upon his neighbors. I just need a little more time to sort out in my mind how I can say to the American people, it's over, finally. Last t is crossed, last i is dotted."

The helpless: Iraqi woman and child get food from G.I.s.

And All Over America, Yellow Ribbons

Before the fighting began, America held a sort of meeting about the question of going to war. Strung house to house with phone wires and broadcast beams, the nation became the vast town hall that the inventors of democracy once envisioned. Debate over war and peace unrolled in coffee shops and classrooms and Congress, in the streets and over dinner and on the factory floor. Everyone had something to say about the gulf, but few people really knew what to think.

By the night the air war commenced in January, CNN had become a persistent, demanding houseguest. Churches began keeping their chapels open past midnight, and Army-Navy stores ran out of gas masks. Pizza orders soared and remained high for weeks as Americans ate at home, close to their TV sets. Yellow became a color of hope, not fear.

By the time the war went to the ground in February, *Rolling Stone* magazine, chronicle of the hip, the skeptical, the avant-garde and the antiestablishment, was running yellow ribbons around the border of its cover. By the time the war ended, President Bush held an approval rating of 91%, and the Second American Century had been proclaimed.

When it all began, that end was nowhere in sight. Rarely in the nation's history had so many people had so much time to make up their minds, with so little success. After the invasion on Aug. 2, most Americans seemed cautiously supportive of the President's actions. Few people thought he was behaving

Families and friends hold a candlelight vigil in Bayshore, N.Y., in support of the troops.

213

rashly in dispatching the first troops to Saudi Arabia, and his approval ratings, sinking under the weight of a faltering economy, climbed 20 points in the aftermath of the invasion. In fact, his standing was so high that hawkish voices in Washington began urging the President to strike quickly to accomplish, in Henry Kissinger's words, the "surgical and progressive destruction of Iraq's military assets." The assumption was that the public, though on board for the moment, would soon grow weary of the whole exercise.

At that point, less than half the American people believed there would actually be a war. But other fears were on the horizon: fears of terrorism, of an even deeper recession, of a conflagration in the Middle East that, once it began to spread, would be impossible to extinguish. In October, while overwhelming majorities still supported Bush's announced goals in the gulf, 70% of the American people said he should not even consider starting a war until economic sanctions had been given time to work. At no point did the American public, the Congress or the media write the President a blank check.

Once the November election was safely tucked away, the President made his second fateful decision, to send an additional 250,000 troops to the gulf. Bush thus forced the American public to confront the possibility that if Iraq would not get out of Kuwait, the U.S. was prepared to go in and push it out. But never did the President make an unequivocal public declaration of intent, or deliver the prime-time rallying cry that some pundits clamored for. He may have been reading the polls, sensing the ambivalence in public feelings about war. "Undertaking to explain our foreign policy in terms of our public opinion," Walter Lippmann once wrote, "is to explain one mystery in terms of another."

By mid-November, people were expressing their confusion about U.S. war aims, about whether the diplomatic efforts were energetic enough, and about the wisdom of moving beyond containment into an offensive position. Bush's approval ratings slipped about 20 points from their August level—though roughly half the President's critics said they thought he was moving not too fast but too slowly. About this time, the demonstrations began, the first antiwar vigils and peace marches and teach-ins. Over the next two months the demonstrators swelled into the hundreds of thousands. At first, said the Rev. William Phillippe of the Presbyterian Church's committee on social witness, it was "not an antiwar movement so much as it is a process question, a sense that we should be debating the issues more before we act."

The news reaches Rockfalls, Ill. Everyone had something to say, but few people really knew what to think.

In December, after Saddam released the hostages he had taken, a majority of Americans were willing to settle for some compromises, if Iraq would withdraw from Kuwait in exchange for concessions on the disputed oil fields. By the time the President and the U.N. Security Council set the Jan. 15 deadline, the public was evenly divided. According to one poll, 45% thought the U.S. should go to war if Iraq did not withdraw; 48% thought we should wait a bit longer to see if sanctions would work. Through all the diplomatic maneuverings, the Baker-Aziz meeting, the brokerage efforts of the French and the Soviets, right up until the very day that the bombing began, Americans gradually came to agree that perhaps diplomacy had been exhausted. "Bush has given ample time for Iraq to leave Kuwait," said John Barry, an insurance underwriter in Troy, Mich. "I think we've got to act according to our word. We've spent too much time and money to just whistle in the breeze and not do anything."

All through the fall, the tone of the debate was sober, reasoned, full of questions and ambiguities. Americans were thinking hard, trying to find answers to some basic questions. Why were we suddenly staring over the brink of a war in a country we had never paid much attention to, breathing fire at a tyrant we had scarcely ever heard of—but had helped to create? "I think it's stupid. I don't like why we're there," said Brian Scanlan, a Boston carpenter, in early January. "But I feel it's inevitable."

Perhaps it was the complexity of the issue—the moral and economic and historical complications—that gave rise to increasing that sense of inevitability. Some, like New York *Times* columnist Anthony Lewis, argued that it would be a just war, but not a wise one. SUPPORT OUR TROOPS—BRING THEM HOME NOW read one sign at a huge Washington peace rally. Prowar forces, by contrast, carried banners saying, WE WANT PEACE, BUT NOT WITH SADDAM. In between the extremes of NO BLOOD FOR OIL and NUKE IRAQ, the middle ground was filled with uncertainty.

Every war trails memories of the past one, and so there was a desperate search for parallels. The handiest was World War II: Saddam was cast as Adolf Hitler, Kuwait as the Sudetenland, and those who favored any negotiated settlement were accused of appeasement. Still more vivid were the invocations of Vietnam. Not another remote and undeclared Third World War, cried some, but others saw different lessons. This time, the generals vowed, we will not underestimate the enemy. This time, the President promised, the officers

"would not fight with one hand tied behind their back." This time the soldiers would not come home to be spat on or vilified.

Many Americans saw the gulf war as a chance to make peace with Vietnam's ghosts, and to make reparations for its failures. With anthems and flags and bells, with care packages and valentines, Americans sought ways of expressing solidarity. In Pine Bluff, Ark., Deborah Hurt sent personal letters and yellow ribbons to nearly 400 fellow Arkansans serving in the gulf. "I had seven brothers; six were in the military, and four served in Vietnam," she said. "I saw what they came home to. I made a promise when I was 16 years old not to let that happen again." Doug Swardstrom, a prowar investment counselor in Los Angeles, vowed that "when these guys come back, we're going to make sure they come back to a hero's welcome. We're going to organize the biggest parade they've ever seen."

In the meantime, there was a parade of gestures, of yellow ribbons, blood donations, hastily drawn wills. A tattoo parlor in Houston reported a 40% jump in business, mostly military designs. A waitress in Rocky Hill, Conn., told her boss he could fire her if he liked, but she would not remove the red, white and blue ribbon she was wearing. Two fraternity brothers at Oklahoma State kept vigil in a tree house to support the troops in the gulf. A disabled Vietnam veteran paid the Arkansas Flag and Banner Co. $45 to make him an Iraqi flag, so he could burn it.

Not all the gestures were symbolic. Military recruiters reported a surge of inquiries in the first days of war. Many callers wanted to be sent to the gulf—particularly, recruiters noted wryly, those who turned out to be overage or underqualified. At some stations, like the Air Force recruiting office in Quincy, Mass., the number of enlistments doubled. "I haven't seen anything like this since I began recruiting," said Technical Sergeant Rick Shellene. "A lot of kids feel it is about time to start standing behind the country, that the country has been knocked for so long."

While there was solace in the symbols, there was also room for a larger political message. Just as peace activists hoped the movement would inspire a new era of social protest, their opponents looked for a return to traditional values. "There's something about saying the Pledge of Allegiance and singing patriotic songs," observed Marilyn Loeffel, president of FLARE, a conservative, interdenominational group based in Memphis, "that makes us reflect on how far we've drifted from those values America was founded on." As ever in a time of inflamed rhetoric, there was plenty of hypocrisy to go around. Adlai Stevenson once noted that "it is often easier to fight for principles than to live up to them." Any claim to patriotism was made grotesque when it was expressed by torching Arab-owned stores, or when it cheered war as long as someone else was fighting it, or protested violently against violence, or drove 900 gas-guzzling miles to march beneath a banner that reads NO BLOOD FOR OIL.

Fortunately, much of the debate was characterized by a new respect for the right to disagree. "War is the gravest moral question a nation can face," said Eduardo Cohen, 41, a former Vietnam infantryman who actively protested the war in San Francisco. "This isn't a time to end discussion." Even the President referred benignly to the protesters, and did not impugn their motives, though Vice President Dan Quayle played attack dog on occasion. This time patriotism would not take sides. Supporters of the use of force had no monopoly on national pride, any more than protesters had sole claim to the desire for peace. A forest of flags rustled above the crowds at rallies across the country, waving, rather than burning. Devotion to

America, peace activists argued, was what inspired them to march, to protest the distraction of war that deflected energy and money and attention from battles being waged closer to home. What was victory worth, they wondered, if returning soldiers could not find a house or a job or health care once the battle ended? "We're saying support the soldiers, bring them home alive," said the Rev. Emory Searcy Jr., "there's nothing unpatriotic about that. There isn't the gulf between the troops and families and the protesters that there was in Vietnam."

In fact, the troops and families were often among the demonstrators. The diversity of dissent made generalization untidy. The rallies absorbed all manner of fringe groups (Lesbian Zionists for Peace, Unitarian Universalists Against Apartheid, and so forth) but they also tapped into mainstream movements that cut across all lines of color, class, age and gender. "Everybody's involved this time," said Paul George, director of the Peninsula Peace Center in Palo Alto, Calif. "We've developed a tradition of working together labor, churches, antinuclear, environmental."

Antiwar demonstrators in Chicago. "War," said one Vietnam veteran, "is the gravest moral question a nation can face."

Some polls found evidence of a gender gap: in the weeks before the air war began, one poll found, 73% of women opposed a war to liberate Kuwait, vs. 48% of men. Some suggested that this was because women were less disposed to fight for, or beside, a country that would not let women vote, or drive. NOW president Molly Yard referred to Saudi Arabia and Kuwait practicing "gender apartheid." Other women agreed that Saddam had to be stopped, but were not convinced that diplomacy had been given a chance.

Blacks were also uneasy about the disproportionate number of African Americans who were fighting in the gulf. Back in August, when 74% of whites approved of sending troops to the gulf, only 41% of blacks agreed. This was partly because of the fear that blacks would suffer a disproportionate number of casualties. As it turned out, the predictions were wrong. Blacks died roughly in proportion to their percentage of the population, and the greatest casualties occurred among pilots, who were mostly middle-class whites. Others noted that if the war deepened the recession, the economic downturn would strike hardest at poorly paid, inner-city workers. "This Middle East venture," said civil rights activist Julian Bond, "erases whatever chance we had of a peace dividend."

The organized clergy made its voice heard, from the street corners and the pulpits, as it rarely had before. A coalition of Protestant leaders called upon churches and the nation "to fast and pray for peace, to pursue every means available of public dialogue and popular expression to find a way out of certain catastrophe." Bishop Walter Sullivan of Virginia suggested that Catholics in the Army should consider laying down their weapons if fighting broke out. A Catholic priest in a poor Chicago neighborhood declared, "If George Bush wants to set deadlines, he could set deadlines on unemployment, apartheid, homelessness. He has been hellbound for months on war. I have never heard a President talk so much war talk in my lifetime."

For a war that was far away, it had a real and profound effect on the daily lives of millions of Americans. (The visible symbols multiplied, flag upon flag, one yellow ribbon unwinding up and down the streets, tied to the antennas of New York taxis.) The Empire State Building was lit red, white and blue as long as the soldiers fought (then turned yellow once they won). Bars that once showed N.B.A. games kept their sets tuned to CNN round the clock. Previously little-known, journeyman reporters—Wolf Blitzer and Arthur Kent and Charles Jaco—became the town criers, sharing each

new piece of news. Strangers struck up conversations on bank lines, in drugstores, in hotel lobbies. When will the fighting start? How long will it last? How bad will it be?

Only fear was consensual. Radio-talk shows were deluged with somewhat hysterical speculation about targets for Iraqi terrorism. Would the Super Bowl be canceled? Could the reservoirs be poisoned? Is Walt Disney World a target, or the Alaska pipeline, or the New York Stock Exchange, where officials outlawed all fast-food deliveries on security grounds? Business travelers who had planned trips overseas put them on hold; vacationers too decided to wait and see. Louisiana officials installed metal detectors at Caddo Parish Courthouse in Shreveport, La. They did not find any bombs, but did recover, in one week, more than 375 knives, a meat cleaver and a stash of crack cocaine.

As the January deadline approached, the fear and the helpless sense of waiting drove many people to church. The war produced a surprising portrait of the nation's faith, a tableau of people praying hard, slipping into chapels for special services during lunch breaks, joining candlelit vigils, seeking moral certainty or moral reassurance. The night before the deadline, parishioners gathered at St. Columba's Episcopal Church in Washington. The congregation had been praying especially for one parishioner: Secretary of State Jim Baker. But that night there was a profound sense of despair and futility. "O God the Father, Creator of Heaven and earth, have mercy upon us," went the reading from the *Book of Common Prayer.* "From violence, battle and murder; and from dying suddenly and unprepared, Good Lord, deliver us."

A few blocks away, 6,000 gathered inside the cavernous National Cathedral, sitting on the floor and packing the aisles under the vaulting stone buttresses. After the service many worshipers lit candles and marched silently through the streets of the capital. The vigil wound past the Iraqi embassy, quiet and dark except for a single light, and ended in front of the White House. Susan Meehan, a Quaker, attended on crutches. "Up at the cathedral they told us to fling our prayers to heaven," she said, "so I'm flinging mine—nonviolently."

On the actual deadline, Tuesday, Jan. 15, the tension reached its peak. Jewish congregations began a daylong fast. Demonstrators in Boston poured red paint on the snow, chanting, "No blood for oil." In Los Angeles high school students performed a skit in which American businessmen plucked dollar bills off the bod-

Yellow became a color of hope, not fear. Nine-year-old Sara Negron ties yellow ribbons on the school fence during a rally.

ies of young people. In Providence a George Bush doll was burned in an oil drum. While thousands chanted through the streets, San Francisco's supervisors declared the city a sanctuary for anyone who chose not to participate in the war. Local opponents took to the streets by the thousands, bearing signs splashed with anger: NO BODIES FOR BARRELS; and KINDER, GENTLER WAR; and THERE IS NO BOOT CAMP FOR WIDOWS.

That Tuesday marked what would have been the 62nd birthday of Martin Luther King Jr., and in Atlanta the day echoed with irony and anger. Organizers of commemorative events had invited General Colin Powell, the first black Chairman of the Joint Chiefs of Staff, to be grand marshal of the celebration, but at the last minute, he declined. He was busy in Washington, he explained. "It's like planning for Christmas and then having a member of the family die," observed John Cox, coordinator of events. "You carry on, but the spirit is not the same."

Although few people actually expected an attack just after the Tuesday-midnight deadline for war, the nation was awake and waiting. By nightfall in Washington, in the park across from the White House, protesters had brought bongos and snare drums and a solitary tom-tom. "Wake Up Bush!" they called, "Don't go to sleep tonight." The crowd carried fat red Christmas candles and the battery-powered ones with flames that don't flicker. By 12:30 a.m. Wednesday, many of the candles had melted into colored pools of wax on the park's sidewalks. A light sprinkle of rain had begun.

Nineteen hours later, the countdown was over. On a Red Line train headed toward the Maryland suburbs, a couple huddled over a portable TV, the sound turned way down. Then the woman gave a sudden cry: "We're at war!" Other passengers rushed over, straining to hear the news, and the woman burst into tears. Her husband turned to explain: "We have a 22-year-old son in the gulf." Meanwhile, over at the aptly named Hawk and Dove, silence fell over the noisy bar as Peter Jennings announced on the TV that America was "at war." One sharply dressed couple looked down from the screen and then at each other, and then raised their glasses in a quiet toast.

When the news came, people hurried home to be with their families. Church bells began tolling in town after town, and phone lines hummed as friends and families called one another, the conversations beginning in the middle, the premises understood. Americans showed a sudden elasticity of attention span; in bars and pool halls and college common rooms, the television stayed tuned to the news. For the next

several hours an entire nation watched news anchors, caught in history's ambush, struggling to tell the story without yet knowing just what it was. There was no time for anything else. In New York City during the next 12 hours, only one person was murdered; a typical night brings five or six dead. Police speculated that even the killers were watching the news.

For all the division, the President's announcement of the start of hostilities was received with respect; it was not that Bush had not heard the voices of protest, only that he did not agree with them. And polls that week showed that 4 out of 5 Americans now approved of Bush's handling of the crisis. "I have my troubles with Bush," said John Barber, a merchant banker in Los Angeles, "but in this instance I feel for him, on his solitary walk around the White House lawn, or as he calls clergymen to ask for their prayers." By and large, even word of the first night's victories was greeted with a respectful restraint, an awareness of the anxiety felt by families of soldiers. Until this was over, there would be few celebrations.

People puzzled over how to behave. Crowds and players at the Orlando Arena, gathered to watch the Orlando Magic play the Chicago Bulls, observed a moment of silence, perhaps conscious that this did not seem to be a time for basketball games. MTV played peace songs from the '60s, while KAZY, the hard-rock station in Denver, switched to round-the-clock news. In Manhattan the colorful crowds of Times Square spread like spilled paint beneath the illuminated news ticker over 42nd Street as bulletins on the attack marched around the building above their heads, one word at a time.

Everywhere, the reports could not come fast enough. There was a national craving for news, despite the saturation coverage, and frustration at the thinness of reports. "I don't think it's going as smoothly as it appears to be," said Andy Ach, an investment banker in San Francisco. "The news seems so sanitized, it's hard to get a sense of casualties or destruction." The morning after the bombing began, the New York *Post*, already hoarse from a week of war cries (KISS IT GOODBYE! screamed the headline in Wednesday's paper, accompanying a photo of Saddam kissing the ground in Baghdad), contented itself with one black word in thick letters 6 in. high: WAR! The *Wall Street Journal* ran a four-column headline, the largest since the Japanese attack on Pearl Harbor. The Houston *Chronicle* was typical of editorial opinion in the South. Saddam, it said, "asked for the war he has gotten. May his God forgive him; we won't."

S/Sgt. Daniel Stamaris salutes as the national anthem is played for returning war prisoners at Andrews Air Force Base.

People sought to find out more. Publishers rushed into stores instant books on the war and the region, such as *Saddam Hussein and the Crisis in the Gulf* and *Unholy Babylon—The Secret History of Saddam's War*. Rand McNally struggled to meet the demand for its maps of the Middle East. In the first week, the company sold more maps than it did of Vietnam in six years of war.

For the families of soldiers, it was a time to seek and lend support. The departure of National Guard and Army Reserve Units had hollowed out countless communities across the country. Camden, Ala., lost one-third of its police force—two of the six officers. In Rock Falls, Ill., the 181 members of the National Guard unit shipped out over the weekend before the conflict began. "So many people used the Guard to supplement their income but never expected to be called," said Carol Siefken, a computer supervisor at the local steel mill. "These are people in their 30s and 40s. Their lives were mapped out. They never expected to be fighting for their country."

In a house across the icy Rock River, Laura Root looked through her newly assembled wedding album.

She was married on New Year's Eve to Tom Root, a local policeman who was just called up. "I have no idea of where he is tonight," she said. "The last thing we talked about was that if he came home with no arms or legs, that if he was turned into a vegetable by chemical weapons, he didn't want to be a burden." She looked at a merry picture of their celebration. "I just married him three weeks ago," she said. "I want 20 more years."

Perhaps the deepest anxiety fell to the children, and not only those whose parents had left them behind. Everywhere, the young were struggling to understand the preoccupation of adults, full of questions too often left unspoken. Many feared not only for their own safety but for that of their parents and of children they did not even know. Zoe Owers, a fifth grader from Concord, N.H., had tears in her eyes when she heard that the fighting had started. "I'm surprised I can't hear anything," she said. Her mother reassured her that Baghdad was far away. "But I thought bombs made a lot of noise," Zoe replied.

The start of the fighting brought a pronounced shift in mood. More and more stores and street corners were

full of signs that simply said: SUPPORT OUR TROOPS IN THE GULF. Though ambivalence remained, many Americans were willing to give the President the benefit of the doubt and to support his policy, albeit conditionally. Then, one by one, the conditions fell away. Those who originally favored sanctions but not bombing soon shifted to support an air war but not an invasion. Betsy Loth, who owns two clothing stores in Watertown, Conn., happily put up peace-rally posters in her stores during the days before the fighting started. But that Thursday morning she took them down. "It's not of my choosing, but we're in a full-fledged war. We should get on with it." Of Bush, she said, "I can't stand the man but I think he did enough."

One crucial ingredient in the stiffening of the public's resolve was the behavior of Saddam Hussein. Few Americans had any illusions that we would have been fighting if Kuwait's main export were papayas. The breadth of the U.N. alliance, the cooperation of the Soviet Union and the support of other Arab nations all made the war strategically viable. But geopolitical analysis about new world orders could not carry a population into war; the appearance of a moral crusade was a different matter. It was the moral ingredient that the President stressed, and that brought his popular support to its highest level ever. It was hard to remain ambivalent in the face of such obstinacy, and such cruelty. Saddam's behavior lent weight to the President's rhetoric. After the war began, Iraqi Scud attacks on Tel Aviv, the fouling of the gulf with oil, the brutal parade of prisoners of war and the continuing reports of atrocities in Kuwait all seemed to confirm the President's assertions that this was a fight about good and evil, not oil and money. "Our patriotic impulse is also a moral impulse," said Professor John Schutz, who teaches a famous history course at University of Southern California called Patriotism and the American Spirit. "I notice that George Bush spends a lot of time in church or on the air saying this is a just war. Vietnam wasn't defined that way."

But maintaining the initial surge of support posed a problem for the White House handlers. Ten days after the air war started, hundreds of thousands of demonstrators converged on Washington and cities across the country. At the time it seemed that the protest movement was gathering steam, not losing it. Though Bush's approval rating was still running at around 75% in the days after the air war began, there was plenty of

Wife and children grieve at funeral of Marine Captain Jonathan Edwards, killed while flying an escort mission in Saudi Arabia.

expert condescension about how much blood the public would bear.

As the ground war drew near in the early days of February, the newspapers and networks focused on medical treatment for trauma and burns, on the elaborate Iraqi defenses and the tens of thousands of lives that would be lost in trying to pierce them. On Feb. 17, thousands of people gathered in Times Square and in other rallies, teach-ins and vigils around the country. These demonstrations were smaller than they had been a month ago, but often more vehement. In New York City former Congresswoman Bella Abzug lashed out at Bush for dismissing Saddam's latest peace plan as a "cruel hoax." "Unless we make our voices heard more effectively," she said, "we may see a ground war very shortly that will take the lives of innocent soldiers and civilians alike."

The American tolerance for heavy casualties or economic hardship, or hardship of any kind, was never tested in a ground war that lasted 100 hours. As for the thousands of Iraqi dead, they were all too easily forgotten. "Any military adventure, however poorly conceived, however dubious the strategic objective, is absolutely validated by victory," said Bruce Babbitt, the former Arizona Governor. "Once we commit to the use of force and it's decisive, then the cost is automatically worthwhile, without any exceptions in the course of American history."

The conclusion of the war brought all sorts of other conclusions as well. This was the end of the "Vietnam syndrome," it was said; the renaissance of presidential leadership; the death of the national Democratic Party; the rebirth of American pride and patriotism. Particularly affected, according to White House pollster Robert Teeter, were the nation's young people. "These are people who have not seen the country either lead or succeed in a big way on anything, for a long time, whether it was Vietnam or economic competition," he said. "Now they've seen us succeed."

Those rather aggressive predictions were crowded out, however, by the simplest and most joyous of images. "It's going to be a hell of a welcome bout," said Jim Schroder, president of the Chamber of Commerce in Oceanside, Calif. Humorist Lewis Grizzard of the Atlanta *Journal and Constitution* called for a national day of gloating. Newspapers whooped in giddy headlines with rows of exclamation points. Bars served free champagne.

The first wave of fathers and mothers of Operation Desert Storm tumbled off huge dark airplanes at Fort Stewart and Camp Pendleton and Travis Air Force Base, and fell into the arms of loved ones and children and anyone else within reach. Well-wishers lined Main Street and the interstates, waving yellow ribbons and flags. Horns honked, lights flashed and whole towns stayed up late in the first wondrous daze of reunion.

In quiet corners were the sad endings: coffins rolling out of the bellies of airplanes, widows clutching folded flags. In all, 232 American soldiers died, an astonishingly low number to historians but a burden of grief to a host of families. The youngest was an 18-year-old private from New Jersey who had joined up right out of high school, five days after the Iraqi invasion. The oldest was a 55-year-old Air Force reserve officer named Carpio Villarreal, who was planning his retirement after this final assignment.

The strangest death was that of Anthony Riggs, 22, an Army specialist who had been back in the States less than 24 hours when he was shot in Detroit in what looked like a robbery attempt. A few days later, his wife and her brother were arrested and charged with conspiring to kill him. "I have no intention of becoming one of this war's casualties," he had written from the gulf shortly before. But he was talking about the wrong war.

Though the situation in the gulf remained explosive over the next several weeks, people were eager to bring their attention home, to take up where they had left off, as individuals and as a nation, some seven months before. The President captured the mood of satisfaction and finality when he went before a joint session of Congress on March 6 for his victory speech. "We went halfway around the world to do what is moral and just and right," he said. "And we fought hard and—with others—we won the war."

Joy and relief in Fort Stewart, Ga.: a warm family welcome for Sgt. James Roark of the 24th Mechanized Infantry Division.

INDEX

PICTURE CREDITS